ALFRED XUEREB

My Days with
BENEDICT XVI

Translation by
Msgr. Larry Spiteri

Revised by
Carmel J. Camilleri

SOPHIA INSTITUTE PRESS
Manchester, New Hampshire

Sophia Institute Press
Box 5284, Manchester, NH 03108
1-800-888-9344
www.SophiaInstitute.com

Sophia Institute Press is a registered trademark of Sophia Institute.

hardback ISBN 979-8-88911-045-3

ebook ISBN 979-8-88911-046-0

Library of Congress Control Number: 2023936177

A special thanks to Dr. Aldo Maria Valli
for your valuable advice.

To Valter and Lucia
with deep gratitude

Dear friends!
God guides his Church, he sustains it always,
especially at times of difficulty.
Let us never lose this vision of faith, which is the one
true way of looking at the journey of the Church and of the world.
In our hearts, in the heart of each of you, may there always abide
the joyful certainty that the Lord is at our side: he does not abandon us,
he remains close to us and he surrounds us with his love.
Thank you!

BENEDICT XVI
General Audience, February 27, 2013

CONTENTS

PREFACE

Msgr. Alfred Xuereb was one of the two personal secretaries to Pope Benedict XVI for five and a half years. To be precise, he was the second secretary, Msgr. Georg Gänswein being the other one. A very discreet person, he always intentionally assumed a low profile so as not to be seen going beyond what was strictly necessary to fulfill his role. However, all of us who are familiar with the Vatican know that he was one of those persons who had been very close to Pope Benedict during the major part of his pontificate. He particularly accompanied the Holy Father very closely in those aspects of daily life that were unknown to the general public because such fell outside the spotlight and television coverage.

His testimony is very precious, for it provides a deep knowledge of the personality of Pope Ratzinger. His approach is completely different from most of the other witnesses. He is aware of this. Eventually, he went beyond his habitual discretion to present us with a diary, which contributes to a rendering that is "a more truthful, more precise and authentic portrayal of both the man Joseph Ratzinger and

Pope Benedict XVI." Without doubt, at the end of reading
his testimony, we do not discover confidential information
on the history of a pontificate, but we are able to understand
better the thoughtfulness and the traits — and therefore the
soul — of a pontiff whose public image was mostly very partial, if not falsified by inevitable simplifications or by inten-
tional modifications.

The relationship between Msgr. Xuereb and Pope Benedict is clearly parental. It is explicitly affirmed in many of the
passages in this diary. We can also add that it is a relationship
that involves a spontaneous harmony between two persons
who have a natural bend toward being discreet, and let us also
say a certain modesty and shyness, which, however, does not
fail to reveal a depth of feeling of great finesse, sometimes
expressed with a certain "ingenuity," that is an unmistakable
stamp of serene and total authenticity.

It is, therefore, an emotionally intense, distinct diary in
which the daily "little things" are more significant than the
"big" ones. The most headline-grabbing events are not entirely absent from the script, but in a certain way remain present
in the background and are rightly relegated to records. This
diary was not written for them. Instead, it recounts conversations carried out at table during ordinary days, the gentle
attentions given to the closest persons at different times of
the day, the very special relationship with a brother almost of
the same age, the atmosphere present during Christmas Eve in
the intimacy of the "papal family," with songs and memories
from his childhood, and so on.

Yes … the "papal family" … in the "apartment." … In reality, every pope is different, and we are convinced that it is good
that it is so! Pope Francis explained to us from the outset of
his pontificate that he had decided to remain at Santa Marta
for the sake of his "psychic balance." This was an important
message that we gladly embraced in its novelty. Evidently, the

"psychic balance" of Pope Benedict elicited different needs that derived from a different story. Msgr. Xuereb helps us to understand the humanity, simple and rich at the same time, within the context of personal and spiritual relationships that accompanied and helped a pope, day after day, to carry out his responsibilities for the universal Church. This is probably the most perennial and intimate value of this diary.

The narrative develops in an orderly fashion. The richest observations are those during the first year, given the fact that the force of new impressions deeply impacted the soul of the diarist. Subsequently it is enriched with quotations from the pope's speeches and remarks. This is done without weighing down the narrative; we realize that the author carefully chooses the themes and the emphases that touched him the most. Understandably, it is particularly the travels that provide a rhythm to the narrative in the passage of time. There is no shortage of pages in which Msgr. Xuereb details his participation in the difficult moments of toil and suffering in the ministry of Benedict XVI. But even the beautiful moments — sometimes forgotten — find their confirmation. The signs of his diminishing strength are discreet and polished; the pages that speak about the renunciation are rich with great and contained emotions.

The continuous tenor of the diary is that of great serenity, of faith in service and prayer. Once we finish reading this diary, we can take it with us as something rewarding. Certainly, the most profound meaning of the entire pontificate of Benedict XVI was rooted in the service of faith. This diary helps us to understand better how this service was actually lived out and implemented each day *in* faith.

Rev. Federico Lombardi, S.J.
President of the Joseph Ratzinger Foundation

A WHITE HELICOPTER

February 28, 2013: This day is destined to become for the Church — but not only for her — a very special date, one that will enter the pages of history: a pope leaves the Vatican having decided to renounce his pontificate on his own initiative.

Behold Pope Benedict! He takes his leave from the papal apartment, his residence for seven years, ten months, and nine days, with no particular ceremony. In a few hours Joseph Ratzinger will become pope emeritus, and the See of Rome will become vacant.

The Holy Father descends to San Damaso Courtyard, where a small guard of honor of the Pontifical Swiss Guard awaits him. More importantly, there stand beside them those persons who have worked with him and for him during all these years. Emotions run high and one is unable to hold back tears. Pope Benedict smiles and salutes everyone with a slight wave of his hand. He walks with the aid of a cane, and it is not hard to read in his face the signs of fatigue. Indeed, his figure seems to be more frail than usual.

A short distance away, a white helicopter of the Italian Air Force awaits the pope at the heliport. Benedict reaches it by a black car, with license plate SCV1, after traveling silently along the Vatican Gardens. Here, there is another salute, another smile, another hand gesture. A banner appears that simply states *Danke*, "Thank you," in the pope's mother tongue. Some seminarians have climbed onto the roof of the minor seminary, where they wave as a well-wishing sign.

Within a few moments, the helicopter heads toward the locale called the Castelli Romani, the Roman Castles. The destination is the pontifical residence at Castel Gandolfo. It is there that, from this evening, Benedict XVI will spend the next few months before he takes up his new and already designated residence at the former monastery Mater Ecclesiae, within the Vatican. He will live there hidden from the eyes of the world.

The helicopter flies above the Eternal City, accompanied by the ringing of the bells of all the churches along the route. Patarina, the historic bell of the Senate Palace, adds its own voice to the occasion. This is the salute of the City of Rome to her bishop. At the Campidoglio Square there are banners being waved with the inscription "You will always remain with us. Thank you." The sky is clear. As the helicopter becomes smaller and harder to perceive as it flies into the distance, the Vatican issues the text of the last tweet of Pope Benedict: "Thank you for your love and support. May you always experience the joy of placing Christ at the centre of your lives."

Among the small group of persons who accompany the pope on board in this short but extraordinary flight is a fifty-four-year-old Maltese priest. His name is Msgr. Alfred Xuereb, though he prefers to be called Fr. Alfred. He has been the second personal secretary of Pope Benedict since September 2007, and he is very much aware that this day also closes a very important chapter for him.

All through this morning, but especially during this short flight, with the amazing spectacle of the historical and monumental beauty of Rome opening up below them, Fr. Alfred's heart and soul have been caught in an overflowing turmoil of feelings. On the one hand, there is a feeling of emptiness and loss, which is perfectly understandable on a human level; on the other hand, there is complete trust in the Lord's designs.

A few days have already passed since he was informed of Benedict's decision. The Holy Father himself, with refined gracefulness, told him the news, and the recollection of this encounter remains embedded in Fr. Alfred's mind in every detail. The pope had called him to his private study and asked him to sit on the other side of the desk, a clear hint that he was going to share some very important information. Benedict XVI, fully aware of the import of the news he was to disclose and the effect it would have on those around him, told Fr. Alfred of his decision with complete calmness and serenity. Although he was stunned, Fr. Alfred's long experience came to his rescue. Deep emotions almost overwhelmed him, but with a great effort he managed to stop himself from exclaiming, "No, Holy Father! Why don't you take a little longer to think it through?" He resisted uttering a word and instead listened, frozen, trying hard to suppress the turmoil within him. When the moment finally came for him to speak, Fr. Alfred managed, with profound difficulty, to assure the pope of his prayers, now more fervent than before, and thanked him for the esteem and trust he had bestowed upon him.

Seemingly trivial recent events now flashed through his mind. He remembered the number of times when the pope, while in the sacristy, prayed for a much longer period before Holy Mass. It was the habit of the pope, at the chimes of the clock at the Cortile San Damaso at seven, to make the Sign of the Cross while pronouncing, "*Adiutorum nostrum in nomine Domini*" (Our help comes from the name of the Lord) so as to signal the entrance to his private chapel to commence Holy Mass. Lately, on some days, despite the chimes striking seven o'clock, Benedict remained immobile and completely absorbed in prayer. At the time, Fr. Alfred intuitively knew that the pope was praying for something very special, but nothing of this magnitude.

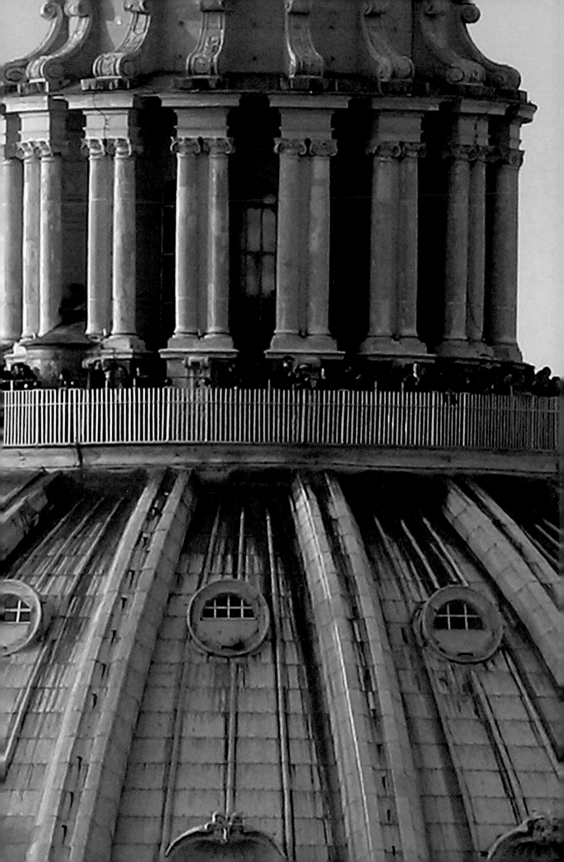

Consequently, as soon as the pope informed his second secretary of his decision to leave the Petrine ministry, Fr. Alfred linked this decision to that prolonged praying before Holy Mass, and it became clear to him that the pope had already gone through his internal struggle, which explained why he was now so serene and calm revealing his extraordinary decision to Fr. Alfred.

The helicopter flies light, as light, one might say, as Benedict's soul. But it is very difficult to describe the emotions Fr. Alfred is going through, dazed as he is by the day's events. He has been with Benedict for five and a half years. He has served him with diligence, been close to him. He was part of that group called the "pontifical family," a term that for him was not only technical but, in truth, also gave a hint of his filial relationship with the Supreme Pontiff. For him the pope was a father, full of attention and tenderness, wise but also humble.

So many images flood back to Fr. Alfred. The days immediately preceding His Holiness's departure have been filled with a profusion of confused and astonished, but deeply moved, cardinals, as Benedict announces in Latin his decision to sacrifice the pontificate for the good of the church.

It was February 11 when the pope rose to say, "After having repeatedly examined my conscience before God, I have come to the certainty that my strengths, due to an advanced age, are no longer suited to an adequate exercise of the Petrine ministry." Later there is the memory of his last general audience in St. Peter's Square. The pope began by saying, "I thank all of you for having come in such great numbers. Heartfelt thanks! I am truly moved, and I see the Church alive! And I think we should also say thanks to the Creator for the fine weather which he gives us even on this winter day."

But Fr. Alfred conserves within himself other, much more personal treasures: the regular morning Mass celebrated by the pope in the chapel of the Apostolic Palace, at times enriched with beautiful homilies; the walks in the Vatican Gardens and at Castel Gandolfo; the foreign travels; the great celebrations; luncheons and dinners either in intimate privacy or in the company of distinguished guests; the moments of prayer or rest; the jovial encounters with Msgr. Georg, the pope's brother; the recollections of the Holy Father of when he was a small boy; his love for animals; the hours of apprehension and others of joy.

Out of this confusion and uncertainty, Fr. Alfred clings, more in hope than conviction, to the belief that soon things will settle down and make sense.

Many things have already been said and written about Benedict XVI, and much more will be added in the future, very often, in Fr. Alfred's view, in a mistaken and uninformed manner. In the main, Joseph Ratzinger has been portrayed as a stern, rigid, and cold, almost insensitive person, dedicated solely to control strict doctrine. However, Fr. Alfred knows otherwise: that it has never been such and that there is another, perhaps hidden, side to Pope Benedict's persona.

And now, in the intimate environment of the helicopter still in flight, the thought that a person so dear to him, so

considerate and caring of those around him, and so assiduous in the implementation of the great responsibilities thrown upon him, is leaving his ministry a respected figure but a misunderstood person, troubles Fr. Alfred to the core. Besides, the wish that the decision to abdicate the pontificate be perceived in the right light starts to grow within him. He knows that it is not, as has been alleged, a decision that lacks courage; rather, it is an act of love for the Church. Most of all, he is aware of the heroic nature of the decision; after all, Fr. Alfred has seen the momentous event play out in front of his own eyes.

For a long time, the faithful secretary remained close to the pope, but silent, unnoticed, almost invisible as his delicate role required. This was the proper thing to do, and he never wished it otherwise, never desiring to stand out or step into the limelight. However, he did keep a diary in which he jotted down events and the sentiments and reactions aroused by them. It is a logbook of personal entries that now, in its own way, has taken the form of a historical record for posterity, which can now contribute to a more truthful, more precise, and more authentic portrayal of both the man Joseph Ratzinger and Pope Benedict XVI.

This diary, this notebook, this narrative from behind the scenes is being made public as a means to tell the truth. It is a small contribution, if you wish, but it carries the stamp of authenticity. Obviously, Fr. Alfred, in his witnessing, does not pretend to impose the exact notion and image of Pope Benedict, but to simply say to readers, "Here is the man whom I had the privilege to know!"

ALDO MARIA VALLI

My Days with
BENEDICT XVI

My Days with
BENEDICT XVI
2007

11 TUESDAY SEPTEMBER

This morning, once I completed my round of salutations to the superiors and colleagues of the Prefecture of the Pontifical Household, where I have worked for about seven years, and the preparations for moving were over, I left my room, number 522, at Domus Sanctae Marthae. I have lived happily there for eleven years. I also gave my parting wishes to the monsignors and personnel at Santa Marta and visited our sisters of the Daughters of Charity in their convent.

On the way to Castel Gandolfo, where I will begin my new service as the second personal secretary to Pope Benedict XVI, I stop to meet a priest friend, Fr. Lino, to share a moment of prayer and, at the same time, to renew my complete dedication to the Virgin Mary. At the end I make my confession before I leave the place.

I arrive in my car at the courtyard of the Apostolic Palace of Castel Gandolfo at 4:50 p.m. I am full of anxiety. Although I have been here many times due to my responsibilities to the antechamber, now everything has changed. However, my nervousness is soon dispelled following the very warm welcome of the personal secretary, Msgr. Georg Gänswein, and the meeting with the four Memores Domini, and above all after the brief audience with the Holy Father in his private study, I immediately feel better. I feel reassured and more at peace.

It was just about a month ago that I was informed that the pope wished to speak with me. I went to see him feeling somewhat anxious. It felt strange to find myself sitting in the same chair that, for a number of years in my role as a prelate of the antechamber, first under John Paul II and then under this same Benedict XVI, I had invited many visitors to sit in to wait for a private audience.

The pope was very clear and direct with me. He said, "As you know, Msgr. Mietek is now going to Ukraine. We were very pleased with him, and I thought that you might be his replacement. I know that you have been to Germany and so know a little bit of German."

I told him that I had been to Münster, where I had done some work in a hospital. The pope told me that he knew both the hospital and the zone in which I had resided, and also the pastor, for he himself had lived in that vicinity during the seventies when he was a university professor. I understood that he wanted me to immediately assume this new ministry. What emotions ran through me!

And now here I am! For the first time, at 6:45 p.m., I go for the recitation of the Rosary with the Holy Father in the gardens running along Villa Cybo. He announces the mysteries, while Msgr. Gänswein and I alternate in leading the prayers. We walk as we pray, and the path ends at the feet of a most beautiful statue of Our Lady. This place is called "the garden of Our Lady" and is very close to the heart of Benedict XVI. He enjoys praying there, surrounded by nature's beauty in the same place that has already witnessed in prayer at least five popes: Pius XI, Pius XII, John XXIII, Paul VI, and John Paul II.

Blessing of a halo with twelve stars for the framework of the Madonna in Gozo (Malta). Private library of the papal apartments in the Apostolic Palace in the Vatican.

According to an affable custom, the gendarmes prepare a basket that contains small pieces of bread for the red fish and the two carps swimming in the pond. After the pope, it is our turn, the secretaries, to throw the bits of bread to the red fish, which very soon gather on our side of the pond. Sitting on the garden benches, we share the serenity of the place while we discourse amongst ourselves.

After Msgr. Gänswein gives me some instructions regarding office matters, supper begins at 7:30 p.m. While I am wishing to contribute something to our table's conversation and searching for something to say, the pope graciously guides the conversation toward the topic of Malta and my past experiences. We watch the news after supper and end the evening with a short walk. After I finish the last prayers and put away my clothes in the closet, I try to sleep ... but it is difficult to do so after the exhilaration of the day!

12 WEDNESDAY SEPTEMBER

Today is my first full day in the secretariat of the Holy Father. The day begins with the celebration of Holy Mass, presided over by the pope. There are in the chapel the butler, Paolo Gabriele, the four Memores Domini, and the consecrated lay persons of the Communion and Liberation movement who look after the papal apartment. I remain in the chapel after Holy Mass for the recitation of Lauds and a few minutes of meditation. The pope stays to pray after the rest of the people leave the chapel.

During breakfast, the pope, being always ready to help me, asks how I have spent my first night in my new quarters. He senses from my hesitant response that things could have gone better. I state that perhaps the "fault" was due to the chiming of the clock in the courtyard. Benedict immediately states that it is possible to stop it, at which I am somewhat embarrassed. I do not wish that the pope has to decree that the chimes should be stopped simply not to disturb the sleep of his secretary! Perhaps I should have been more honest in admitting that I did not sleep due to my deep emotions arising from my new position.

While the Holy Father returns to the Vatican for the Wednesday general audience, I remain working in the office. We see each other again at luncheon, and Benedict informs me that there was at the audience a Maltese choir that gave a great rendition of *Tu es Petrus* (You are Peter). I appreciate that the atmosphere at the table is very genial, and I find the same gentleness during dinner when we mention, among other things, the soccer game between Ukraine and Italy scheduled for this evening, as well as Italian soccer in general. The pope reminisces about an event. He recalls that in 1982, when he had just arrived in Rome, he was surprised by the cacophony of beeping car horns he and his sister heard every Sunday evening, which became louder and louder with each succeeding week. He did not understand the meaning of this until he discovered that it had to do with Rome's soccer fans celebrating their team's victory. All of us burst into laughter! Next, we go for prayer and then off to bed, tired but happy with how the day went.

13 THURSDAY SEPTEMBER

Today, once again, I proclaim the Gospel and serve as an "altar boy" for the washing of hands. I assure the Holy Father during breakfast that I have had a refreshing sleep, perhaps thanks to my orthopedic pillow that I have fetched from Santa Marta.

Although there is much work to do at the office, I have to first hook up the computer and set my desk in order. By way of exception, I perform some service at the antechambers, as I previously did in the Prefecture of the Pontifical Household, but most likely this will be for the last time. I jokingly tell the collaborators that I should receive two salaries. In fact,

"Altar boy" service during Mass in the private chapel of the Apostolic Nunciature in Berlin.

however, there is only one audience scheduled, and it seems that it will not require the presence of one of the antechamber prelates from the Vatican.

It occurs to me that the pope likes to retrace the morning events and meetings while we are at table, doing so with great simplicity and within a familiar atmosphere. And sure enough, to my great surprise, he asks me the results of yesterday's soccer match.

He comes to my office in the afternoon and notes that I am looking at a website on my computer. He stops full of curiosity and exhibits his marvel at modern technology. It is a world almost alien to him, but he has no apprehensions about it.

Later, after the office hours, I take part in the recitation of the Rosary in the garden, followed by the "ceremony" of feeding the small fish with bits of bread. The pope, in a friendly and informal way, directs me to sit next to him instead of on the other bench, and we spend some time in small talk, at the end of which, due to the approaching cold air, the driver arrives with a closed car rather than the open electric one.

There is the usual short walk after supper, and then, having requested leave from the Holy Father, I go back to the office to finish some work.

16 SUNDAY SEPTEMBER

I have a good opportunity during these days to confirm even more that the Holy Father loves to create a family atmosphere among us, his secretaries and the Memores, in that he allows us, especially during meals, to relate some personal anecdotes of a light nature. The pope really enjoys himself, is curious, and shows keen interest in the ensuing conversation. It is wonderful seeing him smiling and joining in and making us laugh with his subtle sense of humor.

Yesterday we watched a DVD on the life of Wolfgang Amadeus Mozart, the composer so much loved by Joseph Ratzinger. When the documentary was over, the pope remained seated, enjoying the closeness of his family. Although he is a great expert on Mozart, he does not impose his views on the group but allows us space to contribute with our own opinions on the subject, adding greatly to the enjoyment of the evening.

During this weekend at Castel Gandolfo there is a gathering of the so-called *Ratzinger Schülerkreis*, comprised of a group of former students of Professor Joseph Ratzinger. The

Bird's eye view of the Apostolic Palace of Castel Gandolfo.

group has been meeting annually since the seventies to discuss theological issues. The pope presents a talk and celebrates Holy Mass inside the chapel of the international Mariapolis Center, which lies a small distance from the Apostolic Palace. The celebration is in German, and I, being the second concelebrant, recite part of the Eucharistic Prayer in German too. Once I finish the prayer, it seems to me that I was understood!

18 TUESDAY
SEPTEMBER

I receive numerous congratulation cards regarding my new position that the Holy Father has entrusted me with. I try to answer all of them. I wish to show my closeness to those who know me, in particular to the priests who were ordained with me and also others from my diocese. I want them to understand that my new position will not distance me from them, but, on the contrary, it is a new way to remain in contact with one another. Anyway, our friendship continues and, possibly, it becomes deeper. Throughout I try to keep in mind the counsel of Don Stanisław, the ex-secretary of John Paul II, now the cardinal-archbishop of Cracow. He told me to remain attentive to the needs of people and to practice great humility. This is the joy of being a priest: be close to others so that they become closer to Christ!

23 SUNDAY
SEPTEMBER

These are very significant and intense days, filled with beautiful experiences. We receive an abundance of spiritual riches from the Holy Father. He keeps us positive and on the right path! One of the Memores tells me that during our conversations at meals, the pope immediately senses whether a joke might have disrupted fraternal charity among those present. I am also advised to be always attentive not to allow any conversation to finish with some comment lacking charity. This morning the pope has a pastoral visit to the nearby city of Velletri. There he is welcomed by Cardinal Francis Arinze, the person who succeeded Joseph Ratzinger as the cardinal with the titular of that diocese, and by Bishop Vincenzo Apicella of the Diocese of Velletri-Segni.

I am in the third car of the papal procession, and I am deeply moved upon seeing all of the people who have come to the streets to salute Benedict. I feel very proud but immediately recall my intention to prefer the crucified Lord and not human vanity. The Holy Father goes to visit the cathedral where he gives homage to the precious icon Cruz Veliterna and then goes to the chapel of Our Lady of Grace for a brief Eucharistic Adoration. Next comes the celebration of Holy Mass in San Clemente Square. I am standing in the background, but I deeply feel the affinity in the encounter between the universal pastor and the people during the celebration of Holy Mass.

This evening, after we return to Castel Gandolfo, the Holy Father decides to take a different route in his walk during the recitation of the Rosary with Msgr. Gänswein and me. In the end, the three of us end up sitting on the same old bench. We speak about the visit to Velletri. We find that all of us have been touched by the enthusiasm of the people, who were moved not only by curiosity but by their sincere desire to be with the pope and listen to his words.

25 TUESDAY SEPTEMBER

My new experience of being with the Holy Father is captivating, and the feeling grows that my efforts to attune myself to Benedict's character and the way he works are bearing fruit. These days also witness the receipt of well-wishes, which express the joy from many at the new responsibilities that have been entrusted to me in the service of the pope. I begin

Benedict XVI in recollection in the Apostolic Palace chapel of Castel Gandolfo before the celebration of Holy Mass.

responding to every writer and try to reciprocate the unmerited privilege of celebrating Holy Mass with the pope every morning by remembering these dear persons during the eucharistic celebration. I know that the knowledge that they are being remembered in the papal chapel brings pleasure to these kind well-wishers and comfort to those experiencing difficulties in their daily struggles.

28 FRIDAY
SEPTEMBER

"I see that the pope is feeling great. His face is relaxed, and these days here have restored him." These are the words of a person who really knows Benedict XVI. She is Sr. Birgit Wansing, a member of the Schönstatt movement and a collaborator with the Holy Father when both of them were at the Congregation for the Doctrine of the Faith.

Sr. Birgit is currently a member of the secretariat of Pope Benedict. She comes over to Castel Gandolfo a number of

First photo: Cat stuffed animal resting on the a window sill of the papal apartment.

Second Photo: Grotto of the Madonna of Lourdes — Vatican Gardens: the pleased pope observes two kittens who had been napping on his cushioned kneeler.

times during the summer months to work on various projects of the personal papal office. When I tell her that the pope frequently recounts to us some pleasant episodes to make us smile, she comments, "When Benedict acts this way, he wants to indicate that he really feels good!"

I recall an anecdote that is indicative of Joseph Ratzinger's sense of humor. As many probably know, Benedict loves cats, but what very few are aware of is that he never had a cat as pope! One day a particular office of the Holy See requested to visit the pope even if it was comprised of "four cats." He immediately comments, "Pity they are not real cats!"

The love that the pope has toward cats is such that even the stuffed cat, resting on a windowsill in the corridor that leads to his room, frequently receives a pat from the Holy Father and at times even a gentle passing comment!

The Holy Father loves all animals — the more intelligent they are, the more he loves them — and he is especially enamored by their gestures. I eventually discover that when he watches television, he is even delighted with advertisements that depict dogs and cats.

29 SATURDAY SEPTEMBER

Today is the feast of the three archangels: Michael, Gabriel, and Raphael. It is a very special day. We are gathered at St. Peter's Basilica for the consecration of six new bishops, one of whom is Msgr. Mieczysław Mokrzycki, whom I have replaced at the personal office of the Holy Father. He is better known as Fr. Mietek, a forty-six-year-old Polish priest. He was for many years the personal secretary of John Paul II before being retained for some time in the same position by Benedict XVI. The other five bishops, called to serve in different capacities in the service to the one Church of Christ, are Fran-

cesco Brugnaro, Gianfranco Ravasi, Tommaso Caputo, Sergio Pagano, and Vincenzo Di Mauro.

We depart from Castel Gandolfo in a helicopter that belongs to the Italian Air Force and arrive at the Vatican ten minutes later to find the prefect of the pontifical household, the substitute secretary of state, and others waiting our arrival. We go to the papal apartment, and for the first time I see the office in which I will be working inside the Vatican once we return from the summer residence.

The Holy Mass is full of emotional moments, especially the moment when the pope rests his hands on the new bishops' heads and later when they bless the assembled congregation. Present are many cardinals, but even many more bishops, among whom is the bishop of my home diocese of Gozo, Bishop Mario Grech, who is about my age and who, like myself, was ordained a priest on May 26, 1984.

Later at lunchtime we talk about the Holy Mass. When I allude to the beautiful homily during which, among other things, the pope said that in the ancient Church the bishops

Benedict XVI's walk in the "garden of the Madonna" in Castel Gandolfo. Here, at the foot of the statue of the Madonna, the Popes, traditionally, conclude Marian prayers.

were defined as being "angels" — to underline that they should be men oriented toward God — the pope thanks me almost timidly, and with a modesty that characterizes him.

During this time the pope is suffering from a hoarse voice, and while we are walking back, I venture to suggest that perhaps he should gargle with lemon juice. I know it to be an old recipe that always works with me. He responds that he has noticed that I possess a strong, low voice. I reply that actually I have a weak voice, which was the reason that, in my home parish choir, I sang with the bass voices. This prompts him to ask me if we have beautiful choirs in Malta, to which I promise that I will obtain for him a collection of my choir's music on a CD. We remain alone for the recitation of the Rosary and, as usual, we walk until we reach the statue of the Madonna, and the red fish pool. As we throw our bits of bread into the water, I notice that the pope looks on engrossed, watching the little fish dart about having a feast.

1 MONDAY
OCTOBER

We are preparing to leave the summer residence and move to the Vatican. Before his departure, the Holy Father greets with great courtesy and gratitude the community of Castel Gandolfo, the *carabinieri*, the helicopter pilots, and the staff at the papal villas.

After the recital of the Rosary in the afternoon, the staff attend the "lucky grab" event at the pavilion — a sort of a cloister within the gardens — which takes place before the pope leaves the summer residence. This is so called as it entails the distribution to the staff of gifts received in the previous months. These are laid across a long table and are up for grabs, so to speak. The children of the staff anxiously await this moment, and the pope himself calls out the names of those drawn first. The director of the villas, Saverio Petrillo, greets the pope in the name of all present, and is kind enough to think of extending to me a welcome to the pontifical family.

Later, after we finish reciting the Rosary, we stop for a minute or two to chat as we sit on the usual bench close to Our Lady "of the little fish." Somehow our conversation ends up with us talking about a Spanish Discalced Carmelite, Fr. Jesús Castellano Cervera, who, incidentally, was the director of my doctoral dissertation. The pope knew him well because he was also a consulter of the Congregation for the Doctrine of the Faith. He wants to know how he died and about the dramatic two-day search in all of the hospitals that was undertaken by the Discalced Carmelite community at the Teresianum on the Janiculum Hill due to the fact that they had not heard from him. It transpired that since the friar did not have any identity papers on his person, he had been taken to the hospital's mortuary to await the discovery of his identity. I confide to the pope that Fr. Jesús frequently gave me sound advice and that without any doubts he would have been pleased to learn of my new appointment in this new service, to which the pope comments that Fr. Jesús must certainly be delighted then in Heaven.

3 WEDNESDAY OCTOBER

The time has come to go back to the Vatican. It is a moment of great emotions for me. I take up residence in the papal apartment for the first time and start on my new duties in a new office. Here I am fortunate enough that I have some people to help me arrange the furniture and organize the books and other personal items that were transferred in cardboard boxes from Santa Marta.

I recall with a smile my hurried transfer from the apartment that I had at my disposal inside St. John Lateran, when I was the secretary of the rector of the university. Now I find myself living in this new home made available to me, and though I am happy, I do not want to attach myself unduly to these magnificent new surroundings. I believe I have learned my lesson well.

The pope continues with his catechesis dedicated to the Fathers of the Church during the general audience. Today, it is Cyril of Alexandria's turn. I am always struck by the pope's capacity to give current significance to past personages and their teachings. One phrase in particular attracts my attention during today's catechesis when, citing *Deus caritas est*, Benedict says, "The Christian faith is first of all an encounter with Jesus, a person who 'gives life a new horizon.'"

6 SATURDAY OCTOBER

I find it very comforting that this afternoon the Holy Father will receive the sacrament of Penance from a religious confessor. He does this on a regular basis and is for me a very inspirational witness.

This evening, while we are having a brief walk after supper, I ask the Holy Father if it is possible for me to celebrate Holy

Confessional regularly used for the Confession of the Pontiff.

Mass at the beginning of the civil New Year in the chapel of the Association of Sts. Peter and Paul. The association, to which I used to be the spiritual advisor, is comprised of Catholics residing in Rome. They are professionals, artisans, students, teachers, and workers who, apart from their personal and professional responsibilities, dedicate the necessary time to various voluntary initiatives. The Holy Father immediately gives me permission and asks if I also have to deliver a homily. I reply in the affirmative and say that I wish to preach about the disciples' request to the Lord to deepen their faith. I comment also that "for a spiritual adviser, there seems to be nothing better than this topic. I want to be able to help the members to purify their motivation. The essential thing is to undergo a journey of faith." He indicates his approval.

14 SUNDAY OCTOBER

It is my birthday, the first one to celebrate in the pope's home. Filled with gratitude to the Lord for granting me forty-nine years of life, I go to Holy Mass, during which I pray for my parents and friends in a very special way. It is a great surprise when, after I have proclaimed the Gospel, the pope moves to the ambo to deliver a homily. Later, on my way to breakfast, I find the pope waiting for me with a nicely wrapped package in his hand, which he presents to me with his best wishes. It is the Maltese translation of his book *Jesus of Nazareth: From the Baptism in the Jordan to the Transfiguration*. He writes a personal note on its first page; what a privilege!

At the Angelus, Benedict addresses the crowd gathered in St. Peter's Square. He speaks on the Gospel's passage, which narrates the healing of the ten lepers by Jesus. He says, "Indeed, the 'leprosy' that truly disfigures the human being and society is sin; it is pride and selfishness that spawn indifference, hatred and violence in the human soul. No one, save

God who is Love, can heal this leprosy of the spirit which scars the face of humanity."

A little later, the pope expresses his preoccupation with the situation in Iraq, from which news of attacks and violence continues to arrive. There are two priests of the Syriac Catholic Archeparchy of Mosul who have been kidnapped and threatened with execution. The Holy Father launches an appeal to the kidnappers and asks for their prompt release. He is very clear with his words: "I once again reassert that violence does not resolve tensions. I raise a heartfelt prayer to the Lord for their liberation, for all the victims of violence and for peace." The pope's apprehension regarding this situation is very evident, but he does not allow his preoccupied state of mind to have an impact on his day's work routine with us.

15 MONDAY OCTOBER

There is a birthday card addressed to me in this morning's mail from Sr. Christine Felder. She is a member of the spiritual community of *Das Werk* (The Work). She informs me that the pope has spoken of me while on the telephone. These are the pope's words: "*Don Alfred ist ein gläubiger und frommer Mann, gibt mir einen ehrlichen Eindruck und hat das richtige Naturell, um sich gut im Appartamento einzufinden. Ich bin sehr froh über diese Wahl, sie war einfach richtig*" — that is, "Father Alfred is a man of faith and piety. He is a genuine person and has the right character attributes to feel good within the living setup at the apartment. I am very happy with his selection, and it was simply the right one." I hold on very closely to this portrait rendered by the pope, and I welcome it as a goal to reach. I will try to do my best to mirror it.

17 WEDNESDAY OCTOBER

During this morning's general audience, the pope announces the creation of twenty-three new cardinals, among whom is Fr. Umberto Betti, a Franciscan to whom I was secretary when he was the rector of the Lateran University. The pope told me of this news a couple of days ago, when we were at table.

Since I was unable to speak personally with Fr. Betti, I sent him a note with Mrs. Wilma, who goes to visit him every morning at the convent in Fiesole. He retired there after he left his favorite convent at La Verna for good. I am truly happy, and I can hardly wait for the moment to see him here, when he is given the cardinal's hat on November 24.

Fr. Betti, born in 1922, is a theologian with vast experience. He participated at Vatican II as a consulter to the Preparatory Theological Commission and then as an expert and theologian for Archbishop Ermenegildo Florit of Florence. The pope has stated that he is elevating Fr. Betti to the dignity of cardinal because he is particularly deserving, due to his work in the service of the Church. How can one disagree with this? One day his brother confided in me that he saw him burdened by work more than many men who work in the fields.

19 FRIDAY OCTOBER

Today, Mrs. Clelia Moneta has come to pay a visit to the pope. After speaking with the pope, she wishes to meet me. She is a lady of simple tastes, a true Roman to the core, who lives in a small apartment at the Congregation for the Doctrine of the Faith. She came to live in the Vatican with her father, who was hired as a porter and had remained living there with her brother Alfredo. Following the death of their father, when an official in charge of the buildings of the Holy See at APSA decided to ask her to relocate outside Vatican City, Cardinal Ratzinger worked out a deal by which she could remain occupying the apartment, having lived there for so long. Alfredo, now quite old, came with her. He was the driver of the then-prefect of the Congregation for the Doctrine of the Faith. I noticed that both Clelia and Alfredo continue to refer to Benedict as "the cardinal." We speak about this visit during dinner. I am struck by the simplicity of the soul of the Holy Father and his availability to elderly visitors.

21 SUNDAY OCTOBER

Benedict XVI admires the "Presepe Bianco" nativity scene on display in the Royal Pontifical Basilica Church of San Francesco di Paola in Naples during the pastoral visit of October 21, 2007.

Today the pope went to Naples for a one-day visit. Apart from the faithful of that diocese, the pope met with some representatives of world religions, assembled there by the Community of St. Egidio. They were to reflect together on the theme "For

a world without violence." During his greeting of the participants at the seminary of Capodimonte, Benedict recalled the encounters of the Prayer for Peace at Assisi in 1986 and 2002, propagated by John Paul II. At the event he issued a very clear admonition: "In the face of a world torn apart by conflicts, where violence in God's Name is at times justified, it is important to reaffirm that religions can never become vehicles of hatred; it is never possible, invoking God's Name, to succeed in justifying evil and violence."

Once back at the Vatican, the pope informs us that the archbishop of Canterbury, Rowan Williams, had inquired about the canonization of Cardinal John Henry Newman. When Williams discovered that there needs to be a miracle, he responded with a very surprising question: "And if the Anglicans unite with the Catholic Church, would that be considered a miracle?" The pope told us that he responded that it would really be a great miracle. Then, after supper, becoming pensive, he returned to the comment of Archbishop Williams and said, "Who knows what he had in mind!"

24 WEDNESDAY OCTOBER

The pope spoke passionately about the great St. Ambrose of Milan during today's general audience. I intuited that he holds him as a model, and I was struck with the passage in which Benedict emphasized that for both Ambrose and Augustine catechesis is inseparable from the witness of life. He stated that, in the end, "the true disciple is ultimately the one whose proclamation of the Gospel is the most credible and effective." This also applies to all theologians. Then the pope referred to Augustine's amazement that Ambrose read in silence — that is, only with his mind. This was extraordinary, as at that time it was advocated that reading should always be done aloud.

One of the Memores Domini asks me if I am comfortable in my new lodgings. I reply that the start of my stay has been excellent and that I am very pleased with this experience as a member of the pope's family. This prompts me to realize that we who live here should not be happy solely because we are living so close to the Vicar of Christ, but even more because living with him is like attending a school of character formation. In fact, his example and words help us to maintain among ourselves a high level of charity and fraternity. Indeed, living with the pope makes us understand that there is never a need to fall into futile talk or act outside the boundaries of charity. It is a very simple fact: we are most fortunate!

Sitting area in the papal apartment. Moment of recreation with the four Memores Domini who assist Pope Benedict.

ALFRED XUEREB

27 SATURDAY OCTOBER

This evening, at the Paul VI Hall, we attended with the Holy Father a concert by the Bavarian Radio Symphony Orchestra and Choir under the direction of the conductor Mariss Jansons. The pope greatly appreciated the rendition of Beethoven's Ninth Symphony — which the pope indicated in his opening greeting as "belonging to the universal patrimony of humanity" — and of the *Tu es Petrus*. Benedict's speech was outstanding. Being well versed in Beethoven, he contrasted the composer's "silent solitude," due to his becoming deaf, with a phrase from the prophet Isaiah that states, "In that day the deaf shall hear the words of a book, and out of their gloom and darkness the eyes of the blind shall see" (29:18). Next, the Holy Father, before thanking everyone with the typical Bavarian expression of "Vergelt's Gott" (a heartfelt thanks), noted that in 1989, the Bavarian Radio Symphony Orchestra and Choir performed the Ninth Symphony under the direction of Leonard Bernstein, on the occasion of the

The two Ratzinger brothers listen attentively at the concert.

fall of the Berlin Wall. They changed the text of the "Ode to Joy" to "Freedom, beautiful spark of God," thereby underlining the fact that "true joy is rooted in that freedom that, basically, only God can bestow," because "He wants to make us — sometimes through periods of emptiness and inner isolation — attentive and capable of 'hearing' His silent presence not only 'above the star-strewn vault' but in the innermost depths of our soul."

The pope's brother, Msgr. Georg, came from Germany especially for the concert. He has been with us for a number of days. It is marvelous to see the interaction between the two brothers and to note the pope's attentiveness toward his older brother, who has health issues.

During these days we celebrate Holy Mass and recite the Rosary in Latin to accommodate Msgr. Ratzinger, who is not well versed in the Italian language.

1 THURSDAY
NOVEMBER

Today, along with the Holy Father, the Memores, and Msgr. Gänswein, I watched a film on the recently restored chapel of the secretary of state, Cardinal Tarcisio Bertone. We visited the chapel yesterday for the recitation of the Rosary and blessing. It is well refurbished and houses some frescoes dating back to 1567 that were originally intended for the chapel of the Pontifical Swiss Guard during the pontificate of St. Pius V. That chapel is better known as the chapel of St. Martin of the Swiss and is located close to the Basilica of St. Peter's. Nowadays it is overshadowed by the colonnade on the right side of St. Peter's Square.

Following the inauguration of the chapel yesterday, Cardinal Bertone hosted us for supper at his apartment on the First Loggia. There was a good atmosphere among us and a lot of cordiality between the pope and the cardinal. Everyone knows very well that the secretary of state worked for many years at the Congregation for the Doctrine of the Faith with the then-Cardinal Ratzinger.

3 SATURDAY
NOVEMBER

As I recite Psalm 4 of this evening's Night Prayer, I remain deeply comforted by the words of the psalmist when he states, "You have given my heart more joy than they have when grain and wine abound." My soul overflows, in effect, with a lively gratitude to God for filling me with His presence, which brings joy, peace, and meekness. These are the fruit of His abiding in me.

I find strength during difficult times in the words of a priest, Fr. Silvano Cola, whom I have known since my seminary days. He wrote in his spiritual testament of wanting "to be entirely in

God, without any wrinkle." If one keeps within oneself feelings and emotions, ideas and projects without entrusting them to Christ, one causes great wounds in one's soul, rendering it less transparent and full of shadows. I want to make this joy as a gift to the Holy Father in my relationship with him.

Following custom, the pope went this morning to the Basilica of St. Peter's to celebrate Holy Mass in memory of the cardinals and bishops who died during these past twelve months. We, the secretaries, stood next to the prefect of the papal household and the archbishop-almoner of His Holiness.

9 FRIDAY
NOVEMBER

This afternoon the Crescenti couple came to Rome to see the pope. They have known Joseph Ratzinger for over forty years — that is, from the time that the future pope came to Rome to participate in the sessions of Vatican II. Their friendship remained intact and even deepened when Ratzinger became the prefect of the Congregation for the Doctrine of the Faith. The then-cardinal in fact officiated at the marriage of their daughter and baptized the two grandchildren who came from the union that he himself blessed. It was also scheduled that he would baptize the third grandchild, but a few days before the birth, Cardinal Ratzinger was elected pope!

The couple recounted all of this to me with great animation. However, when I told them that his papal election must have generated much joy in them, the wife, with tears in her eyes, told me with great sincerity, "Not in the least! We were very sad because we understood that we will not meet as frequently as before!" However, in spite of this, they managed to make frequent visits. It is wonderful to discover this more intimate side of the pope's character, this capacity to keep relationships of friendship alive.

14 WEDNESDAY NOVEMBER

The urn that contains the remains of St. Thérèse of Lisieux was brought to the private chapel of the Holy Father at the end of today's general audience. The reliquary had been brought to Rome during these days to mark the tenth anniversary of St. Thérèse as a Doctor of the Church. It is on a long pilgrimage across the whole of Italy that will continue until the end of the year. We gathered in prayer with Bishop Pierre Auguste Gratien Pican of Bayeux and Lisieux, the rector of the Basilica of Lisieux, and a few more persons to venerate the remains of the sainted Carmelite.

Today also, during the general audience, the pope was presented with an intriguing book by Jeanne Perego entitled *Joseph and Chico*. It is the narration of the life of Pope Benedict XVI by a tabby cat! The amazing thing is that the cat actually exists and belongs to the Ratzingers' neighbor in Pentling in Bavaria.

While we were at table, the pope spoke to us about the pleasant meetings he has had with the author of this book for children, and he revealed to us that, when he was a cardinal, he thought of writing a book on cats once he retired. It was a dream that obviously has remained in the drawer. He commented, "The irony of fate: instead of me speaking about cats, it is the neighbor's cat that speaks about me!" We had a great laugh.

18 SUNDAY NOVEMBER

The Holy Father today reminds the faithful during the Angelus that the Servant of God Antonio Rosmini will be declared "Blessed" at Novara. He enunciates words that manifest his sincere esteem toward the new Blessed, highlighting his contribution to the reconciliation between reason and faith and describing him as "a great figure as a priest and an illustrious man of culture, animated by his fervent love toward God and the Church."

Prior to this, during the morning Holy Mass in his private chapel, the pope shared with us a great homily. We thanked him at table, and I shared with him a point that had particularly touched me, namely that the heavenly Father constantly works to answer our prayers. With this in mind, I mentioned to him a couple whom I know, who had gone into a crisis after the birth of their second girl. I had prayed a lot for them. They recently informed me of the return of serenity in their life and had gone to Holy Mass together to thank God. One can see that God had worked in the recesses of their hearts, blessing them with feelings of reconciliation and forgiveness. The Holy Father seemed pleased.

In the afternoon I asked permission from the pope to go have supper with some friends at their home. He immediately consented, but not only that! The pope asked me if these friends were Maltese and then suggested that I take with me one of the desserts he had received as a gift. My friends were overwhelmed with joy when they discovered that the dessert was sent to them by none other than the pope himself!

19 MONDAY NOVEMBER

There is an important audience today with the members of the Episcopal Conference of Kenya. Benedict is very concerned with the campaigns to introduce even in Africa a distorted idea of the family, based on a global secularized cultural model. He is particularly very

Detail of the majestic Michelangelo's dome of St. Peter's Basilica.

saddened with the attempts to promote abortion. Therefore, he has prepared a forceful speech in which he states that "this direct destruction of an innocent human life can never be justified, however difficult the circumstances that may lead some to consider taking such a grave step."

Benedict will meet in two days' time with members of FAO, the United Nations organization for food and agriculture, and here, too, he will not mince words. He will gently insist that progress cannot be tied solely to a technique but should also be nourished by the value of persons and peoples.

At breakfast the pope asks me how it went with last evening's dinner. I always remain stupefied that the pope, notwithstanding the many commitments of his ministry, manages to recall little things related to his collaborators. I recount to him the joy and gratitude of the family for his greetings and his gentle thoughtfulness. He smiles when I tell him that my friends, before tasting the dessert, wanted to take a photo of "the pope's cake" to keep as a memento.

24 SATURDAY NOVEMBER

Today is a very special day. While the Holy Father presides at the Ordinary Public Consistory, he creates twenty-three new cardinals. Due to bad weather, the ceremony takes place inside St. Peter's and not at the square in front of the basilica. The pope seems very pleased, and I thank him for the new cardinals because they are a great gift to the entire Church. It is the wish of Benedict that the universal Church be represented in the Roman Curia.

As soon as we enter the sacristy, and while the Holy Father is putting on his vestments, I notice Fr. Umberto Betti, with whom, as stated earlier, I had spent time as his secretary during his role as rector of the Lateran University. He is now confined to a wheelchair and in the first row of the candidates to become cardinals. Two of the members of his religious community inform him of my presence, at which point I embrace him, expressing my joy and esteem, affection and gratitude. The old friar, overflowing with emotions, cries quietly.

At the end of the ceremony, the pope decides to go to greet and address the people gathered in St. Peter's Square. He tells them, "Thank you for being here. We feared that it would rain, and so the ceremony was moved to inside the basilica. You remained here, full of courage, and joined us in prayer. I thank you for your prayerful presence, for your participation in this very important step for the Catholic Church. The new cardinals reflect the universality of the Church, her catholicity: the Church speaks in all the languages, embraces all the peoples, all the cultures. All of us, together, form the family of God. And we are united here like a family and let us pray that the Lord blesses these new cardinals who are at your service. And let us also pray that Our Lady accompanies us step by step."

25 SUNDAY NOVEMBER

"As you wear the cardinal's ring, you are constantly reminded to give your lives for the Church." The pope uses these words to address the new cardinals during the beautiful liturgy of the giving of the ring. Benedict is very emotional when he declares, "Venerable cardinal brothers, this is in a distinct way our responsibility: to announce to the world the truth of Christ, which is the hope of every person and for the entire human family. My venerable predecessors, the Servants of God Paul VI, John Paul I, and John Paul II, on the heels of Vatican II, were great heralds of the kingship of Christ in our contemporary world. It gives me great comfort that I can count on you, both as a group and as individuals, to assist me to bring to conclusion this fundamental responsibility of the Petrine ministry."

While waiting to go to the planned luncheon for the Holy Father and the new cardinals, I get a call from home: my father's condition has worsened. I hear my mother crying, and my sister, too, cannot hide her worries. They inform me that they have called the parish priest to administer the sacrament of the Anointing of the Sick to my father. During the luncheon hour, with the assistance of the Vatican Gendarmerie, I search for a flight to Malta. Unfortunately, since it is a Sunday, there is only one flight, and it left earlier in the morning.

26 MONDAY NOVEMBER

News from home states that my father is doing a little bit better. However, I have already decided to fly home notwithstanding. After the celebration of Holy Mass in the private chapel, I converse with the pope, who assures me that he is accompanying me with his prayers. Leaving, he turns back to ask me to convey his greetings to my parents. I deeply appreciate this gesture of exquisite fatherly care.

27 TUESDAY NOVEMBER

I feel serene and pleased that I went to Malta. I will always carry in my heart my father's smile, and the moral support of my mother, sister, and brother-in-law. On my return to Rome, at the very moment when I enter San Damaso Courtyard, I sense the feeling of having returned to my true home. I am surprised to realize that during my short trip to my native Gozo, my thoughts frequently drifted to the daily rhythm with the pope, and I recognize how much I miss it.

1 SATURDAY
1 DECEMBER

It has been customary for some years for the Holy Father to open the sacred time of Advent with the singing of First Vespers inside St. Peter's. Consequently, this being the first day of Advent, we go to the basilica for the occasion in late afternoon. The pope delivers a beautiful homily, and he makes me reflect on the exhortation to await the coming of the Savior, as promised.

The pope tells us that he wants to dedicate his second encyclical, *Spe salvi*, published yesterday, to the theme of hope. He says, "I am pleased to offer it in spirit to the entire Church on this First Sunday of Advent, so that, during preparation for Holy Christmas, the communities and individual faithful can read and meditate upon it to rediscover the *beauty and depth of Christian hope*. This, in fact, is inseparably bound to knowledge of the Face of God, the Face which Jesus, the Only-Begotten Son, revealed to us with his Incarnation, his earthly life and his preaching, and especially with his death and Resurrection. True and steadfast hope is founded on faith in God Love, the Merciful Father who 'so loved the world that he gave his Only Son' (John 3:16), so that men and women and with them all creatures might have life in abundance (cf. John 10:10). Advent, therefore, is a favorable time for the rediscovery of a hope that is not vague and deceptive but certain and reliable, because it is 'anchored' in Christ, God made man, the rock of our salvation." I connect these words to the young woman who anxiously awaits the return of her fiancé from war, and to the mother who awaits the return of her son who disappeared somewhere unknown. Hope springs eternal in such instances, even though human certainty is absent. Likewise, the return of Our Lord rests on a solid promise.

2 SUNDAY
DECEMBER

This morning the Holy Father pays a visit to the hospital of St. John the Baptist of the Sovereign Military Order of Malta. It is located on the Via Nomentana. During his homily, the pope reverts to the theme of Advent and says that "precisely because it is a time of waiting, Advent is a season of hope." Then I recall that the opening words of his new encyclical were those that St. Paul addressed to the Christians of Rome, "*Spe salvi facti sumus* — in hope we were saved" (Rom. 8:24). As I have remained at home, I follow the Holy Mass on television.

Later we visit Cardinal Tarcisio Bertone, secretary of state, at his residence as his guests for a brief concert to mark his seventy-third birthday. The eighty-year-old Maestro Pierluigi Sampietro plays the pianoforte, followed by the girl prodigy Masha Diatchenko, fifteen years old, with her violin. It is a very relaxing break and very pleasant, especially when the maestro takes the floor.

6 THURSDAY
DECEMBER

Today is the feast day of St. Nicholas. In accordance with the Bavarian tradition, our dining table in the papal apartment has been set up in a very special way. There is the spicy bread made by the Swiss Guards, and there are also nuts, peanuts, small chocolates, and mandarin oranges.

The festive family atmosphere prompts the Holy Father to tell us about an episode that happened during his childhood. One day a shining St. Nicholas all dressed in gold arrived at his nursery school at Tittmoning. "We children had no doubt: this was the real St. Nicholas! But, along with the saint, there was a bad man, dressed all in black, and the sisters pretended to keep him at bay, barring him at the doorway. The door was finally closed with a great effort, leaving the bad man outside, and the sisters, turning to us, told us to always be good because, they told us, their strength was in dire straits." All of us have a hearty laugh, but we are also left a little bit thoughtful about the eternal fight between good and evil.

7 FRIDAY DECEMBER

It is customary that on the Fridays of Advent and Lent, the preacher of the pontifical household presents a talk for the superiors at the Roman Curia. It takes place in the Redemptoris Mater Chapel. The pope is present. He, along with his two personal secretaries, follows the homily from the adjacent chapel, dedicated to St. Lawrence, which houses a priceless relic of the martyr.

The Franciscan friar Raniero Cantalamessa is the preacher of the papal household. For this year he chooses the theme "Jesus of Nazareth, one of the prophets?" It is a homily very rich in ideas regarding various opinions circulating about Jesus within and outside the Church, and especially on the so-called third search that is going on in our time. It is referred to as such so as to distinguish it from the "old search," which was inspired by the rationalists and liberals of the eighteenth and nineteenth centuries, as well as from the "new historical search," which, around the middle of this last century, declared the historical Jesus to be unattainable and irrelevant to the Christian faith. These are themes well known by Professor Joseph Ratzinger, who discusses them with great passion, as demonstrated in his books on Jesus.

8 SATURDAY DECEMBER

As I thought it was time that I pay a visit to the Association of Sts. Peter and Paul of which, as I have already stated, I was the spiritual advisor, this morning I join its members in their traditional procession to the Grotto of Lourdes inside the Vatican Gardens. After our homage to the Immaculate Virgin, I pause to greet the members and their families. Later at lunch, the Holy Father asks me how the procession went. He is surprised when I tell him how long it took for the procession, which included the recitation of the Rosary and the singing of hymns accompanied by a band. It started at San Damaso Courtyard, where the association has its headquarters, and moved up toward the gardens along the road of the observatory.

That afternoon, in line with ancient tradition, the Holy Father travels to the Piazza di Spagna as an act of homage to Our Lady. He states among other things that "on this solemn day, the Church once again holds up Mary to the world as a sign of sure hope and of the definitive victory of good over evil. The one whom we invoke as 'full of grace' reminds us that we are all brothers and sisters, and that God is our Creator and our Father. Without him, or even worse, against him, we human beings will never be able to find the way that leads to love, we will never be able to defeat the power of hatred and violence, we will never be able to build a lasting peace." This is the first time that I accompany the pope in Piazza di Spagna. The occasion is well attended, with many people standing on the steps of the Trinità dei Monti and in the square, as well as along the street.

Two private secretaries in Piazza di Spagna, during the act of homage to Our Lady.

One of the Advent wreaths, a traditional custom from Bavaria.

9 SUNDAY
DECEMBER

Some priests and sisters who are members of the spiritual family *Das Werk* (The Work) arrive in the afternoon of this Second Sunday of Advent. They lead the singing of Vespers in Latin in the pope's private chapel, with Benedict XVI presiding. Afterward, in the library on the Third Loggia, all of us join the pope in singing some Advent hymns. There is even one in Maltese entitled "Ejja Fostna Mulej" (Come among us, Lord). They sing the refrain and I sing the verses, and when we finish, the Holy Father shows his desire to learn the meaning of the words of the hymn just sung.

We have received many Advent wreaths from Germany that we set up in various places within the apartment. I am very pleased with this custom, and I have been given one to set up in my room.

23 SUNDAY
DECEMBER

It is the Fourth Sunday of Advent. By now, Christmas is at the door. "Come, Lord, and transform our hearts so that justice and peace will spread across the world." These were the words the pope said to the faithful gathered for the Angelus.

The pressure from my present job these days seems to be more than in previous responsibilities. The correspondence, the telephone calls, and various persons who ask to come by to greet me and to offer best wishes have transformed my days into a continuous exercise of altruism. I take into account that for many the occasion to see me carries the value of feeling closer to the pope. Thus, it is worthwhile to receive every one of them with courtesy and warmth. Pope Benedict is my teacher. Some of my friends laugh when I tell them that I feel unsophisticated next to the pope.

24 MONDAY DECEMBER

After some intense work at the office this morning, the evening vigil of Christmas has finally arrived. This is truly a very special Christmas for me. It is the first time that I experience it with the pope and his family, and I have replied to all those who have invited me to their homes that I will be spending Christmas with the new family that has adopted me.

At 6:00 p.m., the pope sets off to the window of his study to light the candle of peace. Below in the square, there are many people who have come for the inauguration of the Christmas crib, and the pope proceeds to bless them and places the lit candle on the windowsill where it will remain all night.

We dine earlier than usual, after which we gather in the sitting room. The pope himself explains to me that, according to Bavarian custom, the head of the household reads an excerpt of the Gospels and then intones some Christmas carols. He does just that, choosing for a reading the announcement of the birth of the Savior in the Gospel of St. Luke. It is a very impressive ambience, standing there in the dim light, gathered around the fir tree decorated and lit with candles on its branches, listening to the pope singing some Christmas carols. This is a propitious prelude to Midnight Mass, during which I feel a strong spiritual unity with the pope presiding at the Liturgy of the Eucharist. The homily is outstanding, recalling the encounter with God made man, who entered the world's sphere to enable us to meet the heavens and the divine reality. The salient moment is Holy Communion. Jesus, Son of God, be born in me to take away my sins and to save me.

Once the Holy Mass is over, we gather in the room next to the kitchen to share a glass of sparkling wine and a slice of the panettone.

In recollection at the end of the Holy Christmas Vigil Mass in St. Peter's.

25 TUESDAY DECEMBER

Due to the fact that all of us went to bed rather late, we had a later than usual celebration of Holy Mass at the private chapel, where I felt that our singing was more harmonious than usual.

At breakfast we commented on the Midnight Mass, especially about the questions that the Holy Father had posed: "Do we have time for our neighbor who is in need of a word from us, from me, or in need of my affection? For the sufferer who is in need of help? For the fugitive or the refugee who is seeking asylum? Do we have time and space for God? Can He enter into our lives? Does He find room in us, or have we occupied all the available space in our thoughts, our actions, our lives for ourselves?"

Later, at noon, the pope delivers the traditional message in the Hall of Benedictions, which is followed by the greetings, given in sixty-three languages this year, including for the first time the Guaranì language, which is spoken in Paraguay. I feel very close to the Holy Father and look for signs of internal unity with him as I pay close attention to his words. Many, including my relatives, see me on television standing on the famous balcony from which a new pope is announced. It is a beautiful and great feeling to find oneself next to the pope!

The pope's Christmas greetings include one even in the Maltese language, and regarding this, I wish to give some background. A couple of days before Christmas, when the texts of the greetings were delivered, the pope requested that my language should also be included in the list of greetings, which I gladly obliged. Moreover, Benedict also showed his desire to hear from me the right pronunciations of the phrase in Maltese. Once I did so, he commented, "It seems to me that this greeting is very short." I explained to him that the greeting in former years was longer, but it was shortened to help the pope read all of the phrases. The pope, however, preferred the original greeting. Consequently, at the suggestion of Msgr. Gänswein, I called those responsible for composing the greetings to ask them to use the original greeting in Maltese. When the pope read it, he burst into a smile. I felt very proud of this gift being given to my people.

Later this afternoon, we gather again in the sitting room to sing some Christmas carols in the dim light of the candles of the Christmas tree. At a certain moment, while I am sitting relaxed, the Holy Father turns toward me, looks at me, and says, "Your predecessor Fr. Mietek always sang for us some carol from his native land. Do you have any Maltese carol to sing for us?" I go immediately to my office to retrieve some music and the lyrics of three Maltese carols that I recently received. While I sing the verses, the Memores and Msgr. Gänswein sing the refrain with me, which fortunately they rehearsed a couple of days ago. When we have finished singing, the Holy Father, as he did with the Advent hymn, wants to know the meaning of the words.

26 WEDNESDAY DECEMBER

During today's Angelus, taking as his cue the figure of the protomartyr St. Stephen, the pope notes that even in our own times, "we receive news from various parts of the world of missionaries, priests, Bishops, men and women religious and lay faithful who are persecuted, imprisoned, tortured, deprived of freedom or prevented from exercising it because they are disciples of Christ and apostles of the Gospel; at times, they even suffer and die for being in communion with the universal Church or for their fidelity to the Pope." The dimension of martyrdom belongs to the Christian: we are called

The traditional
greeting message
Urbi et Orbi, from the
Loggia of the Blessing,
with greetings in
various languages.

to accept the cross and death, transforming them into an act of love. "What on the outside is simply brutal violence — the Crucifixion — from within becomes an act of total self-giving love.... Violence is transformed into love, and death into life."

Today, once again, we recite Vespers together in the private chapel, and then, like yesterday, we gather in the sitting room to sing some Christmas carols and to listen to a Christmas story. And what a big surprise it is when the Holy Father sits at the pianoforte and begins playing "Ninni la tibkix izjed" (Sleep and cry no more), a lullaby to Baby Jesus that is very popular among the Maltese people! I am profoundly moved.

27 THURSDAY DECEMBER

During the usual daily walk in the Vatican Gardens after praying the rosary, the Holy Father asked me to tell him some Maltese Christmas traditions.

I explained that on the evening of Christmas Eve, there is a simple yet meaningful procession, with the Christ Child carried on the people's shoulders down the main roads. Then there is the so-called "child's sermon" in a square or in church before the start of midnight Mass. Benedict was impressed when I told him that each year this sermon is given by a child around ten years old, who memorizes a text written by the parish priest.

During the walk in the Gardens, the conversation often turns to animals and their world. Today, after telling me that in Germany many prepare little wooden houses to give shelter and food to the birds during the winter, the Holy Father recalled with a hint of sadness, "My mother always fed the birds and, when she had drawn close to death, she wondered with concern who would think of the birds after her." I was left with great admiration for the sensitivity of mother Maria who, even at the time of her death, did not turn her thoughts to herself.

28 FRIDAY DECEMBER

Ever since he was a small boy, the pope has had a great affinity toward Christmas cribs, especially the traditional ones. The dining room has a very special Christmas crib that has been his for many years. It is very moving to see the pope, before luncheon, recall some event from the past every time he passes by this Christmas crib. Some of the little statues go back to his time at his home in Bavaria. There are some sheep that his sister, Maria, covered with wool. One perceives that the pope still has a fondness toward those who gave him some of the statuettes, and as he touches one of them, he recalls the giver's name.

I notice that Benedict's heart fills with joy even more than usual when his brother comes to visit from Germany. He anxiously fusses over him, and it is very moving to see how they dialogue and help one another.

Pope Benedict with his brother Georg, to whom he bears a particular affection.

30 SUNDAY DECEMBER

These days are very intense and there is a lot of work to be done. I go to survey the convent of the Sisters of Schönstatt this afternoon, after the recitation of the Rosary. The pope will go there for a private visit this coming Thursday. The residence, located on Via Aurelia, is very beautiful, sitting in the midst of much greenery, and the community residing there is even more beautiful. I am greeted by each religious, one following the other, the local superior, and Sr. Birgit, who works at the private office of Benedict XVI. They show me the route that the Holy Father will take on his visit.

31 MONDAY DECEMBER

We go to the basilica at 6:00 p.m. for Vespers for the Solemnity of Mary, Mother of God, and the Te Deum to mark the end of the civil year. The pope says in his homily, "Time passes and its inexorable passing induces us to raise our gaze in deep gratitude to the One who is eternal, to the Lord of time." Then he turns to the central theme of his homily, that is, to the participants of the convention for the Diocese of Rome: the pressing needs of education — that is, "the increasing difficulty encountered in transmitting the basic values of life and upright conduct to the new generations." He acknowledges that there are problems, but "it is certainly comforting to note that the work undertaken in recent years by parishes, movements and associations for the pastoral care of the family is continuing to develop and bear fruit."

All of us gather together in the sitting room — the pope, the Memores, and us secretaries — to celebrate the end of the year. We sing, pray, share a glass of *vin brûlé*, and try some typical German Christmas biscuits.

My Days with

Benedict XVI

2008

1 TUESDAY JANUARY

I offer thanks to the Lord for granting me the grace to start another new year and for the innumerable blessings He has bestowed upon me, the last and not least of which is this new responsibility in the secretariat of Benedict XVI. I want to begin 2008 with these words of thanksgiving from my heart, despite some health difficulties.

We celebrate the morning Holy Mass in the private chapel without the pope because he will be presiding at the 10:00 a.m. Holy Mass of the Solemnity of Mary, Mother of God, together with us secretaries assisting but not concelebrating.

The Catholic Church, on the first day of the new year, celebrates the World Day of Peace. The Holy Father has chosen for the year 2008 the theme "The human family, the community of peace," and at this Mass, addressing the faithful who pack the basilica, the pope states, "Today, we are beginning a new year and Christian hope takes us by the hand; let us begin it by invoking divine Blessings upon it and imploring, through the intercession of Mary, Mother of God, the gift of peace: for our families, for our cities, for the whole world."

Recalling in the homily what he has already written in his message, he states, "The natural family, founded on the marriage of a man and a woman, is 'a cradle of life and love' and the 'first and indispensable teacher of peace.' For this very reason the family is 'the primary agency of peace,' and 'the denial or even the restriction of the rights of the family, by obscuring the truth about man, threatens the very foundations of peace.'" Truly powerful and courageous words.

We return to the Apostolic Palace just before noon for the Angelus, which is recited from the private study of the pope. The square is full of people, all waiting for Benedict's words and greetings. His opening words are simply beautiful:

"We have begun a new year and I hope that it may be serene and profitable for all. I entrust it to the heavenly protection of Mary, whom we invoke in today's liturgy with her most ancient and important title, that of Mother of God." Then follow words of thanks and a very special greeting to Italy: "I cordially thank all of those who sent good wishes for the New Year. I wish to single out in a very special way the president of the Italian Republic who conveyed his greetings while addressing the nation on television. I hasten to exchange my best wishes, conveying the best wishes for his lofty mission and for the harmony and prosperity of the beloved Italian nation."

3 THURSDAY
JANUARY

Due to the absence of Msgr. Gänswein, who is visiting his relatives in Germany, my days have become more demanding. However, outpouring my love for the Lord and for the Holy Father has made my burden light.

After the Rosary, as has been foreseen, the pope visits the community of the Sisters of Schönstatt. Following a very warm welcome, there is a liturgical celebration in the small chapel, followed by a surprise for the pope: due to the fact that by now he is unable to go around Rome to view his much-loved Christmas cribs, the sisters project on a screen some photographs of nativity scenes, a much-appreciated virtual tour. After the singing of some Christmas carols in German, as well as one in Maltese, we partake of dinner and return home.

4 FRIDAY
JANUARY

I am honored to accompany the Holy Father as he visits the Dono di Maria shelter, where the Missionaries of Charity of Mother

"Gift of Mary" House, Vatican City. The joyful welcome from novices of the Missionaries of Charity upon the arrival of Pope Benedict.

Teresa of Calcutta help needy persons. We pass through the atrium of Paul VI Hall and are welcomed by a group of novices who render an Indian dance and song. Benedict is touched by both the words of the song and the very happy faces of the novices.

The visit begins in the women's section, where the pope wants to greet every one of the guests. This is followed by having something to eat with the men. Next, he goes to see the sick guests and finally to the church where there are some Fathers of Charity, and many volunteers and their families. The pope returns home very happy. He mentions at luncheon that he wishes the Memores had been present and participated in this beautiful and touching experience.

I assist in a singular event in the afternoon: there is a concert by the Sistine Choir in the Sistine Chapel in honor of the pope's brother, Georg Ratzinger. The chapel's perfect acoustics provide an unforgettable execution of pieces from Perosi, Victoria, Palestrina, and Liberto, the last being the conductor of the Pontifical Chapel Choir. The pope delivers some words of gratitude to the renowned choir at the end of the concert. He encourages the younger singers to imitate Jesus who, from His childhood, sang the Psalms to praise God.

6 SUNDAY JANUARY

"Today, we are celebrating Christ, Light of the world, and his manifestation to the peoples." These are the opening words the pope addresses to the faithful assembled inside the Vatican Basilica for the celebration of Holy Mass on the Solemnity of the Epiphany of the Lord.

Then the Holy Father picks up again the theme of Christian hope: "If true hope is lacking, happiness is sought in drunkenness, in the superfluous, in excesses, and we ruin ourselves and the world. It is then that moderation is not only an ascetic rule but also a path of salvation for humanity. It is already obvious that only by adopting a sober lifestyle, accompanied by a serious effort for a fair distribution of riches, will it be possible to establish an order of just and sustainable development. For this reason, we need people who nourish great hope and thus have great courage: the courage of the Magi, who made a long journey following a star and were able to kneel before a Child and offer him their precious gifts. We all need this courage, anchored to firm hope."

I take great courage from the words of the prophet Isaiah proclaimed in the first reading of the Holy Mass, which we secretaries celebrated in the private chapel, in the presence of the Memores. The same reading is repeated at the Holy Mass, celebrated by the pope in St. Peter's, which I assist in. The words were "Then you shall see and be radiant, your heart shall thrill and rejoice; because the abundance of the sea shall be turned to you" (Isa. 60:5). The light and the glory that enveloped the Messiah at His Incarnation are certainly extended to us, His ministers, and to all the baptized through the great gift of the Holy Spirit! Listening to these words, I feel my heart expand with joy for the high dignity with which I have been clothed.

Today I remember, in a special way during the Holy Mass, my brother Patrick on the eleventh anniversary of his premature death.

7 MONDAY
JANUARY

I have scheduled for today my departure for Malta, where I plan to spend five days at my parents' home, specifically to visit with my ailing father. With ticket in hand and my luggage prepared, I am ready to go. However, at this late hour, Msgr. Gänswein explains to me how important it is for him to go to Fribourg to participate at the funeral of Archbishop Oskar Saier, who ordained him to the priesthood. So I willingly agree to change my plans and postpone my departure by a week, which pleases both Msgr. Gänswein and the pope, who appreciate my flexible availability. Despite this unforeseen change in my plan, my heart is full of joy.

Msgr. Georg Ratzinger will leave tomorrow to return to Regensburg, Germany. It was wonderful to see the two brothers together, as they share a great love toward one another. Joseph is always helping Georg, who is three years older and, in addition to having poor eyesight, has some trouble walking.

9 WEDNESDAY
JANUARY

We had a great scare today. After breakfast, the gendarme in service at Sixtus V Courtyard calls to alert us that smoke is coming out of the window of the private chapel. All of us run to the chapel, where we find the Christmas tree and the Christmas crib, made of cloth, in flames. We put out the flames in a few minutes. Meanwhile the fire brigade is called, and they finish off the operation. The Holy Father is very disappointed that his Christmas crib, decorated with statuettes dressed in typical Bavarian outfits, lays destroyed. He immediately begins to think of how to replace it.

10 THURSDAY
JANUARY

Msgr. Gänswein is out of town. Therefore, I accompany the Holy Father at this morning's audiences. One of them is for the administrators of the city of Rome, of the province, and of the region of Lazio. The pope, even on this occasion, again asks for the respect of the human person and for the protection of the family, which is founded on a marriage between one man and one woman. Next, he underlines the need to concretely deal with the scourge of poverty, which not only has found its way even to the urban suburbs but is also beginning to manifest itself in other contexts. The pope's words are very powerful when, recalling the murder of Mrs. Giovanna Reggiani at Tor di Quinto, he says that "here especially, constant and concrete interventions are required that go far beyond the emotion of the moment, which has the twofold and inseparable purpose of guaranteeing the safety of citizens and assuring everyone, particularly immigrants, of at least the minimum indispensable for an honest and dignified life."

During the afternoon, after the Rosary, the Holy Father reiterates his appreciation that I chose to postpone my visit to Malta.

13 SUNDAY
JANUARY

The ceremony of the Baptism of thirteen babies taking place this morning inside the Sistine Chapel is simply beautiful. The pope himself administers the sacrament on this Solemnity of the Baptism of Our Lord. We, the secretaries, participate in the papal chapel after celebrating Holy Mass in the private chapel. At lunch the pope looks very pleased and comments, "Today the Church has thirteen new Christians!"

There is a nice incident at the end of Holy Mass in the Sistine Chapel. The Holy Father, on becoming aware that his Fisherman's Ring had slipped off his finger, asks one of the pontifical masters of ceremonies to look for it. As we are later watching the news on television, the incident is reported, at which the pope, enjoying himself, lets out a laugh.

Benedict wanted to use at the Baptism the seashell that was a gift from Mayor Veltroni of Rome. He also decided that the monstrance that was a gift from the president of the province of Rome, Enrico Gasbarra, will be used for the Eucharistic Adoration during the upcoming spiritual exercises.

The Christmas festivities end in the afternoon with the praying of Vespers together and later with listening to the last part of the Christmas concert of Bach with the participation of the Domspatzen Choir of Regensburg.

23 WEDNESDAY JANUARY

October 18, 2003: Pope John Paul II greets Cardinal Joseph Ratzinger during a general audience in the Paul VI hall in the Vatican.SJ

Now and again, we have a guest for lunch, and yesterday it was the turn of Cardinal Paul Josef Cordes, president of the Pontifical Council Cor Unum. Today we have as a guest Cardinal Stanisław Dziwisz, the current archbishop of Cracow and the former personal secretary of Karol Wojtyła. He tells us some news regarding John Paul II, specifically about the many graces that people, in and outside Poland, receive through his intercession. A Polish gentleman told him of the healing of his twin sons. The doctors had told him of the certain death of one of the twins, but the father took them to the parish priest. When the priest placed one of John Paul II's zucchettos on the twins, they were healed, an act that science cannot explain. Next, he recalls for us the day when the pope died, of his serenity and total absence of fear. According to Cardinal Dziwisz, the pope, to the very end, wanted to do everything that he always did: the Holy Mass, the Liturgy of the Hours, and Eucharistic Adoration. He had also asked that they read to him a section of the Gospel of St. John, beginning with chapter 9 and onwards, after which he asked to be left alone. The famous "let me go" can be interpreted in this sense: after he greeted everyone, he felt the need to remain alone in the proximity of his encounter with the Lord.

24 THURSDAY JANUARY

Today the Holy Father invites for luncheon Archbishop Mieczysław Mokrzycki, who worked at his secretariat until my arrival. Benedict shows great interest in the archbishop's first experiences as the coadjutor archbishop of Lviv of the Latins in Ukraine. Fr. Mietek, as he is generally known, talks about his first Christmas in Lviv and of some meetings in the diocese that he now serves.

27 SUNDAY JANUARY

As has been happening for these last few years on the last Sunday of January, the youths who participate in the Caravan of Peace promoted by the children's Catholic Action are present for the Angelus. A small representation has been escorted to the papal apartment to free two white doves from the window of the pope's study. A boy and a girl, Andrea and Federica, appear at the window, next to the pope. Federica, speaking for everyone, reads a brief message. Next follows the freeing of the doves, something that is always unpredictable. The Holy Father shows great warmth toward these young people. During our chat at lunch, the pope is very pleased to learn that one of the doves released this morning decided to rest on top of the Cross of Christ, which is at the top of the basilica's façade.

31 THURSDAY JANUARY

At lunch the conversation revolves around the feast of the Shipwreck of St. Paul, which the Maltese residing in Rome celebrate with a Holy Mass on February 10. The pope is very interested to learn where the eucharistic celebration will take place. When I explain that chapter 28 of the Acts of the Apostles is read during the Holy Mass because it speaks of the shipwreck of St. Paul, he asks whether Malta is mentioned in that passage. While I answer in the affirmative, I note that the pope is not convinced. He says that the name of the island does not appear in the Greek text. I remain perplexed but do not wish to contradict him. Sure enough, however, that evening, during supper, the pope returns to our discussion. He says that he looked up the text and realized that he was mistaken: the Greek text does mention Malta. I reply with a good dose of humor, "Thank goodness, because I almost began to lose the faith that St. Paul brought us!" All of us have a good laugh. I am struck with the magnanimity of this theologian pope, greatly versed in Sacred Scripture, who has no fear to admit that he was mistaken and corrects himself in front of everyone.

3 SUNDAY
FEBRUARY

Apart from being the day of the Lord, today marks also the feast of St. Blaise. Thus, at the end of Holy Mass, the pope is the first to receive what is called "the blessing of the throat" with two lit candles crossed over one another. Then he imparts the blessing on each of us. Afterward the pope informs me that this blessing is not exactly for the protection of the throat from colds, as is commonly believed, or from fish bone or other things that might prevent breathing. He explains that the holy bishop Blaise, who lived in Armenia during the third century, was a doctor, and it is known that he prayed for the recovery of persons and animals who were wounded either by a bone or a thorn in the throat.

4 MONDAY
FEBRUARY

Benedict XVI is highly esteemed by intellectuals and politicians for his exceptional cultural finesse and his clarity in search of truth. One of his great admirers is the former president of the Italian Republic, Francesco Cossiga, who loves sending the pope letters that contain very affectionate words. The pope, as a gesture to express his gratitude, has invited him to join us for today's lunch. I greet him before we sit at table. Since he knows I am from Malta, Cossiga shares with me some anecdotes about some of his Maltese friends, among whom is our former president, Vincent Tabone. He tells me that Tabone, being a doctor, cured some vision disorder suffered by Queen Elizabeth when she was staying in Malta at the time she was still princess. The luncheon is marked by a long speech by the president, during which, at one point, he hits his glass and spills the wine across the table. Without losing a beat, he states that in Sardinia, his native land, this is considered a good omen!

Later, on our walk in the Vatican Gardens, we reminisce about our luncheon. Everyone agrees that President Cossiga loves to talk and frequently skips from one topic to another, a sign of his joy at being able to dine with the "great theologian," as he usually refers to the pope, when speaking to us secretaries by telephone. All of us have a warmhearted smile.

6 WEDNESDAY FEBRUARY

Today is Ash Wednesday. The pope did not celebrate Holy Mass in the morning, because he will be presiding at Holy Mass at Santa Sabina Basilica on the Aventine. We proceed to the Church of St. Anselm in the afternoon to begin the introductory ritual, and then we continue toward Santa Sabina, where Holy Mass is celebrated.

The pope delivers a very beautiful homily, which contains some references to the encyclical *Spe salvi*. During the celebration I have the privilege to receive the ashes from the

Cardinal Jozef Tomko, priest of Santa Sabina, imposes the ashes on the Pope.

Holy Father with a great feeling of joy knowing that I will share this Lenten season with the pope!

Speaking of the rite, the pope tells us that when he was still a seminarian, it was customary to receive the ashes in the form of a dough that remained visible on one's forehead through the day as a sign of adhering to the penitential aspect of Christian Lent.

10 SUNDAY FEBRUARY

We pass this week, starting from this evening until Saturday, with the Holy Father in spiritual retreat. The retreat master this year is Cardinal Albert Vanhoye, a French Jesuit who is well known by Joseph Ratzinger. The former was the latter's very close collaborator for over ten years, from 1990 till 2001, in his role of secretary to the Pontifical Biblical Commission. He is considered to be one of the greatest students in biblical exegesis, specialized in the study of the Letter to the Hebrews.

We gather for the recitation of the Rosary at 4:00 p.m. This time, due to tomorrow's feast of Our Lady of Lourdes, we pause by the statue of Our Lady inside the Vatican Gardens and pray for the grace to obtain the indulgences proposed by the Apostolic Penitentiary on the 150th anniversary of the Marian apparitions.

The theme of the spiritual retreat, "We welcome Christ as the High Priest," is inspired by the Letter to the Hebrews. Following exposition of the Blessed Sacrament and the chanting of Vespers, Cardinal Vanhoye presents a meditation on how "God spoke to us" (Heb. 1:1–2). The Letter to the Hebrews is more than an epistle because it seems to be a homily in which is presented the centrality of Christ the Priest, who introduces man to a new form of communication with God. It speaks of a glorious Christ, "the sovereign

Benedict XVI thanks Cardinal Albert Vanhoye SJ, preacher of spiritual exercises to the Roman Curia.

Lord of all things." Next, the author of Hebrews presents Him with two dense and significant terms. While past prophets were presented as men chosen to speak of God to the people, Christ is "the refulgence of God's glory and imprint of His being." Being the Son of God, Christ radiates the divine glory through His Incarnation. While the face of Moses reflected the glory of God after he has spoken with Him, Christ is not simply a reflection but the imprint of His substance. There is a direct contact and an authentic radiation between Christ and the Father. We are very pleased with Fr. Vanhoye because he is offering us very rich ideas to meditate on during these spiritual exercises. We maintain our reflective mood during the meals by listening to sacred music.

11 MONDAY FEBRUARY

Cardinal Vanhoye, in today's meditation, reflects on the fact that Christ is the Son of God, as well as our brother. By taking on the humble form of our human existence, He was not spared any suffering or temptation throughout His life up to His death. He is shown as being merciful by assuming our human frailty. The glory of Christ is not that of a soldier who has defeated his enemy. Rather, it is the glory of that love with which He offers Himself on the Cross so as to reconcile us with the Father. Having washed human beings clean of their sins, Christ established a new creation, reestablishing for us our communion with God.

13 WEDNESDAY FEBRUARY

We continue our spiritual retreat, assisted by the silence that is maintained at all the meals and throughout the day. Cardinal Vanhoye explains to us how our reconciliation with God was established through the sacrifice of the High Priest who had offered Himself as the sacrificial victim of expiation.

The term *sacrifice* actually signifies "making sacred." Jesus, our High Priest, by offering His body in sacrifice underwent a sacred suffering and death. He fought and defeated death by His own death and Resurrection, and now lives gloriously forever. We have been clothed with this glory by our participation in His new priesthood. It is useless to speak to a dead person because he neither hears nor speaks, and thus it is impossible to establish a relationship. However, by making death sacred and redeeming it, Christ reopens the way to communication. We die in Jesus, and we live in the risen Christ.

15 FRIDAY FEBRUARY

The full communication between man and God, brought about through the offering of Christ on the Cross, renders Christians a privileged status when compared to the old Hebrew people. The blood, which was shed by the High Priest, making Himself the victim, has bestowed on us the right to enter the heavenly tent. On the other hand, the people of the Old Covenant were only allowed to enter up to the precincts of the temple courtyard and not into the actual building itself. Furthermore, the simple priests could not cross into the sanctuary of the Holy of Holies. The only person allowed to do so was the High Priest and then only once a year. There was a separation between the priest and the victim. But now, with Christ, the priest is the actual victim.

Thus, Christians, who through their Baptism participate in the priesthood of Christ, are able to offer themselves as an oblation to God and enter into an intimate communication with Him. This innovation reveals the profound desire of God to allow us to enter into an intimate relationship with Him. Seeking to please God does not mean to conform to a fixed code, but to unite oneself to His will and to allow God to continuously mold us. Cardinal Vanhoye perceived that "at times Christian preachers present many moral exhortations but not enough theological exhortations, which are the most important."

16 SATURDAY FEBRUARY

The spiritual exercises for the Roman Curia finish with today's meditation. The final topic is about the heart of Jesus, the channel of God's mercy toward men, and the union of the priest to the heart of Jesus.

Cardinal Vanhoye explains that in the Old Testament, the rite was not bound to the heart. The priest had the task of doing what was prescribed, without involving himself interiorly. On the other hand, in the New Testament, the offering to God in the name of the people also presumes the offering of one's self, as the High Priest Jesus has done. He offered His heart to the priests so that they, in turn, will offer their own hearts to others. The cardinal continues, saying that Christian life essentially consists in receiving the heart of Christ so as to acquire the same longings.

The Holy Father, at the end of the spiritual exercises, exits from St. Lawrence Chapel, where he listened to the meditations. While thanking the retreat master, he also shares a thought with all those present. He explains that from where he had been sitting, he was able to look at the figure of Christ, kneeling in front of Peter in the act of washing his feet. He says, "This image spoke to me and helped me to understand that the heart of a

priest must be similar to the heart of Jesus, who implores Peter to allow Him to pour into him the mercy of the Father." The red apparel of the kneeling Christ recalls how the divine mercy has come to men through the blood of Christ, offered in His Pas-

Detail of the mosaic by Fr. Marko Rupnik SJ in the *Redemptoris Mater* chapel, Apostolic Palace, Vatican City.

sion and death. As one who participates in the priesthood of Christ, the priest of the New Covenant receives a new heart, the heart of Jesus, and becomes the dispenser of saving mercy.

The pope goes on to say to the present cardinals and bishops, "But I was unable not to meditate on the figure of Peter with his finger pointing to his front. It seems to be that this gesture expresses the difficulty that Peter — and all the disciples — has in trying to understand the surprising news of the priesthood of Christ, that it is a priesthood of lowering oneself, of solidarity with us, and thus opens the access to the true Sanctuary, the Mystical Body of Christ." Thus, in order to grasp the true meaning of the new priesthood, it is always necessary to constantly listen to Jesus and to receive a new heart, the very heart of Jesus, as the center of the mystery of the New Covenant.

Cardinal Vanhoye is the pope's guest at luncheon. He tells us about his many commitments across the world, despite the fact that he is already eighty-five years old. His efforts to evangelize are truly admirable!

18 MONDAY FEBRUARY

A question frequently crosses my mind during the spiritual retreat: "Am I certain that it was the Lord who led me here, to have this extraordinary experience with the Holy Father?

Why did He do this to me?" I feel that all that I experience is like a school of formation — what is the Lord preparing me for? He knows that I do not aspire to great things, except to do His will. Even if I do not know what He wants of me, the awareness that He is forming me gives me strength to face, with even more faith, difficulties, sufferings, and the daily labor of life.

I call a person who worked with me in the Secretariat of State to wish him a happy birthday. He tells me that the Lord had His plans for me and that what I am experiencing will be of service. I remain struck by these words, for they match the feelings that I received from on high and welcomed into my heart.

21 THURSDAY
FEBRUARY

Due to the unavailability of the two prelates of the antechambers, I attend to the Second Loggia with the Holy Father to do some of their work. It's a good feeling to return to the locale in which I served for over four years — that is, until I was called to take on the responsibilities at the personal secretariat of His Holiness.

25 MONDAY
FEBRUARY

Msgr. Gänswein has left this morning with Domenico Giani, the commander of the Vatican Gendarmerie, to carry out an inspection at Bolzano and Bressanone. The Holy Father, in fact, has expressed his wish to go there for a few days of rest next summer.

The Holy Father makes me feel at ease even when we are together all alone. I accompany him this morning during the audiences, later for the Rosary in the afternoon, and finally to watch the news on television.

29 FRIDAY FEBRUARY

I have been asked again this morning to accompany the Holy Father to the audiences. Before I leave, I am shown how to assist the Holy Father in putting on the rochet, the mozzetta, the stole, and the pectoral cross. Today the pope receives the new ambassador from the United States for the presentation of the credential letters.

When we go to recite the Rosary in the gardens, I help the Holy Father put on his white jacket and scarf. These simple gestures create a very pleasant rapport between us, and the Holy Father appreciates our gentle concern in his regard.

An amusing incident occurs during the audience for the participants of the plenary assembly of the Pontifical Council Cor Unum. As is the custom, the person who heads the group called into audience delivers a brief opening greeting to the Holy Father in the name of all those present. This fell to the president, Cardinal Paul Josef Cordes. While in the process of standing up, he realizes that his eyeglasses are missing. One of the cardinals sitting next to him lets him borrow his eyeglasses. But when Cordes puts them on, he still is unable to read the text. Another cardinal does the same thing, but without success. The whole thing is now taking a rather long time, and so the pope, from his chair, offers poor Cardinal Cordes the use of his eyeglasses ... and these fit his eyesight perfectly! The entire hall bursts into laughter, followed by applause.

Obviously, the pope still needs his eyeglasses back so he can read his own speech. At the end of the speech, Cordes's eyeglasses are found; they had slipped under his chair. The pope cannot help himself relating the episode to the Memores during luncheon.

1 SATURDAY
MARCH

I participate this morning at the Ordinary Public Consistory, during which the Supreme Pontiff proclaims four new saints, as well as elevates to the presbyteral rank some cardinal deacons. In the afternoon we proceed to Paul VI Hall, from which the Rosary is transmitted via satellite to a number of university student groups gathered in different countries across the world. It is wonderful to see the enthusiasm of those young people as their group is identified. Most of all, it is great to see the smile on the pope's face, obviously very happy to see young people united in the Marian prayer.

Ordinary Public Consistory, March 1, 2008.

3 MONDAY MARCH

The pope today inquires about the outcome of my outing the previous evening with some friends I knew during my years as an assistant pastor at their parish. His fatherly interest is very dear to me. He also asks me if there were stalls of fish sellers and if I came across any dogs.

6 THURSDAY MARCH

The ecumenical patriarch Bartholomew I of Constantinople is invited for lunch today while on his visit in Rome. After a moment of prayer in the chapel of Pope Urban VIII on the Second Loggia, the pope and the patriarch go to the apartment, accompanied by a number of cardinals, among whom are Kasper and Sandri.

The patriarch, during luncheon, has some very courteous words for the pope. He thanks him for all the kindness the Catholic Church shows toward small churches, such as the Orthodox one in Turkey. At the end of lunch, the Holy Father extends an invitation to the patriarch to come to Rome for the feast of Peter and Paul. Bartholomew not only accepts but asks the pope if they can meet together at the Church of St. Theodore, a church donated to the Orthodox by the Catholic Diocese of Rome. The pope willingly accepts.

7 FRIDAY MARCH

As soon as I inform the Holy Father, while at table, that Cardinal Umberto Betti is eighty-two years old today, he immediately asks me to convey to him his most cordial best wishes. The cardinal collaborated for many years in the role of consulter at the congregation of which Cardinal Ratzinger was the prefect, but by now Fr. Betti has been sick for a while. Consequently, he is very moved when I tell him later of the caring attention by the Holy Father in his regard.

13 THURSDAY MARCH

The Diocese of Rome provides a penitential liturgy for the youth in preparation for Easter. Many confessors participate in it, including the Holy Father. The celebration is aimed at inviting all the faithful because it is a time of immediate preparation for the Pasch of the Lord, a time that brings to conclusion the penitential journey of Lent. It is a propitious moment for penitential reconciliation so those confessing can be rendered clean for the celebration of the Easter mysteries.

The pope hears confessions in St. Peter's Basilica for about forty-five minutes, during which six young people render their act of confession to him.

16 SUNDAY MARCH

Holy Week begins today. After the celebration of Holy Mass in the chapel of the apartment, we proceed to St. Peter's Square for the liturgy of Palm Sunday. Today also happens to be World Youth Day on the diocesan level.

The Holy Father's homily is beautiful, especially when the pope, taking his cue from the scene of the festive reception of Jesus in Jerusalem, says, "Dear friends, let us join at this moment the procession of the young people of that time — a procession that winds through the whole of history. Together with young people across the world let us go forth to meet

Jesus. Let us allow ourselves to be guided toward God by him, to learn from God himself the right way to be human beings. Let us thank God with him because with Jesus, Son of David, he has given us a space of peace and reconciliation that embraces the world with the Holy Eucharist. Let us pray to him that we too may become, with him and starting from him, messengers of his peace, adorers in spirit and truth, so that his Kingdom may increase in us and around us."

Something particularly new struck me! The pope explained that the changing of money at the entrance of the temple in Jerusalem was due to the fact that, since a coin had the depiction of the Roman emperor, a worldly figure, the coin could not be used to purchase cattle destined to be sacrificed.

20 THURSDAY MARCH

Today is Holy Thursday. The blessing of the holy oils and chrism takes place during the celebration of Holy Mass at St. Peter's Basilica, when any priests concelebrated. I am struck by what the pope says during the homily regarding one's dedication to service: "No one is closer to his master than the servant who has access to the most private dimensions of his life. In this sense 'to serve' means closeness, it requires familiarity. This familiarity also bears a danger: when we continually encounter the sacred it risks becoming habitual for us. In this way, reverential fear is extinguished. Conditioned by all our habits we no longer perceive the great, new and surprising fact that he himself is present, speaks to us, gives himself to us. We must ceaselessly struggle against this becoming accustomed to the extraordinary reality, against the indifference of the heart, always recognizing our insufficiency anew and the grace that there is in the fact that he consigned himself into our hands. To serve means to draw near, but above all it also means obedience."

21 THURSDAY MARCH

The rite of the Veneration of the Cross takes place this afternoon inside the Vatican Basilica, where the pope sits on a raised throne right across from the bronze statue of St. Peter. Due to the great number of people participating in this rite, only a few have the possibility of going up to the papal altar to kiss the cross. I am very much aware of the privilege of being included in this number, and so I try my best to live this moment of deep devotion by making an act of contrition.

The pope presides at the Way of the Cross at the Coliseum in the evening. This is always a very moving and inspiring event. In spite of the pouring rain, it is admirable to see a large crowd below us. Throughout the whole time the pope

Traditional *Via Crucis* of Good Friday at the Colosseum presided by the Pope.

stands under the protection of a canopy and follows the Way of the Cross from the Palatine Hill. His final words to the faithful are "This is the truth of Good Friday: on the Cross, the Redeemer has restored to us the dignity that belongs to us, has made us adoptive sons and daughters of God whom he has created in his image and likeness. Let us remain, then, in adoration before the Cross. O Christ, crucified King, give us true knowledge of you, the joy for which we yearn, the love that fills our heart, thirsty for the infinite. This is our prayer for this evening, Jesus, Son of God, who died for us on the Cross and was raised up on the third day. Amen."

22 SATURDAY MARCH

The Easter Vigil begins at 9:00 p.m. and finishes around 12:30 a.m. This requires a great effort from the pope, but it seems to me that he takes it on serenely.

Magdi Allam is among the newly baptized, when he takes the name Christian. At the time of the baptismal rite, I am not aware that this person is a journalist and a politician.

Before retiring to bed, we assemble in the room off the kitchen for a piece of sweet bread in the form of a dove.

23 SUNDAY MARCH

A very rainy Easter Sunday. Holy Mass is celebrated in St. Peter's Square during unceasing rain. It is also cold, and I am worried about the Holy Father's health. At the end of the occasion, the pope finishes his Easter message with the *Urbi et Orbi* blessing in many languages.

Before Holy Mass, the Holy Father asked me to repeat for him once again the way the greeting should be pronounced in

Maltese, to make sure that he knew it well. He is an extraordinary man! He has a thousand things to think about, but never fails to give attention to such matters.

At lunch, Benedict seems very happy, despite the inconvenience caused by the rain. Later on in the afternoon, we leave for Castel Gandolfo. We will be staying there until next Sunday.

24 MONDAY MARCH

At the end of the Rosary the joyful "ritual" to feed the goldfish.

I love staying again at Castel Gandolfo. After breakfast, we start working on the preparations for the recitation of the Regina Coeli, which is scheduled for every Easter Monday, otherwise called "the Monday of the Angel." The courtyard of the Apostolic Palace has been renovated, and now the window from which the Holy Father appears for the prayer at noon has been converted into a balcony.

Despite the bad weather during these days, Benedict is in good humor. At the end of his talk, he even makes an off-the-cuff joke. He says, "Even the sun has managed to make a short visit at this moment. A happy and holy Easter to you all!" The crowd applauds and shouts joyfully with great affection.

We gather in the garden in the afternoon for the recitation of the Rosary. Afterward there is the usual offering of small pieces of bread to the small fish that occupy the pond in front of Our Lady's statue.

25 TUESDAY
MARCH

Cardinal Tarcisio Bertone comes this evening for supper, accompanied by two of the sisters who look after him. He has come to report to the Holy Father of his recent visit to Armenia and Azerbaijan. As usual, the cardinal secretary of state is very cheerful. He takes a photo with the Holy Father, wearing a typical Azerbaijani headdress and, at his insistence, we secretaries also have to put on an Azari hat for a picture.

27 THURSDAY
MARCH

These last few days I've been very busy with a large quantity of mail that arrived and accumulated between Holy Saturday and the Monday of the Angel.

We have two guests for luncheon, Alfred and his wife, Maria. As has already been stated, Alfred worked for many years as a driver at the Congregation for the Doctrine of the Faith. The Holy Father holds him in high esteem and knows his family very well.

The pope asks me during our walk after lunch whether, during my recent visit to Malta, I had the chance to take some photographs of the cats in my parents' garden. I went

to Malta to vote in the national elections. I had mentioned to him my intention to take these photos some time ago, and he remembered my promise, and he wanted to know when he could see them! It is true that Benedict has a soft spot for felines, but I know that he did this for my own enjoyment.

In the evening, I feel the need to cheer him up and relieve the tension I sense in him due to the speech he is scheduled to deliver at the UN during his upcoming visit to New York. He is spending a lot of time thinking of this speech. As a way to distract him, I mention the last phone call of President Cossiga, which covered a number of things. I also talk about the occasion when I met the president in the Vatican. Discovering that I was Maltese, he had joked, in his usual way of overstating things, that he knew everything about Malta, which left me embarrassed as to how I should answer. The Holy Father smiles knowingly.

There was another light moment this morning. I was expected to remove the zucchetto from the Holy Father's head at the beginning of the Eucharistic Prayer. Since this was not my usual task, I remembered to do so only at the end of the Our Father. Following Holy Mass, while in the sacristy, after I had apologized, the Holy Father, in order to defuse the situation, told me jokingly, "If it had been Cardinal Noè, he would have fainted!" Cardinal Virgilio Noè, former archpriest of St. Peter's Basilica, was the master of ceremonies for Paul VI and, for a brief period, also for John Paul II. He was famous for his precision during any liturgical service. At breakfast, we told the Memores what had happened, knowing that such pleasant episodes create a serene environment around the pope.

Pope Benedict always shows his good-heartedness in not mortifying anyone on those occasions when someone seeks pardon for some unintentional mishap. On the contrary, he always finds a way to provide us with an excuse by using such a phrase as "All right, but it was only for a very short time!" It's a way of saying, for instance, "It is true that you forgot to remove the zucchetto, but it lasted for a short time because you fixed the oversight!"

Speaking about his delicate way of excusing us, I wish to narrate an episode that highlights this fact and that I will try to put into practice. One afternoon, the pope, as usual, was in his study at a time when I happened to be alone in the secretariat. At one point the porter called me to say that a priest, visiting Rome, had missed his return flight home and was asking for my assistance. I went down to the concierge to see how the matter could be resolved. At that very moment, Pope Benedict, in a manner altogether out of character, left his office and, if my memory serves me well, went to look for a pencil. When I returned upstairs, I felt mortified that the pope had not found me in my office, and I apologized as soon as I met him later for the Rosary. That evening, before going to bed, I was in the process of repeating my apology when he interrupted me and said something like "There is no need to apologize again, for it has already been accepted and there is no further need to think about it." I learned a great lesson that I will keep in mind whenever someone tries to repeat an apology, so as to spare him further mortification.

28 FRIDAY MARCH

In the wake of what happened yesterday regarding a "liturgical oversight," the Holy Father during breakfast this morning says in a self-deprecating way, "Finally, this morning I remembered that I should add the double Alleluia at the end!" Holy Mass during the Easter Octave ends with a double Alleluia, and the pope does not always remember to do this.

Today the sky is clear, and the air is fresh and crisp after so many days of incessant rain and overcast skies. As usual we took the path that leads us to Our Lady's statue while reciting the Rosary. The little fish immediately gathered to feast on the bits of bread.

30 SUNDAY MARCH

Overnight we change to summertime. The Holy Father delivers a beautiful homily in the morning. He explains that for the Jews the last day of the week is what in our culture is the seventh day. However, due to the Resurrection of the true Son, it has become the first of the eternal day. Then he speaks about the way the Risen One greeted His disciples: "Peace be to you!" The Lord, with these words, reconciles them with Himself and God after He was abandoned and betrayed. This greeting continues to be the opening words of every liturgy, enabling us to receive the new life that He bestows upon us.

The pope explains that the phrase "He breathed on them" recalls the living breath that God gave to the first man made from clay. The risen Christ gives us the Holy Spirit who makes us new. It is the Spirit that gives us the vigor of a new life. With regard to the greeting of peace that Jesus repeated in the end, the Holy Father highlights the point that in this way the Master had invited His disciples to freely offer the forgiveness of sins in His name, as they themselves received it. Thus, the disciples of Christ were not closed within themselves when contemplating the mystery of Christ but were invited to witness and to bring new life to others.

I remain ever grateful for these authentic lessons that the Holy Father shares with us. Although he is not obligated, he gives with extreme generosity and uses his vast experience to edify us spiritually and to help us grow in our understanding.

We prepare our luggage for departure in the afternoon and take the helicopter to the Vatican in the evening. Afterward we dine together and then continue to put our things in order.

2 WEDNESDAY APRIL

The pope celebrates Holy Mass in St. Peter's Square to commemorate the third anniversary of the death of Servant of God John Paul II. It is broadcast live by Rai Uno, with about forty thousand people present in the square on a beautiful and bright day. The pope speaks about the supernatural qualities of John Paul II, as well as his human qualities. I can sense with certainty that many graces have come down today from Heaven through the intercession of John Paul II, and I comprehend, absorbed in prayer, that he teaches me how to suffer for the good of the Church and of the world, as he did in such an exemplary manner.

Cardinal Stanisław Dziwisz and Archbishop Mokrzycki are the guests at lunch. Both of them were private secretaries to Pope John Paul II. During the ensuing conversation, the Holy Father shows particular interest in their pastoral ministry in their respective dioceses, those of Cracow and Lviv.

In the evening the recitation of the Rosary is done at the Vatican Grottoes, where John Paul II is buried, and transmitted on huge screens in the square for the gathered crowd of about four thousand people.

3 THURSDAY
APRIL

During the usual walk that we make after the Rosary, the pope and we secretaries talk about the conference on Divine Mercy that is underway in Rome, which the pope deems to be a very good initiative. He comments that if one does not reflect on the depth of mercy, one risks remaining on the level of simple devotion, as has happened in the case of the cult of the Sacred Heart of Jesus. The Holy Father reminds me that the Jesuits greatly promoted the pedagogical aspect and that a pope, Pius XI, issued an encyclical on the subject entitled *Caritate Christi compulsi*. While doing some research on this, I also come across another encyclical of Pius XI, entitled *Miserentissimus Redemptor*. It speaks about the act of reparation to the Most Sacred Heart of Jesus. I am very grateful to Pope Benedict for his clarification.

6 SUNDAY
APRIL

Today we celebrate Holy Mass a little bit later than usual. The guest at lunch is Christoph Schönborn, the archbishop of Vienna, who updates us on the conference on Divine Mercy being held at the Lateran Basilica. The complete harmony with the pontiff is very evident and much appreciated.

I go for a walk with some friends at the harbor of Fiumicino in the afternoon, and on my return, the pope asks me if the fish market took place, but it is always closed on Sundays.

7 MONDAY APRIL

Since I do not feel well this morning, I skip breakfast, and sure enough, the moment the Holy Father sees me, he immediately inquires about my well-being.

At lunch, the pope informs us about this morning's audiences, beginning with the one with the president of the Bishops' Conference of Venezuela. The bishops of that country are very concerned with the way President Chavez is dealing with the Catholic Church. It is feared that the recent attacks with the use of explosives on the papal nunciature are related to a climate of hostility toward the Church. According to some, the Venezuelan president wants to create a state church, similar to the so-called patriotic church in China. The pope looks very sad and concerned about this situation.

Icon of the "New Martyrs" depicting the witnesses of the Faith in the 20th and 21st centuries, written by Renata Sciachì of the Community of Sant'Egidio and venerated in the Basilica of San Bartolomeo all'Isola.

The pope visits the Basilica of St. Bartholomew on Tiber Island in late afternoon to mark the fortieth anniversary of the establishment of the Community of Sant'Egidio. The basilica safeguards the memory of the martyrs of the twentieth century in accordance with a decision taken by John Paul II. Pope Benedict poses a question: Why did these brothers and sisters of ours, by suffering martyrdom for the Faith, not seek the precious good of their life at any cost? The reply is very simple, though incomprehensible in the absence of the light of faith: they sacrificed themselves as witnesses to Jesus, the same Jesus who said, "Greater love has no man than this, that a man lay down his life for his friends" (John 15:13).

There are seven altars in the basilica. They are dedicated to the martyrs of Communism and Nazism and to those killed in America, in Asia, in Oceania, in Africa, in Spain, and in Mexico.

12 SATURDAY APRIL

On our usual stroll, the pope comments on how many times every day he has to sign congratulatory messages prepared by the Secretariat of State for bishops, cardinals, and other persons for various events. He then adds that when he received the best wishes of the pope for his twenty-fifth anniversary of episcopal ordination, he thought that the letter was personally written by the Holy Father. He comments with a sigh, "I was truly naïve."

There are no audiences today. This enables the Holy Father to prepare for the imminent trip to the United States.

14 MONDAY APRIL

Finally, the pictures depicting the cats at my parents' garden in Malta were printed, and today I bring them to the table for the pope, who holds on to them for a long time. He looks truly pleased and shows a lot of sympathy toward the cats, especially one that is quite fat. During such moments I bring to mind those people who depict Pope Ratzinger as a cold and severe man: if only they could get to know him as he truly is!

15 TUESDAY APRIL

We depart for the apostolic visit to the United States today. The pope is well prepared and confident.

Here we are leaving on an Alitalia plane at noon, after the usual ceremonial best wishes. We the secretaries, along with Mr. Paolo Gabriele, the secretary of state, and the archbishop substitute of state, are at the front section of the plane preparing to welcome the pope. We are treated extremely well, and all the cabin crew members go out of their way to be of every possible assistance. Those persons who are on their first papal flight are allowed to pause next to the Holy Father for a photo. Since this is my first time on such a flight, my name is also called out. Noting my embarrassment, the pope encourages me to sit close to him: "So your mother can also see this!" Following lunch, the pope rests for a while in a place specifically reserved for this purpose.

During the flight the pope takes several questions from journalists. When he is asked for a comment on the cases of sexual abuse by clergy, he replies very pointedly, "It is a great suffering for the Church in the United States and for the Church in general, for me personally, that this could happen. If I read the history of these events, it is difficult for me to understand how it was possible for priests to fail in this way in the mission to give healing, to give God's love to these children. I am ashamed and we will do everything possible to ensure that this does not happen in future. I think we have to act on three levels: the first is at the level of justice and the political level. I will not speak at this moment about homosexuality: this is another thing. We will absolutely exclude pedophiles from the sacred ministry; it is absolutely incompatible, and whoever is really guilty of being a pedophile cannot be a priest. So at this first level we can do justice and help the victims, because they are deeply affected; these are the two sides of justice: one, that pedophiles cannot be priests and the other, to help in any possible way the victims. Then there is a pastoral level. The victims will need healing and help and assistance and reconciliation: this is a big pastoral engagement and I know that the Bishops and the priests and all Catholic people in the United States will do whatever possible to help, to assist, to heal." Now I understand why I saw the pope more than usually absorbed in his thoughts and prayer on the eve of our departure.

The flight takes about ten hours. In the last stretch of the flight, we fly over Canada. It is still covered with snow, and while admiring the white sheet covering the surface, I fondly recall all of the people whom I met during the months I spent helping out at the secretariat of the apostolic nunciature in Ottawa.

The arrival in the United States is right on time — that is, 4:00 p.m. Washington time. President George W. Bush, accompanied by his wife, in an exception to the established protocol, comes to meet the arrival of the plane to welcome

Flying to the United States for the Apostolic Journey.

the pope. We are taken by limousines to the nunciature in cars that are well appointed but very uncomfortable to enter and exit. We will be staying at the nunciature until Friday morning. I visited the United States last May for family reasons, and I am very glad that I am able to return in the company of the pope. There are a lot of cheering people along the way to the nunciature. This seems to negate, as always, those views that, on the eve of our departure, had stated that the pope will receive a cold reception due to the clergy pedophile cases.

16 WEDNESDAY APRIL

This morning we celebrate Holy Mass privately in the nunciature chapel. Then we are taken to the White House, where the welcome is particularly festive since today is also the pope's birthday. He is eighty-one.

The first part of the ceremony takes place on the White House south lawn. The sunny day makes everything all the more pleasant. Following two brief speeches by Bush and the Holy Father, there is a parade of soldiers dressed in vintage uniforms. At the end, all four thousand people present join together in singing "Happy Birthday to You." Benedict appears very pleased and moved.

On the White House balcony with President George W. Bush and the First Lady.

A special guide — the First Lady, Laura Bush — during the visit to presidential residence.

The second part of the program is held indoors. While the pope and President Bush conduct their private meeting in the study, we are shown around the various halls, admiring the furnishings and the beautiful view through the huge windows. The First Lady accompanies us, and we are able to chat a little and also take some photos with her.

The American cardinals and the president of the USCCB have been invited to join us at lunch in the nunciature. I am seated next to Apostolic Nuncio Celestino Migliore, permanent observer of the Holy See at the United Nations in New York.

Later in the afternoon we proceed to the National Shrine of the Immaculate Conception. Here too we are greeted by a sea of people, both in the proximity of the shrine as well as along the principal streets. Sung Vespers begin at 6:00 p.m. in the crypt with all of the American bishops present. While in the sacristy, I approach the Holy Father as he is putting on his vestments and discreetly offer him my comb to straighten his hair, for it had been put out of place during the drive in the open-air car. He gives it two taps and then leaves it as is. It is clear that he and his hair do not get along!

There is an image of Our Lady of Ta'Pinu in the crypt. She is much venerated in my homeland of Malta, and I am pleased to have been able to pray in front of the image, brief though this might have been.

2008

17 THURSDAY APRIL

This morning a Holy Mass is scheduled at the Washington Nationals stadium, one of the most important venues in the United States. The pope is welcomed by an immense crowd along the streets and outside the building, and the stadium itself is filled to capacity. During the Mass the congregation's participation in the liturgy is outstanding, and many people receive Holy Communion. I notice that the pope is very impressed, and it is obvious that he is very pleased.

Archbishop Donald William Wuerl explains to us that the faithful's participation is the result of very careful preparation done at the parish level, where everyone had been invited to confess. Without any doubt, there is a sincere love for Pope Benedict.

Today also, beginning at 6:00 a.m., a great number of priests made themselves available to hear confessions of the

Solemn processions for the celebration of the Holy Mass in the stadium.

faithful in various parts of the stadium. This went on for about three hours, with no break whatsoever.

We proceed to the Catholic University of America in the afternoon for a meeting with the world of Catholic educators. Immediately following, we go to the Pope John Paul II Cultural Center for a meeting with the representatives of other religions. If I am permitted to say so, this second meeting seems subdued, and participation, I might say, is rather dull.

By the end of the day, Benedict is tired but beaming and very uplifted by the reception he is receiving.

18 FRIDAY APRIL

After the morning Holy Mass, the Holy Father, with his usual kindness, wants to greet the entire personnel at the Washington Nunciature before leaving, by an Alitalia plane, for New York, where a busy program of activities awaits him. We are transferred to Manhattan by helicopter, and during the flight the Holy Father appears to me to be particularly concentrating due to the demanding speech he is to give at the UN. There he is greeted by very loud applause when he enters the hall.

In his speech the pope is very clear in upholding the principle of the responsibility to protect, an increasingly important characteristic of the role of the United Nations. He states, "Every State has the primary duty to protect its own population from grave and sustained violations of human rights, as well as from the consequences of humanitarian crises, whether natural or man-made. If States are unable to guarantee such protection, the international community must intervene with the juridical means provided in the United Nations Charter and in other international instruments. The action of the international community and its institutions, provided that it respects the principles undergirding the international order, should never be interpreted as an unwarranted imposition or a limitation of sovereignty. On the contrary, it is indifference or failure to intervene that does the real damage. What is needed is a deeper search for ways of pre-empting and managing conflicts by exploring every possible diplomatic avenue, and giving attention and encouragement to even the faintest sign of dialogue or desire for reconciliation." At the end of the speech, the applause of the diplomatic representatives assembled in the hemicycle is altogether good and substantial.

Together with the Chief Rabbi Arthur Schneier.

Later the Holy Father looks very satisfied and relaxed during lunch. From the start, he had deemed the meeting at the United Nations as being very important, especially as it was the place that had welcomed Paul VI and John Paul II, and he knew that every one of his words would be closely scrutinized.

We make a visit to the synagogue of Park East in New York in the afternoon, where the Jewish community receives him with great courtesy and gratitude. The chief rabbi, during his welcome address, makes reference to the pope's angelic face that conquers hearts, at which a lady, presumably a Jewish woman, turns to me and whispers, "It is true. He has the face of an angel!" As I answer, "He is always like this," I think of how extraordinary the experience is when one can live close to this angel, as in my case.

The pope starts his speech with the Jewish greeting, "Shalom," and continues to express his respect and esteem for the Jewish community of New York. The Jewish community's parting wishes are particularly warm as we leave the synagogue, and one person of the Jewish faith even goes so far as to kiss the pope's hand.

Next, the pope participates in an ecumenical encounter at the nearby Church of St. Joseph. But even this one, if truth be told, seems a little subdued.

19 SATURDAY APRIL

Priests and religious men and women wait for the pope for the celebration of Holy Mass at St. Patrick's Cathedral this morning. Once again, the pope is received with great warmth, something that has been constant throughout the journey. The Holy Father encourages the priests to remain faithful to the ministry they have received and thanks them for their collaboration with the bishops. Today is the anniversary of the election of the pope to the Petrine ministry, and this renders the celebration more solemn and joyful.

The pope goes to St. Joseph's Seminary this afternoon. He first meets some children with special needs, accompanied by their relatives, after which he joins a crowd of thirty thousand youths and seminarians on an expansive green lawn. The reception is awesome, and the pope greets those present with simplicity and gratitude. He seems to be a little embarrassed with the show of so much affection toward him. One could say that he truly wins over everyone's heart.

The German embassy at the United Nations offers the pope a short concert, following our dinner at the nunciature. Even if he is tired after a long day, Benedict really enjoys the concert — he loves classical music!

ALFRED XUEREB

20 SUNDAY APRIL

Today is the last day of Benedict's visit to the United States. All of the Americans, even those not Catholics, are deeply touched with the decision to visit Ground Zero, the enormous crater left as a consequence of the tragic collapse of the Twin Towers, and to pray there in silence in remembrance of all the victims who died as a result of the terrorist attack of September 11, 2001. Benedict meets with some relatives of the victims as well as some of those who survived. The overcast sky and the chill in the air contribute to the somber and moving atmosphere of the encounter.

Afterward a Holy Mass is held in the afternoon at Yankee Stadium, which is jam-packed. The faithful present

A moment of recollection at Ground Zero in honor of the victims of the September 11, 2001 attack.

participate on a grand scale, moving the pope, during the
homily, to compliment the people of the United States for the
growth of the Catholic fold. However, he also recommends
respect and obedience to the proper authority. Then he continues, "Here, in this land of freedom, I want to proclaim
forcefully that the Word of Christ does not eliminate our
aspirations for a full and free life but reveals to us our true
dignity as children of God and encourages us to fight against
everything that enslaves us, starting from our selfishness and
from our passions."

We are transferred by helicopter to John F. Kennedy Airport directly after the celebration, where the vice president
was present for the farewell ceremony, departing on time to
Ciampino Airport in Rome. While in flight, I relive, full of
emotions, all the stages of the trip just concluded. Above all,
the most captivating moment for me was when the Holy Father
received in the nunciature chapel five victims who had been
sexually abused by members of the clergy. I was present at the
encounter. I watched firsthand the pope expressing with passionate emotions his deep sense of shame regarding the betrayal

of priestly ministry. I also noticed that the five people were deeply touched meeting the pope and speaking to him so freely. When the Holy Father left, the victims embraced one another and wept for joy. The planning for the meeting remained a secret so as not to transform it into a media spectacle. Once made public, the encounter was well received by the American press, which served to highlight all that the Catholic Church, in particular the Archdiocese of Boston, was doing to help the victims of clergy sexual abuse. As stated earlier, the pope, during the outgoing flight to the United States, had consented to respond to some of the journalists' questions on this subject, reaffirming that there is no place in the Church for those clerics guilty of certain crimes. The words were very clear and set the trip on the right track.

23 WEDNESDAY APRIL

We celebrate the Holy Mass of St. George since today marks his feast. This is to celebrate the name day of both the pope's brother, who arrived yesterday to celebrate with us, and Msgr. Gänswein. The Memores sing a song and set a special luncheon for the occasion. We even have a cake in the form of a defeated dragon being struck in its throat by the spear of St. George!

24 THURSDAY APRIL

To mark the third anniversary of the papal election, the president of the Italian Republic, Giorgio Napolitano, took the initiative to hold a concert in Paul VI Hall in honor of the pope. The Giuseppe Verdi Symphony Orchestra and Choir of Milan, under the direction of Oleg Caetani, perform musical

Paul VI Hall: Concert on the occasion of the third year of the pontificate of Pope Benedict offered by the President of the Italian Republic, George Napolitano.

pieces by Luciano Berio, Johannes Brahms, and Ludwig van Beethoven. Benedict is delighted by the occasion. After heartily thanking the president and the members of the orchestra and choir, he speaks about the spiritual value of the art of music, uniquely called to instill hope in the human spirit, sometimes wounded by its earthly condition. This comment makes me understand better the Holy Father's love of music. He explains, "There is a mysterious and deep kinship between music and hope, between song and eternal life: not for nothing does the Christian tradition portray the Blessed in the act of singing in a choir, in ecstasy and enraptured by the beauty of God. But authentic art, like prayer, is not foreign to everyday reality although it requires us to 'water' it and make it germinate if it is to bring forth the fruit of goodness and peace."

22 MAY
THURSDAY

After a slight indisposition, I am back at work. The Holy Father himself suggested that I take some days off to convalesce. I spent those days with some cleric friends at Grottaferrata. The pope has just barely seen me in the sacristy when he asks me about my health. I put his mind to rest with my response that all is well.

I quickly see to the mail that awaits me at my office, after which we go to St. John Lateran in the afternoon for the celebration of the feast of Corpus Christi. Benedict explains that the reason for this celebration is that "we kneel in adoration in front of the Lord." This is because "adoring the God of Jesus Christ, who out of love made himself bread broken, is the most effective and radical remedy against the idolatry of the past and of the present. Kneeling before the Eucharist is a profession of freedom: those who bow to Jesus cannot and must not prostrate themselves before any earthly authority, however powerful. We Christians kneel only before God or before the Most Blessed Sacrament because we know and believe that the one true God is present in it, the God who created the world and so loved it that he gave his Only Begotten Son."

There is the traditional procession from the Basilica of St. John Lateran to the Basilica of St. Mary Major after Holy Mass, with the pope on a vehicle specially set up for this precession. He remains in absolute silent meditation in front of the Blessed

Sacrament throughout the procession. The people standing down the street are also silent and prayerful. However, I get the impression that the Holy Father is so concentrated on the Eucharistic Lord that he is oblivious of the crowd.

25 SUNDAY MAY

At today's Angelus, the pope takes his cue from the feast of Corpus Christi to speak of the Eucharist, which he defines as "the school of charity and solidarity." He goes on to say, "The one who is nourished on the Bread of Christ cannot remain indifferent before the one who, even in our day, is deprived of daily bread. So many parents are barely able to obtain it for themselves and for their own children. It is an ever greater problem that the International Community has great difficulty in resolving. The Church not only prays 'give us this day our daily bread,' but, on the Lord's example, is committed in every way to 'multiply the five loaves and the two fish' with numerous initiatives of human promotion and sharing, so that no one lacks what is necessary for life."

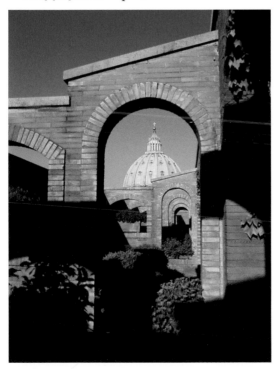

View of the dome of St. Peter from the terrace of the papal apartment.

In the evening there is a gathering on the terrace of the papal apartment at 7:00 p.m. It is to enact a *Maiandacht*, a liturgical Marian devotion that is carried out during May. Some male and female members of *Das Werk* are present.

We recite the Rosary, sing hymns, and pray in front of a painting of Our Lady decked out in flowers. The Holy Father wears a surplice and the mozzetta for this occasion. It is not done simply as a formality; rather, for him, in these instances, the essence is in the substance.

26 MONDAY MAY

Today is the twenty-fifth anniversary of my ordination to the priesthood. My usual custom has been to celebrate a Holy Mass early in the morning at the Chiesa Nuova on the tomb of St. Philip Neri. But today I have the privilege of celebrating the Holy Mass of the Anniversary of Priestly Ordination with the Holy Father. The pope asks me many questions regarding the actual day of my ordination. He wants to know why that specific day was chosen, how many of us were ordained, and where and what these priests who were ordained with me are doing now. After lunch, Msgr. Gänswein and the Memores, having renewed their best wishes, present me with a straw hat similar to the one the Holy Father uses during our walks to protect him from the summer sun.

29 THURSDAY MAY

After every journey overseas, the pope invites for lunch, in two separate groups, all those who were involved in its organization. He expects their comments and an appraisal. Some bishops are here today, among them Archbishop Harvey and Cardinals Bertone, Levada, Stafford, Filoni, and Sandri. Apart from reflecting on the journey to the United States, they also talk about the upcoming papal journey to Sydney for the occasion of the World Youth Day.

The Holy Father decides to share with all of us during supper some observations of that meeting, stating that without any doubt, the main catalyst in the positive outcome of the apostolic journey to the United States was Divine Providence. Then the talk shifts to other papal trips. When he mentions the one to Poland in 2006, I pluck up courage to ask him what he thought about the famous rainbow that appeared across the sky at Auschwitz during his prayer at the concentration camp. It happened two years ago on May 28. "Holy Father," I say, "for me the rainbow appearing in the background exactly at the time of your speech and prayer is no mere coincidence." The pope agrees that "even that was a sign of Providence." One other person at table recalls that journalists present had compared that episode to the rainbow that appeared to Noah after the deluge. The pope simply smiles, but I think that even he is convinced it was a sign from above. On that occasion, Benedict had spoken about reconciliation. It is now very touching listening to him say, "Pope John Paul II went there as a son of the Polish people. I went there that day as a son of the German people. For this very reason, I should and must echo his words: 'I could not fail to come here. I had to come.' It was and is a duty before the truth and the right due to all who have suffered there. It was for me a duty before God to come here as the successor of Pope John Paul II and as a son of the German people — a son of that people over which a ring of criminals rose to power by false promises of future greatness and the recovery of the nation's honor, prominence and prosperity. But this was also done through terror and intimidation, with the result that our people were used and abused as an instrument of their thirst for destruction and power. Yes, I could not fail to go there. On 7 June 1979 I went as the Archbishop of Munich Freising, along with many other Bishops who accompanied the Pope to Auschwitz-Bierkenau, listened to his words and joined in his prayer. In 1980 I went back to that dreadful place with a delegation of German Bishops, appalled by its evil, yet grateful for the fact that above its dark clouds the star of reconciliation had emerged. This is the same reason why I went back during those days: to implore the grace of reconciliation — first of all from God, who alone can open and purify our hearts, then with the men and women who suffered there, and finally for the grace of reconciliation for all those who, at this hour of our history, are suffering in new ways from the power of hatred and the violence which hatred spawns."

31 SATURDAY MAY

Today the feast of the Visitation of the Blessed Virgin Mary is celebrated at the Vatican. It is also the commemoration of the Immaculate Heart of Mary. Furthermore, it is the end of the Marian month, and so there is the procession in honor of Our Lady in which many faithful take part. Since this year is the 150th anniversary of the apparitions at Lourdes, and the Vatican Gardens would not accommodate the huge number of participants, it was decided to hold the prayer service in St. Peter's Square. The procession begins at 8:00 p.m. with the recitation of the Rosary. The Holy Father arrives one hour later to share a reflection and impart his blessing. Benedict tells those present, "Going beyond the surface, Mary 'sees' the work of God in history with the eyes of faith. This is why she is blessed, because she believed. By faith, in fact, she accepted the Word of the Lord and conceived the Incarnate Word. Her faith has shown her that the thrones of the powerful of this world are all temporary, while God's throne is the only rock that does not change or fall. Her *Magnificat*, at the distance of centuries and millennia, remains the truest and most profound interpretation of history, while the interpretations of so many of this world's wise have been belied by events in the course of the centuries. Dear brothers and sisters, let us return home with the *Magnificat* in our heart." I always feel moved by the Marian devotion of Pope Benedict, this highly refined and profound theologian who, at the same time, is so modest and humble.

4 WEDNESDAY JUNE

These days I feel with particular intensity the father–son relationship with Pope Benedict and am strengthened by it. I try my best to follow his example in being thoughtful and available to everyone, especially in little things.

I inform the pope this evening of the surgical intervention undergone by the attorney Gianluigi Marrone, sole judge of the Vatican City State as well as the president of the Association of Sts. Peter and Paul, to which I was the spiritual advisor. The pope asks me to convey his best wishes and to assure him of his prayers. Since I know that his recent surgery produced a lot of psychological stress, I call Gianluigi to inform him of the pope's caring concerns and also to encourage him. He is deeply moved and asks me to thank the Holy Father.

The Pope greets the members of the Association of Saints Peter and Paul and their president, Atty. Gianluigi Marrone.

5 THURSDAY
JUNE

During the usual brief walk that we make with the Holy Father, I take the opportunity to inform him of the deep gratitude of the attorney Marrone. I also inform the pope about the grave illness that befell Fr. Joshua Muscat, a young priest from Gozo serving at a parish in the outskirts of the city of Turin. The pope wants to know more and asks me many questions about the young priest. He is greatly taken by the story of this priest who went to Nichelino to replace a priest, again from Gozo, at the same diocese who died prematurely. Now this priest has been stricken with a tumor. The pope never shies away from getting involved in the personal circumstances of people that are brought to his attention, even when they live far away. There is never an instance when he sees such things falling outside the exigencies of his office and its related responsibilities. This is another example of openness and availability for all of us to emulate.

7 SATURDAY
JUNE

We have some cherries with dinner this evening, and I notice the Holy Father lining up the pits on a dish, placing them in groups of three in a row. I am intrigued as to why he has done this until I see him counting them at the end. I conclude that this is his way of keeping tally of how many he has eaten. Although this may seem to be a rather insignificant act, in fact it says plenty about him and his methodical style. It allows him not only to control himself but also to maintain a good, healthy diet. By the way, the pope quips that it is common knowledge in Germany that this is done to avoid any unpleasant consequences and furthermore recommends not drinking water after eating cherries. I will keep that in mind!

28 SATURDAY JUNE

We go to St. Paul Outside the Walls in the evening for the celebration of First Vespers on the Solemnity of Sts. Peter and Paul and to initiate the Pauline Year that will last until June 29, 2009. It marks the two thousandth anniversary of the birth of the Apostle to the Gentiles.

Gift to the Pope from the Ecumenical Patriarch of Constantinople, Bartholomew I.

It is exciting to see the pope and the fraternal delegates from other Christian creeds unite together at the tomb of St. Paul. He was born some two thousand years ago at Tarsus in Cilicia, in today's Turkey. The pope observes that today we are not gathered "to reflect on past history, irrevocably behind us." Instead, "Paul wants to speak to us — today. That is why I chose to establish this special 'Pauline Year': in order to listen to him and learn today from him, as our teacher, 'the faith and the truth' in which the reasons for unity among Christ's disciples are rooted." Following his greetings and thanks to everyone, beginning with his friend the Ecumenical Patriarch Bartholomew I of Constantinople, Benedict delivers a homily that for all effects is a true and precise presentation on Paul and his relevance today. He chooses to end it with the words Paul wrote to Timothy from prison as he faced imminent death: "'With the strength that comes from God bear your share of hardship which the Gospel entails,' the Apostle said to his disciple (2 Tim. 1:8)." Then he adds, "The task of proclamation and the call to suffer for Christ's sake are inseparable. The call to become the teacher of the Gentiles is, at the same time and intrinsically, a call to suffering in communion with Christ who redeemed us through his Passion. In a world in which falsehood is powerful, the truth is paid for with suffering." Perhaps Benedict is thinking of himself as well.

30 MONDAY JUNE

Although the Holy Father does not follow soccer matches, he often asks about the results of a match of a previous day. Since he has said many times that he was never sports oriented, I suspect that he does so to stay in tune with us.

Last Saturday I was able to observe better how much the Holy Father makes himself available to those who come to meet him. Despite the already oppressive heat, he accepted the suggestion of saying a word or two to every person who would be introduced to him at the end of an audience. I was worried about him because he was very tired. Nonetheless, he met every one of them with a smile and very courteously. He meets this responsibility not as if it was some kind of detail or something to be added on, but rather as an integral part of his ministry.

We went to St. Peter's Basilica yesterday for the celebration of Holy Mass on the feast of the Patrons of Rome, Peter and Paul. Patriarch Bartholomew I of Constantinople was present once again, this time with an Orthodox delegation. The pope delivered another one of his beautiful homilies, during which he greatly encouraged all Christians to heal the Body of Christ, which is torn by divisions. During the course of the ceremony, the pope bestowed the pallium on forty-one archbishops. This is a collar made out of white wool, which symbolizes a sheep being carried by the shepherd on his shoulders, and it is the prerogative of metropolitan archbishops to wear it as a symbol of their jurisdiction in communion with the See of Peter.

Some days ago, while at table, we were talking about the importance of the primacy that unites the dioceses (known as particular churches) to the person of Peter. We highlighted the fact that the Anglican Church, which does not recognize the Petrine primacy, is deeply divided on some red-hot issues such as gay unions and the ordination of women priests and bishops. We also commented upon the inner yearning felt toward the pope by the thousands and thousands of people from around the world as affirmed by the ever-increasing crowds that take part in each Wednesday general audience and at the Sunday Angelus. It is a true fact that there is no other important or famous person in the world who is able to attract people with the same efficacy. However, Benedict, on such occasions, neither comments nor shares his thoughts. He does not want to risk falling, even involuntarily, into an act of pride. He considers everything to be a gift from Divine Providence.

12 SATURDAY JULY

We are again traveling today. This time our journey takes us very far away. Soon after Holy Mass, celebrated each morning in the private chapel of the Apostolic Palace of Castel Gandolfo, we board the helicopter for Fiumicino. From there, we embark on an Alitalia flight to Australia where the Holy Father is scheduled to take part in the World Youth Day events. I am initially anxious during the first moments of the flight due to it being so long. However, I soon calm myself down. On the other hand, Benedict seems to be very comfortable and confident.

According to many observers, the issue of sexual abuse will be brought up even during this trip. But we must not allow ourselves to be conditioned by what is written in the media. Benedict, being ever so serene, inspires everyone. This is confirmed at the press conference held on board the flight. After he says, "I am going to Australia with feelings of joy," he gives a detailed reply to Auskar Surbakti, a journalist for the SBS Australian television network, who asked him if he was going to speak about the problem of sexual abuse and would he issue an apology. He states, "It must be clear, it was always clear from the first centuries that priesthood, to be a priest, is incompatible with this behavior, because the priest is in the service of Our Lord, and Our Lord is holiness in person, and always teaching us." He goes on to state, "There are things which are always bad, and pedophilia is always bad. In our education, in the seminaries, in our permanent formation of the priests, we have to help priests to really be close to Christ, to learn from Christ, and so to be helpers, and not adversaries of our fellow human beings, of our Christians. So, we will do everything possible to clarify what is the teaching of the

Church and help in the education and in the preparation of priests, in permanent formation, and we will do all possible to heal and to reconcile the victims. I think this is the essential content of what the word 'apologize' says. I think it is better, more important to give the content of the formula, and I think the content has to say what was insufficient in our behaviour, what we must do in this moment, how we can prevent and how we all can heal and reconcile." The pope replies in English with not a moment of hesitation. Everything is clear in his mind because everything is clear in his heart.

13 SUNDAY JULY

I managed to sleep for about four hours on the plane, and this is a long time for me when I travel. We landed at Darwin this morning for a stopover. The Holy Father, accompanied by very few people, got off the plane on this military base and we had a cup of coffee. We flew out of the base an hour and fifteen minutes later. The climate at Darwin is tropical. Despite being winter, the temperature at that hour was close to 86°F. I am a little concerned about the pope. He is eighty-one years old and keeps going. Is not all of this a little tiresome for him? I am praying more intensely.

After long hours of flying, we land at Richmond, in the vicinity of Sydney. At the end of a brief welcoming ceremony, we are immediately transferred to Kenthurst Study Centre, which is forty kilometers from Sydney. The residence is entrusted to the Prelature of Opus Dei for putting on conferences, spiritual retreats, and other activities involving Christian formation. The pope will stay here to rest for a day or so before he embarks on the multiple activities of the WYD.

Standing in admiration of the natural beauty that surround the Kenthurst Study Centre, not far from Sydney.

The welcome by our Australian friends is particularly warm. They even go so far as to rent a cell phone to make outside calls so that we may feel a little less confined. We visit the house, and we go to the very beautiful chapel to celebrate Holy Mass in the evening. Beginning today, and until next Wednesday, the stay of the Holy Father at Kenthurst Study Centre will be strictly private, and therefore there will be no public meetings.

16 WEDNESDAY JULY

Today some young people from the Sydney Zoo come to Kenthurst Study Centre, bringing with them some typical Australian animals for the Holy Father to see. Benedict's expressions are unforgettable as he, all smiles and full of wonder, pets a small koala bear, a python named Sebastian, a six-month-old kangaroo, a baby crocodile, a porcupine, and a multicolored parrot. "This is very big!" says the pope to the young man who holds the python very close to himself. The pope has caressed all of the animals and he receives a gift of a plush koala. After we recite the Rosary in the afternoon, he comments about this morning's animals. However, after the pope refers to the animals as "cute," he, in his usual humorous way, observes, "Yes, but not all!" Indeed, some of the reptiles looked really scary!

After the celebration of the daily Holy Mass, with some fifteen people participating, Benedict greets those responsible for the structure and leaves with them a gift of a chasuble and a painting depicting Our Lady. He tells them, "This gift is for you. I thank you for your exquisite hospitality."

Benedict XVI pets
a little koala.

17 THURSDAY JULY

The pope celebrates Holy Mass this morning in private at the chapel of St. Mary's Cathedral House of Sydney. The chapel is dedicated to Mary MacKillop, the first Australian to be declared "Blessed." She lived from the end of the nineteenth century through the beginning of the twentieth century. She is the foundress of a religious community.

We visit the governor general at his residence at 10:00 a.m. Afterward, finally, the WYD in Sydney is opened in a very festive and spectacular way by first meeting some young indigenous Australians who dance for the pope. This is followed with the crossing aboard a boat, the Sydney 2000, from Rose Bay to the Barangaroo Pier, East Darling Harbor. Some youths join us on the boat, while more than two hundred thousand await the pope's arrival at the other end. The pope repeatedly goes on deck during the crossing to greet the youths who crowd various parts of the harbor. The organizers never imagined that the opening of the WYD could be as joyous as this.

The pope says, "What a delight it is to greet you here at Barangaroo, on the shores of the magnificent Sydney harbor, with its famous bridge and Opera House." Then he immediately reflects on and gives homage to the indigenous Australians: "I am deeply moved to stand on your land, knowing the suffering and injustices it has borne, but aware too of the healing and hope that are now at work, rightly bringing pride to all Australian citizens."

The festive atmosphere does not impede Benedict from speaking with the youth in a very clear way. Multi-ethnic Australia is a land of freedom and tolerance, but we must pay close attention to not ever separate freedom and tolerance from truth, a separation being fueled by the notion widely

The Pope on the vessel, Sydney 2000, during the transfer to Barangaroo Pier, East Darling Harbor, Sydney on the occasion of World Youth Day XXIII.

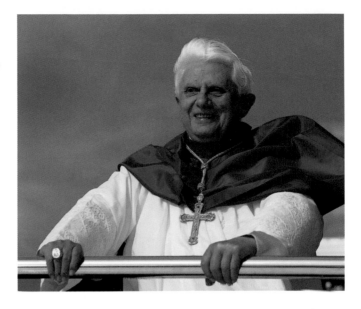

held today that there does not exist an absolute truth that guides our lives: "Relativism, by indiscriminately giving value to practically everything, has made 'experience' all-important. Yet, experiences, detached from any consideration of what is good or true, can lead, not to genuine freedom, but to moral or intellectual confusion, to a lowering of standards, to a loss of self-respect, and even to despair."

The Holy Father looks tired during supper, but also very pleased with the entire day.

18 FRIDAY JULY

We participate in an ecumenical encounter in the crypt of the cathedral. The pope greeted some heads of other churches and Christian confessions and the members of the New South Wales Ecumenical Council. Then he delivers a speech. I must say that it all takes place in a rather detached atmosphere as well as in a setting that is not sufficiently well lit. Following this meeting, the Holy Father meets with the representatives of other religions in the chapter hall. In my opinion the speeches delivered by the rabbi and the imam were very respectful toward the pope personally as well as toward his ministry.

Later, the youths enact a beautiful live Way of the Cross along the principal streets of the city, which is a unique event in the history of this city. The Holy Father recites the prayer of the first station from the cathedral's square, before going down to the crypt to follow the other stations via television.

The meeting between the Holy Father and a group of young people this evening is very significant. They reside in a rehabilitation community at the University of Notre Dame. The speech of the pope is very touching when he makes reference to the parable of the Prodigal Son and hints at the search of true love. Benedict speaks to those young people as a father: "Material possessions, in themselves, are good. We would not survive for long without money, clothing and shelter. We must eat in order to stay alive. Yet if we are greedy, if we refuse to share what we have with the hungry and the poor, then we make our possessions into a false god. How many voices in our materialist society tell us that happiness is to be found by acquiring as many possessions and luxuries as we can! But this is to make possessions into a false god. Instead of bringing life, they bring death."

19 SATURDAY JULY

This is a very special day for the Catholic Church in Australia and for Cardinal George Pell, archbishop of Sydney. Today the pope celebrates Holy Mass at the cathedral, consecrates the new altar, and meets with the clergy and seminarians of the archdiocese.

Holy Mass is very moving, and its celebration is accompanied by wonderfully executed hymns. The Holy Father decides to include a statement about the clergy sexual abuse cases in the official text of his homily. He reiterates that these crimes must be condemned unequivocally and be brought to the attention of justice, and that the Church remains very close to all the victims. Here is one significant passage: "I would like to pause to acknowledge the shame which we have all felt as a result of the sexual abuse of minors by some clergy and religious in this country. Indeed, I am deeply sorry for the pain and suffering the victims have endured, and I assure them that, as their Pastor, I too share in their suffering. These misdeeds, which constitute so grave a betrayal of trust, deserve unequivocal condemnation. They have caused great pain and have damaged the Church's witness. I ask all of you to support and assist your Bishops, and to work together with them in combating this evil. Victims should receive compassion and care, and those responsible for these evils must be brought to justice. It is an urgent priority to promote a safer and more wholesome environment, especially for young people."

We just have time for a hurried dinner and next here we are at the Randwick Racecourse, for the prayer vigil with young people. Half a million young people await the pope!

Christian witness is the center of Benedict's reflection: How can we be consistent and effective faithful witnesses of Jesus in a world that is divided, fragmented, and frequently indifferent? The response to the question, as usual, is very clear. If we think of basing everything on our own efforts and not the action of the Holy Spirit, we are heading toward failure: "Friends, when reciting the Creed, we state: 'We believe in the Holy Spirit, the Lord, the giver of life.' The 'Creator

Spirit' is the power of God giving life to all creation and the source of new and abundant life in Christ. The Spirit sustains the Church in union with the Lord and in fidelity to the apostolic Tradition." Even in this festive atmosphere, the salient moment is altogether silent: everyone is silent during the Eucharistic Adoration.

20 SUNDAY JULY

Today marks the last day of the WYD. We travel to the heliport of Victoria Barracks after breakfast. The Holy Father boards the helicopter, which, before landing, first circles above the young crowd waiting for him at Randwick for Holy Mass. Meanwhile, the rest of us go ahead by car to await his arrival. We are all dressed up for Holy Mass, and while waiting for the arrival of the Holy Father, I go to greet some priests who are sitting in the first row. They are very welcoming and in an exuberant mood. They tell me that they themselves, like all the young people, have slept in the open air. The weather has been a great help so far, but today there are clouds in the sky. The pope administers the sacrament of Confirmation to some young people during Holy Mass.

The questions the pope poses to all those present are as usual very direct: "What will you leave to the next generation? Are you building your lives on firm foundations, building something that will endure? Are you living your lives in a way that opens up space for the Spirit in the midst of a world that wants to forget God, or even rejects him in the name of a falsely conceived freedom?"

I admire the courage of Benedict, who never tries to simply say what pleases young people. Here is his beautiful conclusion: "Through the loving intercession of Mary,

Mother of the Church, may this Twenty-third World Youth Day be experienced as a new Upper Room, from which all of us, burning with the fire and love of the Holy Spirit, go forth to proclaim the Risen Christ and to draw every heart to him! Amen."

21 MONDAY
JULY

This morning's Holy Mass is celebrated in the private chapel of the archbishop of Sydney. The pope has invited four people, two men and two women, who years ago were victims of clergy sexual abuse. As in the United States, the Holy Father wants to speak with each individual on this occasion. He takes their hands in his own, listens very carefully to their narrative, and consoles them, assuring them of his spiritual closeness. He promises to continue to pray for them, for their families, and for all victims. It is a fatherly gesture with which he wants to demonstrate for the umpteenth time his solicitude toward all those who have suffered from sexual abuse. It is all conducted in a climate of great respect and sincere feelings. After he greets representatives from the WYD, we head for the airport for the flight back home.

Before leaving Cathedral House, I do something that is an exception to the rule, a brief interview on a Maltese radio station in Sydney. I consider it a way of sharing witness with the many Maltese immigrants in this land. The interview is done over the telephone, but it has to be repeated all over again because the lady interviewer, perhaps caught up in the emotions of the moment, has accidentally erased the first recording.

I must say it seems to me that, throughout the highly demanding WYD celebrations, the Holy Father remains serene and is pleased with how things are being carried out. A very nice incident takes place during one of the walks the pope and we secretaries routinely take after meals. On reaching the end of the passageway in front of the cathedral, the pope spots a couple of policemen standing next to their parked motorcycles, and Benedict, smiling, raises his right hand to greet them. Continuing on our walk and returning back to the place where we saw the policemen, we are surprised to see that now there are four of them. The pope again greets them with his raised hand and a smile. We proceed along the perimeter line of the cathedral's wall for a third time, and once again we find the policemen waiting for the pope to greet them. But this time they are six! It is a great witness of the pope's humanity toward everybody, knowing full well that the officers are not even Catholic.

The police inform us that they were very impressed with the way the young people behaved. In fact, we have seen during these days that one can be joyful without being vulgar and that young people can act as such if their joy is rooted in an authentic faith. During the initial days, the police officers understandably were very formal, but it was great to see that as the days went by some policemen became very friendly with the young people.

After a brief farewell ceremony, we climb into a Qantas jumbo jet to make our return to Rome. We land at Ciampino at 10:45 p.m. Italian time on Monday, and on arriving at the Apostolic Palace of Castel Gandolfo, we find the Memores, who welcome us back with great joy. We celebrate with a glass of beer, after which we are given the schedule for tomorrow morning's Holy Mass.

21 THURSDAY AUGUST

The Pope's brother, Msgr. Georg Ratzinger, receives honorary citizenship of the Municipality of Castel Gandolfo at the hall of the Swiss Guards inside the Apostolic Palace of town overlooking Lake Albano.

The brother of the pope receives the Honorary Freedom of the town of Castel Gandolfo in the hall of the Swiss Guards inside the Apostolic Palace. I am on duty and seated on a stool next to the pope's throne. After the mayor and Msgr. Georg Ratzinger deliver their respective speeches, the pope takes the floor. He eulogizes his brother lovingly, saying, "From the beginning of my life, my brother was to me not only a companion but also a trusted guide." These words reveal that his brother, Georg, was always considered precious for his enlightened counsels and good example, and indeed remains so.

29 FRIDAY AUGUST

As has been done since 1977, there is also a gathering this year of a group of former students of Professor Joseph Ratzinger, the so-called *Ratzinger Schülerkreis*. They come together to exchange ideas in a climate of friendship. The theme chosen by the pope for this year's meeting is "Conversations on Jesus." One of the participants, Cardinal Archbishop Christoph Schönborn of Vienna, is already in Rome and has come to have lunch with us today. There is also a discussion about the upcoming apostolic journey to Lourdes.

I notice that the Holy Father is very relaxed these days, and I sense more deeply his fatherliness when the two of us are alone.

Above: Pope Benedict with his brother Georg during the usual walk after lunch in the garden of the Moor in the Apostolic Palace of Castel Gandolfo.

This is especially so during our walks when we always find something to talk about. The pope's brother usually joins us after the Rosary, but only on the way back since he has difficulty walking.

Speaking of walks, on one of these evenings the pope, seeing a pine cone on the road, kicked it off the path. I must say that I was surprised with this and spontaneously asked him, "Holy Father, did you ever play soccer?" He immediately replied, "Never, because in my young years soccer was considered a worldly game."

Below: Pope Benedict concluding the Rosary in the Pontifical Villa Garden.

12 FRIDAY SEPTEMBER

We celebrate Holy Mass very early this morning so that we can leave on time from Fiumicino Airport. Today the Holy Father embarks for Paris and Lourdes for the last scheduled trip for 2008. The pope decided to personally go and pray at the Grotto of Massabielle on the occasion of the 150th anniversary of the apparition of Our Lady to Bernadette Soubirous. He also reasoned that the occasion presented him with the opportunity of stopping at the French capital to meet the Church in France, the civil authorities, and the world of French culture.

Benedict appears serene throughout the flight, and in a gesture of great esteem toward the Holy Father, we find President Sarkozy welcoming us at Orly Airport. The pope is at the Élysées at 12:30 p.m. to meet with the French state authorities, after which we are driven to the nunciature, which will be our home during our time here.

In the afternoon, the Holy Father meets the representatives of the Jewish community in France, which takes place in one of the nunciature's halls. Afterward we go to the Collège des Bernardins for the scheduled encounter with the representatives of the world of culture and letters. The college was built by the Cistercians and the late cardinal Jean-Marie Lustiger transformed it into a center for dialogue between Christian wisdom and modern culture. If I may say so, the Holy Father's choice for the theme of the speech is simply brilliant! Many expected it to be a reflection on contemporary Christianity. However, he chooses to concentrate on the origins of Western theology, which are tied to monasticism. Thus, he is able to demonstrate that the roots of European culture lie in the research undertaken by men who were not seeking to promote philosophical theories nor put forward any political proposals but were simply searching for God.

I believe that this speech will remain a milestone of the pontificate of Benedict. This is indicated with his final words: "*Quaerere Deum* — to seek God and to let oneself be found by him, that is today no less necessary than in former times. A purely positivistic culture which tried to drive the question concerning God into the subjective realm, as being unscientific, would be the capitulation of reason, the renunciation of its highest possibilities, and hence a disaster for humanity, with very grave consequences. What gave Europe's culture its foundation — the search for God and the readiness to listen to him — remains today the basis of any genuine culture."

The Holy Father, following this encounter, presides at Vespers with the priests, religious, and seminarians in the majestic Notre-Dame cathedral. He gives an outstanding final greeting to the young people gathered in the square outside for the prayer vigil. When we return to the nunciature, even though the Holy Father seems tired, he goes to the window to give a brief greeting to the festive crowd assembled outside the building and desirous of seeing closely the bishop of Rome.

13 SATURDAY SEPTEMBER

Before today's Holy Mass, the pope visits the Institut de France where representatives of five academies are assembled: the Académie francaise, the Académie des inscriptions et belles-lettres, the Académie des sciences, the Académie des beaux-arts, and the Académie des sciences morales et politiques. After delivering a brief speech, the pope uncovers a commemorative plaque of the encounter.

The pope celebrates an enthralling Holy Mass with a crowd of more than two hundred thousand participants at

the Esplanade des invalides. This is an exceptional number for a metropolis like Paris that is known for being so profane and secular. The congregation includes people who have come from nearby places specifically for this celebration, which, all things considered, proves that those who claim the Church in France is dying are mistaken.

We leave for Lourdes in the afternoon. On landing at Tarbes-Lourdes-Pyrénées Airport, we take the helicopter to St. Joseph's Hermitage, and soon after we go to visit the Church of the Sacred Heart, where Bernadette was baptized. Afterward we visit nearby Cachot, where the very poor Soubirous family lived for some time.

Benedict XVI, arriving at the Esplanade des Invalides.

To the right, the Pope is drinking the miraculous water in the Lourdes grotto like a simple pilgrim.

On the facing page, in Grotto of Massabielle in Lourdes.

Finally, here we are at the Grotto of Massabielle where the Holy Father, despite the rain, does what all pilgrims do — he drinks the water from the fountain and lights a candle to Our Lady. In its simplicity, it is a moving moment.

After supper we go back to the sanctuary complex for the concluding part of the traditional Marian procession with torches, *aux flambeaux*, which is always arresting. The Holy Father himself explains the significance of the torches and the candles: "Lourdes is one of the places chosen by God for his beauty to be reflected with particular brightness, hence the importance here of the symbol of light. From the fourth apparition onwards, on arriving at the grotto, Bernadette would light a votive candle each morning and hold it in her left hand for as long as the Virgin was visible to her. Soon, people would give Bernadette a candle to plant in the ground inside the grotto. Very soon, too, people would place their own candles in this place of light and peace. The Mother of God herself let it be known that she liked the touching homage of these thousands of torches, which since that time have continued to shine upon the rock of the apparition and give her glory. From that day, before the grotto, night and day, summer and winter, a burning bush shines out, aflame with the prayers of pilgrims and the sick, who bring their concerns and their needs, but above all their faith and their hope."

14 SUNDAY SEPTEMBER

The Holy Father presides at Holy Mass this morning at *la prairie du sanctuaire* of Lourdes, where thousands of pilgrims participate. Later in the afternoon he meets with the French bishops. With a polite and fatherly tone of voice, he speaks of central and sensitive subjects, such as the ministerial priesthood, catechesis, and the indissolubility of Christian marriage.

After the meeting, we return to *la prairie* for Eucharistic Adoration. The Holy Father delivers a very touching meditation, many times repeating the invitation that Jesus extends to everyone: giving ourselves to Him. I feel as if the Holy Father is speaking to me personally! Thus, kneeling in front of the Blessed Sacrament, I renew my consecration.

I write a few postcards after dinner, even to those from whom I have not heard for a long time. Then I feel the urge to return to the grotto and there, kneeling, I trust to Mary my work in the service of the pope and my entire life.

15 MONDAY
SEPTEMBER

The bags are packed. We thank the very kind ladies who have hosted us at St. Joseph's Hermitage. Next, we leave for the final Holy Mass, dedicated to the sick, which is being held at the esplanade. We stop along the way at the Oratoire de l'hôpital de Lourdes where Bernadette had been hospitalized and made her First Holy Communion. The Holy Father spends time in prayer inside the hospital chapel.

Holy Mass is celebrated in an atmosphere of great recollection, with us secretaries only a few steps away. Benedict administers the sacrament of the Anointing of the Sick to some ill persons during the celebration, when tenderness toward those who suffer is very touching. Next, he thanks all of those who in one way or another put themselves at the service of the sick: "The service of charity that you offer is a

Lourdes, 15 September:
Closing Mass on
the esplanade,
dedicated the sick.

Marian service. Mary entrusts her smile to you, so that you yourselves may become, in faithfulness to her Son, springs of living water. Whatever you do, you do in the name of the Church, of which Mary is the purest image. May you carry her smile to everyone!"

After the end of Holy Mass, we board three helicopters, which take us to the airport for the farewell ceremony with the participation of the French prime minister François Fillon. We land at Ciampino at 3:15 p.m. and head for the Apostolic Palace of Castel Gandolfo, where the Memores joyfully welcome us back. I have forgotten to refer to an amusing incident that happened yesterday at *la prairie*. In the morning, in the sacristy, I noticed a boy of about twelve years of age dressed up as an altar server. Perhaps he knew someone in security and managed to get this far. He had written a letter to the pope and managed to hand it to me. There he was again in the afternoon, and this time he had a camera with him. So I took the initiative to let him inside so as to greet the pope along with those ministers who served during Eucharistic Adoration. The pope spoke with him like a doting grandfather. That young boy was ecstatic, and my heart was full of joy.

30 TUESDAY SEPTEMBER

We return today. The bags are ready for our return to the Vatican. I already feel nostalgic. I feel more relaxed at Castel Gandolfo, for the atmosphere there is quite different. The panorama is beautiful. It is enough to look through a window, and seeing the lake below elicits a great feeling inside. I take some photos as a reminder.

In the afternoon, the Holy Father takes his leave from the workers at the pontifical villas and their families. After

The view from the terraces
of the Apostolic Palace
of Castel Gandolfo.

he personally greets each of them, he gives the go-ahead for the traditional fishing for goods, an event much anticipated especially by the children. The tradition to distribute amongst the workers the latest gifts given to the pope goes back to the time of Paul VI. It all really gives the feeling of belonging to a huge family. We arrive at the Vatican at around 5:30 p.m. We recite the Rosary on the terrace and then go in for dinner together.

14 WEDNESDAY OCTOBER

I turn fifty today. Once again, the Holy Father shows me the loveliness of his perceptive fatherhood. Msgr. Gänswein, the Memores, and the valet all join to sing me a song at breakfast. The Holy Father's brother is also present.

The pope wasn't satisfied with just giving me his best wishes earlier in the sacristy. I now see him entering the dining room with a package in his hands, and, beaming with pleasure and repeating his best wishes, he hands me his gifts: a really beautiful wooden statue of Our Lady with the Child, and a special edition of the book *Chi crede non è mai solo* (He who believes is never alone). The book is a collection of his speeches during his visit to Bavaria in 2006. The dedication reads: "To Monsignor Alfred Xuereb with my blessings, on his fiftieth birthday. B. XVI." My eyes well up with tears as I gratefully receive the gifts.

Lunch, prepared by the Memores, consists of a lot of wonderful things, including a cake and a bottle of sparkling wine at the end. Feeling a little embarrassed, I very warmly thank everyone.

Once on the terrace for the usual walk, I tell the pope how much I appreciate his gifts, and he, without any sentimentality, replies, "You deserve them." He makes me understand that he is very well aware of the sacrifices we willingly accept day after day to be close to him. I want to tell the pope that he owes me nothing, but rather it is us who are in debt to him. But, in the emotion of the moment, a lump in my throat stops me from saying anything.

21 TUESDAY OCTOBER

I will remember this day for the rest of my life. It started with my phone ringing at 6:30 a.m. It is my sister, Sylvia, weeping, informing me of the death of my father. Though I am stunned and speechless, a deep sense of serenity descends upon me at that very moment and never leaves me throughout the day.

I descend to the sacristy and inform the Holy Father of what has happened. He immediately becomes composed in prayer and recites the Requiem. He then asks for my father's name and invites me to put it in the Collect of the deceased for that day.

I begin the traveling preparations right after Holy Mass, greatly assisted by our gendarmerie, who go as far as getting me a plane ticket as well as a car to take me to the airport. The pope leaves me with the words "Please convey my condolences to your mother and to the rest of the family. Once you come back, we will celebrate a Holy Mass together for your father." His words prove of great comfort to my mother, to us siblings, and to our relatives.

17 MONDAY NOVEMBER

The Holy Father wakes with a touch of cold today. When we ask how he feels and if he still has a headache, he replies that "that never goes away." I have heard it mentioned that the Holy Father suffers from migraine headaches, but this is the first time I personally hear him say it. The pope never complains and carries out every task without reference to any health issues. This is a great example to me and a source of encouragement to take heart when I feel a little under the weather. In any case, despite the headache, the Holy Father is pleased to host Archbishop Reinhard Marx of Munich, a very outgoing and jovial person by nature.

18 TUESDAY NOVEMBER

Entering the elevator this afternoon to go for the usual walk and the recitation of the Rosary, the Holy Father asks to have a shorter walk due to the continuing headache. He also confides in us that he has been unable to work at his usual pace due to the pounding migraine. Nonetheless, when he gets into the car, he greets both the driver and the gendarme on duty in his usual warm way, without giving any hint of his not feeling well. He even forces himself to make some witty comment while at table. He tries to go beyond his difficulties by giving more of himself to others.

25 TUESDAY NOVEMBER

I have been feeling for a while the need to get some time off to recover my energies, and today I decide to discuss this with the pope. So I ask to speak with him. Benedict receives me in his study with a smile and asks me to sit on one of the two chairs in front of the desk. Then, to my great surprise, he comes around the desk to sit on the other chair next to mine. I can immediately see in his eyes his readiness to listen to whatever I have to say. In fact, I hardly begin expressing my request when he, without allowing me to finish it, agrees immediately. Once again, I witness firsthand the great humanity of Joseph Ratzinger.

6 SATURDAY DECEMBER

This year, too, on the day of St. Nicholas, we find the breakfast table laid out in a special way with dried fruits and mandarins and decorated with real leaves. The traditions of Bavaria remain very close to the Holy Father's heart. St. Nicholas and the inevitable wicked Knecht Ruprecht pay us a visit in the evening. Their role is carried out by two Swiss Guards who afterward extend their best wishes to the Holy Father and to the rest of us.

14 SUNDAY DECEMBER

It has been the tradition that on the Third Sunday of Advent we are visited by a group from *Das Werk* to sing some hymns. But this year, it is all of us who, along with the Holy Father, proceed to their recently renovated residence.

We recite Vespers in the chapel, and afterward we spend an hour or so in the library, singing hymns. I am asked to sing in Maltese the song "Ejja Fostna Mulej" (Come among us, Lord). The evening concludes with an excellent supper.

24 WEDNESDAY DECEMBER

This evening, the vigil of Christmas, the Holy Father lights the candle of peace at the window of the Apostolic Palace. Below, many people gather in prayer in the square.

We have an early supper this evening, and afterward we gather to sing Christmas carols and exchange greetings in the TV room. The Holy Father reads an excerpt from the

The lighting of the peace candle.

Gospels on the birth of Jesus. We also sing a carol in Maltese, "Hallelujah, twieled il-Messija" (Alleluia, the Savior is born), to the great pleasure of the Holy Father. It is a wonderful atmosphere, due in part to the presence of a stunning Christmas tree that is adorned with small candles and other decorations.

I experience a strong feeling during the Creed at Midnight Mass, when we profess "*et incarnatus est*," and at the moment of Holy Communion.

25 DECEMBER
THURSDAY

Christmas Mass is celebrated together in the private chapel. Later at noon, the pope delivers his Christmas message and then bestows the solemn *Urbi et Orbi* blessing from the center balcony of the Vatican Basilica. We assemble together in the afternoon for the singing of Vespers, and afterward we sing some Christmas carols in the TV room.

Solemn blessing Urbi et Orbi from the central Loggia of the Vatican Basilica, December, 25, 2008.

My Days with

BENEDICT XVI

2009

1 THURSDAY
JANUARY

When finance is only concerned about profits on a short-term basis, it becomes something dangerous for everyone. The pope supplies an admonition in the message for the 42nd World Day of Peace (fighting poverty to build peace). It is a document written with an eye on the severe crisis that has hit the world economy. When financial activities are guided by self-centric goals, ignoring the common good, the consequences can be devastating.

The document contains a thorough analysis of the current situation and does not bend to sociological techniques. The pope notes that the current food crisis is not the result so much of a shortage of food, but rather from profiteering and by a structural deficiency of political and economic institutions capable of addressing needs and emergencies. He follows this with an appeal that all nations should be guaranteed equal possibilities to have access to the global market that frequently nowadays is a mechanism that increases the disparity between rich and poor. This is a problem especially in Africa, which has a severe issue due to its almost complete dependence on the exportation of commodities (which are largely controlled by foreign conglomerates with their own interests) for its export revenues, and hence to feed its people. Globalization should be regulated because it is inconceivable that commercial mechanisms alone would produce justice. The risk is that the reality of one who has a full stomach is similar to that of a house surrounded by a vast desert dominated by suffering.

The new social situation should be faced with the preferential option for the poor. At this point, Benedict addresses the demographic problem: this state of affairs is not resolved by reducing birth rates, as a dominant school of thought would have us believe in the West, where there already exists a genuine "extermination"

The Sternsingers
(Star Singers) present
the Offertory of
the Gifts during the
Eucharistic liturgy.

of human lives through abortion. It can be resolved by stopping
the foolishness of the arms race, which drains precious resources,
otherwise available to development projects. Thus, it is funda-
mentally important to secure a world economy that works within
a legal framework against imbalances and injustices.

Benedict explains that there is also moral, spiritual, and
affective poverty. While there is frequently "moral underde-
velopment" in wealthy countries, there are also cultural im-
pediments that do not allow progress in poor nations. The
underlying reason in all of these cases is the marked absence
of the recognition of human dignity.

The pope asks that we consider poverty from the eyes
of children. When one does so, priorities emerge with great
clarity: commitment to education, access to vaccines and
medical care, the availability of drinking water, safeguarding
the environment, the caring for and formation of mothers, the
defense of the family and the stability of relations within it.

3 SATURDAY
JANUARY

It is an annual custom that the pope gets invited by the small Schönstatt community during the Christmas holidays. Sr. Birgit is a member of this community. The pope is expected to go to the community's residence on Via Aurelia for a pleasant evening.

The gathering begins with prayers in the sisters' chapel and then continues in the large hall of the residence. We sing many carols, alternating between German, Italian, and Latin, as we stand beside the beautiful Christmas tree. There is a Christmas atmosphere, something that really pleases Pope Benedict. Next, Sr. Birgit reads a charming story that everyone loves. It is about a little angel who, as he was still very small, was dismissed by the other angels from joining them in their standing orchestra, which offered a musical homage to the Holy Family. They gathered together, full of joy, inside the grotto of Bethlehem and began playing. But Baby Jesus did not stop crying. Despite the fact that the angels tried their best to cheer up their special guests, Baby Jesus could not fall asleep and was restless in the arms of His Mother. At a certain point, the Virgin Mary noticed the little angel at the back of the group with his flute in his hands and half obscured by the other angels. She beckoned him to come forward and play his flute for Jesus. To everyone's surprise, Baby Jesus, hearing the sweet sound coming from the little angel's flute, stopped crying, closed His eyes, and slept serenely.

After Pope Benedict gives us a brief Christmas reflection, we proceed to the dining table, which is already set for a frugal dinner.

However, before we sit down at table, a nice incident happens that is worth telling. A few days ago a picture of a "Symbol of the Father" was discovered in the Holy Father's storeroom. It was set in a triangular frame and had at its center an eye, which depicted the fatherly goodness of the triune God, a theme venerated throughout the Schönstatt movement. Pope Benedict thought of giving this "Symbol of the Father" as a gift to the sisters' community in Rome. He assigns me to hang it high in the sisters' dining room, and there is already a ladder set beneath the two nails in the wall where I was asked to hang the picture. It is not as easy as it looks though, because I have to put the two rings of the frame into the nails, which the frame itself prevents me from seeing. The sisters become somewhat anxious, perhaps even Pope Benedict himself. He gets closer to the ladder to direct me with his hands as to how to proceed. All of us, including myself, are relieved when the picture is finally put in place and we can calmly proceed to have dinner.

22 THURSDAY JANUARY

Some members of the media are stating that the Vatican is about to issue a decree through which the pope will withdraw the excommunication of the Lefebvrite Richard Williamson and three other bishops ordained by Archbishop Marcel Lefebvre in 1988 without the approval of the Roman Pontiff. In fact, the decree already exists and is dated January 21. It deals with a provision signed by Cardinal Giovanni Battista Re, prefect of the Congregation for Bishops. It does not concede restitution of full communion to the Society of St. Pius X, which was founded by Archbishop Lefebvre. Nonetheless, the four bishops are reintegrated in the Catholic Church as a sign of good will. Benedict XVI is extending his hand as a sign of mercy so as to avoid further festering of this open wound and prevent its spreading. The pope is impressed by the abundance of vocations flourishing within the fraternity and thinks that healing the separation will benefit everyone.

However, at the time that Benedict revokes the excommunication of the four bishops, he is not aware of a circumstance that the international press brings to light. Bishop Williamson, in the course of an interview some time ago, made incredible statements that deny Nazi crimes, going so far as to deny, among other things, the very existence of gas chambers for the extermination of Jews.

Consequently, Benedict XVI becomes the target of a harsh media campaign. He decides to meet it head-on by making public on March 10 the letter he had sent to his brother bishops across the world to explain the meaning of his decision. The pope acknowledges in the letter that there were errors in communication and affirms that no one in the Vatican was aware of the declarations of Williamson regarding the Holocaust. With great humility and sincerity, he states that it would have been enough to search the Internet to avoid this grave mistake, but regrettably this was not done. In any case, the pontiff wants to emphasize his great regret for the way this matter was handled. A gesture of mercy toward the four pastors, ordained illegitimately but also validly, was interpreted as a denial of a long journey of dialog and friendship with the Jews, and what was supposed to be an invitation for reconciliation with a division of the traditional group within the Catholic Church became a source of friction between the Vatican and our Jewish brothers.

Benedict XVI is sincerely grieved by these misleading and malicious interpretations. He quotes St. Paul's Letter to the Galatians: "'But if you bite and devour one another, take heed that you are not consumed by one another.' I am always tempted to see these words as another of the rhetorical excesses which we occasionally find in Saint Paul. To some extent that may also be the case. But sad to say, this 'biting and devouring' also exists in the Church today, as expression of a poorly understood freedom."

There is no doubt that during these days the pope is living through one of the most difficult moments in his pontificate, and we of his household, like his collaborators in the Curia, are very close to him emotionally and spiritually.

13 FRIDAY FEBRUARY

Pope Benedict is delighted with the news that the estimable Order of the Knights of Malta wishes to enroll me among its members as an "honorary Conventual Chaplain." The ceremony takes place this morning inside the order's church of Santa Maria all'Aventino. It is presided over by the grand master, Fra' Matthew Festing, assisted by the members of the Sovereign Council.

When I return to the apartment, the Holy Father is very interested to learn what took place at the ceremony and who attended. I recount how the grand master very solemnly put around my neck the Collar pro Merito Melitensi and presented me with the certificate of my appointment. Also sharing in the same ceremony was the induction into the order of the archdukes of the Austria-Este royal family, being welcomed as Knights and Dame of Honor and Devotion. Benedict is very pleased and, asking to see the badges, he recommends that I frame the parchment representing my appointment.

24 TUESDAY FEBRUARY

Yesterday morning I informed the Holy Father of the death of the attorney Gianluigi Marrone. I have frequently updated the pope over these last days with the progression of the grave illness that has overtaken the single judge of Vatican City. Pope Benedict had asked me to convey to him his blessing and the assurance of being especially remembered during the recitation of the Rosary. He was very pleased when I told him that Marrone, moved by such a manifestation of good will, asked me to inform the pope that he was offering his suffering for the good of the Church and for the Supreme Pontiff. I knew Gianluigi very well when I had the privilege of collaborating with him during those years when I was the spiritual assistant advisor of the Association of Sts. Peter and Paul at the Vatican, of which group he was president.

The funeral services take place this afternoon at the Basilica of Santa Maria in Trastevere. It is packed to capacity with many distinguished representatives attending. A number of persons deliver speeches. They are members of the Italian Chamber of Deputies, where the attorney Marrone served as the head of the legal department and of the cabinet of the president; members of the tribunal of Vatican City; officials of various departments of the Holy See; and especially many members of the association.

Before I go to the ceremony, Pope Benedict asks me to convey his condolences to the wife and two children and to assure them of his closeness and his prayers. At the end of the funeral rites, I read the telegram that the Supreme Pontiff sent under these sad circumstances.

Once I return home, the pope wants me to tell him all about the funeral.

9 MONDAY MARCH

Today Benedict XVI goes to visit the Campidoglio, the head-quarters of the Commune of Rome. He receives a very warm and friendly welcome. The pope, during his speech, renews "the assurance of the fatherly attention that the Bishop of the Catholic community prays not only to its members but also to all Romans and all who come to the Capital from various parts of Italy and the world for reasons of religion, tourism or work, or to settle, integrating themselves into the fabric of the City."

Perhaps, while enunciating these words, Benedict is also thinking of himself at the time he came to Rome in 1962 for Vatican II. He arrived as the theological expert of the arch-bishop of Cologne, Cardinal Josef Frings. It was at this time that he first started to get to know Rome.

After the pope is welcomed by the mayor of Rome, Gianni Alemanno, and the entire municipal council, he delivers an address focusing on the changes that have taken place in the metropolis, due especially to the arrival of so many people belonging to different cultures and faiths, and acknowledges that "integration is sometimes a very arduous and complex endeavor." He goes on to state that at the same time, however, it is certain that "Rome will be able to find the strength to demand respect for the rules of civil coexistence from all and to reject every form of intolerance and discrimination." Next, he highlights the economic difficulties of so many persons and families and calls on the city administrators to commit themselves to the expression of solidarity and generosity, which are values "deeply rooted in the hearts of Romans."

The pope welcomes the praiseworthy initiative of the municipal administration, who wish to dedicate to Benedict XVI the center on Inviolatella Borghese Street, which will provide formation and support for disadvantaged youth.

17 MARCH
TUESDAY

Today Pope Benedict lands in Yaoundé after six hours of flight to begin his thirteenth apostolic journey outside Italy. This is his first visit to Africa, and he will visit Cameroon and Angola. As usual, the pope is serene, though he is very mindful of the delicate nature of this mission.

It is a journey full of great expectations because the pope will visit two nations during a worldwide economic crisis that has many implications for poor countries. It goes without saying that the Supreme Pontiff does not go to Africa with a political-economic agenda, but with a religious program that deals with faith and morals. One of the fundamental elements in this crisis is precisely a deficit

A festive welcome for Pope Benedict by Cameroonian people.

in the ethics of economic structures. Ethics should not be treated as something "outside" the economy, but rather as something "within," for it should be understood that no economy functions properly if it does not retain within itself an ethical component.

The pope reiterates to the journalists traveling with him on the aircraft that he intends to speak about God and the great spiritual values of the Christian lifestyle as a way to contribute to the overcoming of the crisis and to the renewing of the economic system from within. This is the central point of the true crisis. He will appeal primarily for a Catholic solidarity and that of all those who recognize their responsibility to today's human society. The Church is the font of great hopes, along with many concerns. Hopes spring from the enormous potential of these peoples, the signs of growth, and the natural religiosity of Africans. On the other hand, concerns arise from the poverty that continues to spread, the social imbalances and injustices, the corruption, and the spreading of religious sects.

19 THURSDAY MARCH

Today is the Solemnity of St. Joseph, husband of the Virgin Mary. It is also Benedict XVI's name day. He celebrates it as a day filled with a very heavy agenda.

While reading the press reviews, we realize that the media has focused its attention on the reply the pope gave to a French journalist during the flight to Africa. It regarded the problem of AIDS, unfortunately very widespread in Africa, and the Church's denial of the use of contraception. Is not the Church's stand unrealistic and ineffective?

The pope's response is crystal clear: "I would say the opposite. I think that the most efficient, most truly present player in the fight against AIDS is the Catholic Church herself, with her movements and her various organizations. I think of the Sant'Egidio community that does so much, visibly and also behind the scenes, in the struggle against AIDS, I think of the Camillians, and so much more besides, I think of all the Sisters who take care of the sick. I would say that this problem of AIDS cannot be overcome merely with money, necessary though it is. If there is no human dimension, if Africans do not help by responsible behavior, the problem cannot be overcome by the distribution of prophylactics: on the contrary, they increase it." Benedict then explains that the solution consists in a two-pronged approach: the humanization of sexuality, whereby there is a return to the dimension of the gift of reciprocal fidelity, and that of solidarity and concrete assistance to those who are sick.

The press, however, seizes on a single concept from the pope's argument, and quoting it out of context as being very dismissive (pope: no condoms), generate a series of very harsh reactions, even from the UN, the governments of Germany and France, and the Belgian Chamber of Deputies. So, yet again, Benedict finds himself embroiled in a controversy, despite what he has said. Thus, the many important topics that are the center of the journey end up being overshadowed.

Another reason Benedict is in Africa is to entrust to the local bishops the working document, *Instrumentum laboris*, for the African Synod to take place at the Vatican during October. The document is being delivered in Cameroon, where Catholics form less than 27 percent of the population. On the other hand, the visit to Angola, where Catholics represent about 55 percent of the population, is being singled out for the ceremonies marking the five hundredth anniversary of the first evangelization of that nation.

28 TUESDAY APRIL

The city of L'Aquila and other places in the Abruzzo were stricken by a strong earthquake during the night of April 6, 2009. It claimed more than three hundred lives. Strong shock waves were also felt at the Vatican. As soon as Benedict is informed of the great suffering provoked by this dramatic event, he decides to show his personal solidarity with the victims by visiting the stricken places. The trip will take place on April 28. His visit is truly that of a father who consoles his children, inviting them also to use the spiritual strength gained through prayer for their recovery.

Upon arriving at Onna, a village reduced to a heap of rubble, the pope says, "I would like to embrace you one by one with affection." Then he recalls a saying dear to the local population, "There are still many days behind the Gran Sasso," and encourages everyone to have hope by relying on the strength of spirit typical of Abruzzo.

Inside the Basilica of Collemaggio, in L'Aquila, Benedict venerates the remains of Pope St. Celestine V and leaves on

the tomb the pallium that was bestowed on him at the beginning of his pontificate. This is an episode that, some years later, would be interpreted as a prediction of a historic decision. Next, the pope prays in silence in front of the students' residence where eight young people died.

Benedict XVI venerates the remains of Celestine V kept in the Basilica of Collemaggio.

The meeting with the faithful and with the staff in charge of the relief efforts takes place in front of the school of the Guardia di Finanza, the same where the funeral services of the victims were held on March 10. The image of a small white coffin of a child, placed atop that of his mother, had been transmitted across the world and had evoked deep emotion.

Benedict says, "Solidarity is a deeply civil and Christian sentiment and is the benchmark of a society's maturity. In practice, it manifests in rescue work, but it is not only an effective organizational machine: there is a soul, there is a passion, which derives precisely from our people's great civil and Christian history, both in institutional forms and in voluntary work." Then he gives some advice: the civil community is being called upon to make "a serious examination of conscience to ensure that the level of responsibility never diminishes."

8 FRIDAY MAY

Today Benedict leaves for another trip, as important as it is
desired. He goes to the Holy
Land. Preceded by the compli-
cations arising from the lifting
of the excommunication of the
four traditionalist bishops, the
timing of this trip is worrisome, especially due to many political implications. But beginning with his responses to the
journalists on the flight to the Holy Land, the pope is very
clear on where things stand: this journey is being undertaken
exclusively for religious motives. As to matters regarding the
problem of peace, he affirms, "We are convinced that God
listens and that he can act in history. I think that if millions of
people — millions of believers — all pray, this is truly a force
that influences and can contribute to moving forward the
cause of peace."

First of all, there is the dramatic situation with the Christian communities that in many instances are constrained to
abandon the Middle East. The pope is very much aware of
this misfortune, but he encourages all to try to stay so as to
give a hand to reconciliation.

Irrespective of the fact that the pope is very clear about
the reasons for this journey, there is always someone who
tries to manipulate his words to present them under a bad
light. This happened when Benedict went to the Holocaust
memorial, Yad Vashem, to pay homage to the victims of the
Shoah. Some members of the press reported that the pope
did not explicitly refer to Nazism for the tragedy and did not
include the responsibility of Christians, and they accused him
of leaving this out and of being partial. Fortunately, there

147

were also reporters who pointed out that the pope was very decisive when he denounced anti-Semitism, which "continues to show its ugly head in many parts of the world."

12 TUESDAY MAY

The pope meets the grand mufti, along with the leaders of the Islamic community. The meeting takes place in Jerusalem, at the Dome of the Rock, the most ancient Islamic monument in the Holy Land. He reaffirms the determination of the Catholic Church in its desire to continue to work to overcome past misunderstandings and conflicts and to move forward by setting a path of sincere dialogue aimed at building a world of justice and peace for future generations.

Next, the pope makes a courtesy visit to the Hechal Shlomo Center in Jerusalem. Pope Benedict, as bishop of Rome, addresses the highest representatives of the Jewish faith. He speaks words of encouragement for the continuation of an effective dialogue and reiterates the irrevocable commitment of the Catholic Church to the road that leads to a "genuine and lasting reconciliation."

His praying in silence at the Western Wall of Jerusalem is very touching. It is the most sacred place for the Jews. Benedict inserts a prayer among the stones in the Western Wall.

Silent prayer at the Wailing Wall, where Pope Benedict placed a prayer between the stones of the wall.

13 WEDNESDAY MAY

Pope Benedict meets a Palestinian mother and her child hosted in the refugee camp by Aida.

Pope Benedict's pilgrimage would not have been complete without a visit to Bethlehem, the city of David and the place where Jesus Christ was born.

The Christian presence in Bethlehem has been reduced from 72 to 12 percent in a few years. During his visit to Bethlehem and to the Aida Refugee Camp, the pope personally touches the reality of the Palestinians who live in conditions of constant exasperation due to the wall that prevents their freedom of movement, with serious repercussions on employment, education, and health care. The pontiff denounces these conditions and asks for the Palestinian people to be able to live in a sovereign state with specific borders recognized internationally.

There is an appeal for justice at the end of the journey. Benedict states that only the practice and honoring of justice can secure a long-lasting peace. This is the approach that the Holy See, through its diplomatic and pastoral activities, seeks with determination.

24 SUNDAY MAY

Pope Benedict XVI's message for the World Social Communications Day is entitled "New Technologies, New Relationships: Promoting a Culture of Respect, Dialogue, and Friendship." As happens every year on the feast of St. Francis de Sales, patron of communications, the pope dedicates a reflection on the means of communication. This year, 2009, the pope focuses especially on the so-called digital generation, highlighting the potential of the new technologies in favor of a better understanding between people and social groups. The advances in technology are presenting opportunities that were unthinkable up to a short time ago, and the young are their primary benefactors. The appeal to the producers is passionate and aimed to induce them to feel committed to respect human dignity, while the new generations are strongly advised to think that this "is not just a succession of events or experiences: it is a search for the true, the good and the beautiful."

Today is the feast of the Ascension of Our Lord into Heaven. Since the pope is the sixteenth one to carry the name of St. Benedict, who died in 547, he makes a visit to the abbey of Nursia in homage to its founder. Though it is a short visit, it is full of meaning because Pope Ratzinger has never hidden the fact that for him St. Benedict is genuinely an example and point of reference. The pope delivers a homily during Holy Mass in the piazza, which henceforth will be called Benedict XVI. The pope reintroduces the Benedictine heritage: "We hear resonating St Benedict's appeal to keep our hearts fixed on Christ, to prefer nothing to him." Monte Cassino is a sacred place that Pope Benedict XVI describes as "the cradle of spirituality and of European culture" and "the birthplace of the roots of European Christianity." After the inauguration

Tribute to the fallen during the visit for the 65th anniversary of bombing of the monastery of Montecassino.

of the House of Charity, as a way to mark the sixty-fifth anniversary of the destruction of the monastery, the pope prays
at the tomb of the saint and speaks once again of peace. He
states that everyone should contribute to the establishment
of peace, for this is truly a gift from God that, nevertheless, is
a gift entrusted to the responsibility of humankind.

21 SUNDAY JUNE

Pope Benedict embarks on another journey in Italy. This time
he is destined for San Giovanni Rotondo, in the province of
Foggia. Here the mortal remains of Padre Pio of Pietrelcina
have rested since September 23, 1968. He is the friar with the
stigmata whom Pope John Paul II canonized in 2002.

This city in Puglia is overflowing with excitement for the
papal visit. Thousands of people have come from all over Italy
in homage to this humble Capuchin who spent his life at the
altar or inside the confessional. The pope says that the life of
Padre Pio, even with its vicissitudes and misunderstandings by
Vatican authorities, "teaches us that only a soul closely united
with the Crucified One succeeds in communicating the joy and
riches of the Gospel even to those who are remote."

During this visit, the pope stops at the Home for the Relief
of Suffering. It is the hospital Padre Pio wanted to serve as a place
of science as well as one of prayer and especially of welcome.
The meeting with the sick, their families, the medical personnel,
nurses, administrators, and managers allows Benedict XVI to
emphasize the spirit the holy friar strongly desired to undergird
this establishment, a structure in which one can see in practice
that the commitment to care for the sick "must never be separat-
ed from filial trust in God, who is infinitely kind and merciful."

Padre Pio was a tireless confessor and just as great a minister
of the sacrament of Reconciliation as St. John Mary Vianney,

better known as the Curé d'Ars, whom the pope proposes as the person of reference at the beginning of the Year for Priests. This celebration was initiated just two days before the visit to San Giovanni Rotondo, and the year will conclude in June 2010. It is something Benedict XVI has wanted, as one can see from reading in the letter of convocation for the Year for Priests: it is "meant to deepen the commitment of all priests to interior renewal for the sake of a stronger and more incisive witness to the Gospel in today's world." And, in Pope Ratzinger's judgment, the most applicable words for this task are precisely those of the saintly French priest: "The priesthood is the love of the heart of Jesus."

29 MONDAY JUNE

This is a very important day. It is the feast of Sts. Peter and Paul. The pope has signed his third encyclical, *Caritas in veritate*, his first of a social nature. It is a long-awaited document that has been revised several times in the light of the economic crisis that has engulfed the whole word. The document is addressed not only to Catholics and believers but "to all people of good will." In line with Benedict XVI's personal style, it contains not only criticisms but also practical advice for "an integral human development." It deals with "a further contribution which the Church offers to humanity in its commitment to provide a sustainable advancement that carries full respect for human dignity and the concrete needs of everyone."

The text of the encyclical was polished during the months of the financial crisis. It argues that recent events have demonstrated the need for a global "structure" that is able to deal with these new phenomena.

Faced by global interdependence, there is the urgent need to activate an authority that is recognizable and respected. According to the pope, the issue underlying the worldwide crisis is a world of economy and finance that lacks morality. When human activities dismiss the moral principle, we end up with nothing but exploitation and destruction. It is clear by now that the management of companies, at all levels, cannot have as their objective instantaneous selfish interests. All is lost when we lose sight of the common good. The pope reiterates in the encyclical the Church's approval of the market economy but on the condition that this does not become some source of legitimacy for the dominance of the strong over the weak, of the rich over the poor. The market is only an instrument and is not an end. In any case, the intervention of public authorities may be necessary in some situations specially to remedy inequalities.

10 FRIDAY JULY

Benedict XVI, just a few days after he signs the encyclical, receives for the first time at the Vatican the president of the United States, Barack Obama. The latter is one of the people who can most of all bring about a world government for the economy and finance identified with justice and solidarity. It is a very cordial meeting. The new president was born in 1961 and entered the

Benedict XVI receives US President Barack Obama and wife, Michelle, at the Vatican.

White House this past January. He embodies many hopes that are not restricted to Americans. There are many topics discussed during the meeting. They range from the economic crisis in the Middle East to the aid in the development of poor countries and the issue of drug trafficking. The pope gives the president a copy of the new encyclical at the end of the meeting. President Barack spontaneously thanks the pope, saying, "Thank you, Holiness. Now I have something to read on the airplane." Who knows if the president, while en route to Africa, has had the opportunity to read the papal document!

18 SATURDAY JULY

While taking some days off to rest in Malta, I am very alarmed with the news that Pope Benedict has broken his right wrist due to a nasty fall in his bedroom while spending a few days of vacation in a mountain chalet at Les Combes.

I immediately call him by telephone, and he personally assures me that he feels well and that he has every intention to remain on the mountain as originally scheduled. The pope accidentally fell during the night in a place with which he was not familiar. In accordance with his typical gracefulness, he did not want to disturb his sleeping secretary, and he went to celebrate Holy Mass in the chapel the following morning as if everything was normal. It was only during breakfast that he expressed his discomfort due to intense pain. He was subsequently taken to the hospital in Aosta for an evaluation. An X-ray showed a multiple fracture of his right wrist. He underwent a twenty-five-minute surgery with local anesthesia to treat the fracture. The surgery was very successful, and he will be able to resume writing and playing the piano with no problems after an adequate time of rehabilitation.

Recovery after a fall in Les Combes, during a short rest in the mountains.

Pope Benedict wanted to be treated like any other patient in the hospital. So he waited for his turn to be taken to the operating room. In the meantime, there was an emergency surgery for a patient suffering from peritonitis. The medical doctors who took care of the pope described him as "a patient who is calm, serene, and without any complaint."

10 MONDAY AUGUST

I am willing to interrupt my vacation at home. But Pope Benedict convinces me not to do so, while assuring me that he is making good progress with the help of physiotherapy. When I return to Rome, I am shocked to see the pope with his arm in a cast and to realize that I have to assist him even in simple daily chores.

For a few days the pope has not been able to put on the alb for Holy Mass. Instead, after putting on the stole and the chasuble over his white cassock by himself, he leaves the rest to one of us, his secretaries, including breaking the Sacred Host at the appropriate time. Despite his limitations in movement, he never loses his serenity and frequently makes jokes about himself. The funniest moments are when I help him button up his soutane. I usually start from the bottom, while he buttons from the top going downwards. There have been a few occasions when I inadvertently skip a buttonhole, only to realize this at our meeting point, which means having to undo some buttons and start again. However, when we are able to complete the task successfully, he compliments me by saying in German, "*Erfolg*. Success." We have a great laugh.

21 FRIDAY AUGUST

Finally, the day has arrived to remove the cast from Pope Benedict's wrist! A small medical team, led by the orthopedic surgeon Dr. Vincenzo Sessa, waits in a room equipped for surgery in the Apostolic Palace of Castel Gandolfo. The procedure takes about ten minutes, and at the end the two metal pins that kept the fractured bones together are removed. The surgeon frequently asks the Holy Father if he is able to endure the pain, and the latter nods to continue.

Once the entire procedure is completed, I accompany Pope Benedict to his room while the medical team starts putting the medical instruments back in place. I return to escort them on their way out, and they tell me of their great admiration for the high level of endurance the pope exhibited during the entire procedure. They inform me that usually, in similar cases, the patient emits some cries of pain, but the pope remained calm throughout the time, looking on with meekness.

6 SUNDAY SEPTEMBER

Today the pope embarks on his sixteenth journey in Italy. He is going to visit Viterbo and Bagnoregio. The latter has a special significance for Joseph Ratzinger, for Bagnoregio is the home of St. Bonaventure, who, along with St. Augustine, had a profound influence on the human and spiritual formation of the pontiff. While the doctoral thesis of the young Ratzinger in 1953 was on St. Augustine (whose remains are contained in an urn in Pavia, which the pope visited two years ago), the future pope's dissertation for his university teaching credential was on Bonaventure. It led to the publication of a book in 1959 that presented a new interpretation of the thought of the "Seraphic Doctor," especially regarding the concept of divine revelation, understood as the way through which God communicates Himself to the human creature.

The city of Viterbo itself occupies a very important place in the history of the Catholic Church. It is sufficient to recall that it was here that the first conclave took place, and that fifty popes have visited this city over the centuries, eighteen of them lived here, and four are buried here.

The theme of the visit, "Confirm your brothers," fits the pastoral style of Benedict XVI very well. The local people give him a warm welcome, and there is a sense of celebration and great friendship in the air. The affection of the people toward this humble and somewhat shy pope is tangible.

It is a pity that Benedict XVI cannot administer Holy Communion — the aftermath of breaking his wrist constrains his hand movements.

26 SATURDAY SEPTEMBER

The recitation of his breviary during the flight to the Czech Republic.

The pope leaves for the Czech Republic today. It is his thirteenth international trip. Pope Benedict XVI's words make news even before his airplane lands in Prague. While talking with journalists during the flight, the pontiff says, "I would say that usually it is creative minorities who determine the future, and in this regard the Catholic Church must understand that she is a creative minority who has a heritage of values that are not things of the past, but a very lively and relevant reality." The expression "a creative minority" will become one of the most typical phrases of Benedict's pontificate. The pope is very much aware that in the West to be a Christian has become being part of a minority, but he also knows that numbers are not the whole story. One can be a minority on the quantitative level and, nevertheless, have a clear awareness of the contemporary cultural, religious, and moral challenges. Benedict, during this journey, will launch various appeals to search for the truth and to safeguard Christian values. He states in the presence of political authorities that "Europe is more than a continent. It is a home!" It is a "spiritual homeland" built on the heritage of faith that may not be erased, for this would otherwise entail the loss of that freedom that is ever so fragile and that the countries of Eastern Europe have laboriously recovered from. He will also say to Catholics that it is not enough to identify themselves as believers but that they must be credible and always ready to be witnesses to Christian principles and ideals in every context.

5 MONDAY
OCTOBER

"All our analyses of the world are insufficient if we do not discover that underlying corruption and evil is a mistaken relationship with God." These are the words coming from the heart of Benedict XVI that he pronounced to the almost 250 bishops who are gathered today inside the Vatican for the synod dedicated to Africa, a vast continent. The pope explains that Africa is infected by two viruses: the first arrived from the West and is due to materialism combined with relativistic and nihilistic thought; the other is partly imported and partly indigenous, and it is religious fundamentalism that is being fueled by political and economic interests. The pope recalls for the benefit of the African bishops that the Catholic community, if it really wants to confront and eradicate these two viruses, must first of all undertake a path of purification. What is necessary is recognizing one's own sins and "knowing ourselves in the light of God," for "only in this light can we know ourselves, can we also understand what is evil in us and thus perceive all that must be renewed, transformed." The horizontal analyses, sociological in kind, are important to help us understand these phenomena, but a Catholic must not stop with these. One must always ask oneself what God is calling one to. This off-the-cuff talk comes from the pope's heart and concludes with an appeal: there is a need for the African society to be open, to break down barriers that still exist among the tribes and ethnic groups and religions; it is necessary to open oneself to make room for God's love.

Benedict, as he enjoys doing, shares his impressions during luncheon by showing his joy for the newly inaugurated synod, which he perceives as a bearer of graces for Africa and the entire Church.

8 SUNDAY NOVEMBER

St. Peter's Basilica: Joseph Ratzinger, Metropolitan Archbishop of Munich and Freising, gratefully greets Pope Paul VI during the ordinary public consistory of June 27, 1977.

Today Benedict XVI will visit Brescia and Concesio, the native town of Paul VI, who was pope from 1963 to 1978. He was Giovanni Battista Montini, and Joseph Ratzinger

feels that the two have many things in common: their shy character, their great love for the Church, their dedication to defend doctrine, their confrontation with modern culture.

It is a rainy day. Nonetheless, thousands of people show up to see the pope and to participate at Holy Mass, which is celebrated in Brescia in the square aptly called Paul VI.

The homily focuses on the theme of the Church. Benedict suggests that the Bride of Christ always walks "poor and free," as Montini had wished. Then he recalls the words Paul VI addressed to the students of the Pontifical Lombard Seminary in 1968 at a time of great social upheaval and open protests by young people. The pope from Brescia stated that, unlike some might think, the pope is not called to make sensational gestures, perhaps even breaking with the past, but only to remain close to Jesus.

Meanwhile, Benedict XVI has taken an important step forward with his apostolic constitution *Anglicanorum coetibus*, which bears the date of November 4, 2009. It regards Anglicans who in recent years have expressed their desire to return to full communion with Rome. This document is another eloquent gesture of Pope Ratzinger in favor of Christian unity.

21 SATURDAY NOVEMBER

The Sistine Chapel enjoys an unparalleled setting. It is here that the pope receives about three hundred artists to commemorate the tenth anniversary of the "Letter to Artists" of John Paul II and the forty-fifth anniversary of the meeting with Paul VI. The invited guests represent the arts from every corner of the earth. The pope greets them by stating, "At this gathering I wish to express and renew the Church's friendship with the world of art, a friendship that has been strengthened over time; indeed, Christianity from its earliest days has recognized the value of the arts and has made wise use of their varied language to express her unvarying message of salvation."

Pope Benedict, who has a deep artistic awareness, plays the piano, and likes classical music, expresses his belief that beauty and hope go hand in hand, and he asks artists to be the

guardians of beauty because "beauty, like truth, brings joy to the human heart" and leads us "to grasp the Whole in the fragment, the Infinite in the finite, God in the history of humanity."

We speak about some aspects of this joyful encounter while we are at table. We recall the touching invitation of one of the artists, who asked the pope to leave free the day on which he will celebrate his wedding anniversary.

24 THURSDAY DECEMBER

We gather together on Christmas Eve in the sitting room around the Christmas tree with lit candles, as we have done in previous years to listen to the Holy Father reading the Gospel passage on the Nativity of Jesus. This is a very solemn moment for him, almost a liturgical act. After we finish singing carols, the pope reaches under the tree for a very old, hand-painted wooden box. He opens it, and there inside is an infant Jesus with blond

161

hair, dressed in rich clothing. The
pope, visibly emotional and happy,
declares, "Now it is Christmas!" He
has been waiting for this day for a
long time. I know this fact firsthand
as I had already heard him say on
June 25, "Christmas will be here in
six months!" This is a feast that he
especially awaits.

But the actual Christmas celebrations have a distressing start.

The curly-haired Child,
who for so many years
accompanied the
Christmas holidays with
Joseph Ratzinger.

There is an aggressive attack on the pope. As the procession is
moving along the central nave of St. Peter's Basilica, a young,
mentally unstable Italo-Swiss woman manages to leap over the
barricade, throw herself onto the Holy Father, and pull him
down as she holds on to the pallium. The commander of the
Vatican Gendarmerie, Dr. Giani, immediately gets hold of her.
A scream arises from the crowd. I am petrified. I immediately
think the worst, but the pope stands up and, although shaken,
seems fine. He dismisses the suggestion that he take a few minutes to recollect himself before continuing with the Holy Mass.

The one who gets the worst of it is the eighty-six-year-old
Cardinal Etchegaray, who is also knocked down. He suffers a
femur fracture, is taken to Gemelli Polyclinic, and will have
to undergo surgery in the next few days.

Holy Mass continues in the normal manner as if nothing
has happened. The pope delivers his entire homily with no
problems, even if occasionally his voice sounds a little hesitant
due to breathlessness.

After the celebration, we return to the apartment. The
Holy Father seems serene. He even joins us in the room next
to the kitchen for a slice of panettone and sip of sparkling
wine. He does not comment upon the incident.

My Days with

BENEDICT XVI

2010

26 TUESDAY JANUARY

Today is a tranquil day, as sometimes happens with those Tuesdays when there are no scheduled audiences. Msgr. Gänswein goes about his other tasks. Thus, I am left alone with the pope, experiencing firsthand his solicitude and his fatherly approach in my regard. The first secretary was also absent last Wednesday, and it fell to me to be next to the Holy Father during the Wednesday general audience. Although I am no expert at this, I was very tranquil because I sense that the pope wishes me well.

On our way back to the apartment, I take the opportunity to offer some directions regarding the use of the elevator's telephone. As it happened, the elevator broke down yesterday and we were stuck inside. Therefore, it is good that the pope knows what to do in case of a new emergency. If this happens when he is alone, or is with his older brother, it would not be a pleasant experience.

The Holy Father never misses an opportunity to let us know how much he appreciates our service. A few nights ago, after we watched the news, he told us that he was somewhat dizzy, but then he was himself again and still wanted to climb up to the terrace for our usual walk. He said to us secretaries, "After all, I have two guardian angels!"

28 THURSDAY JANUARY

We talk about a recently published book on Servant of God John Paul II. It stated that the pope did penance by stretching out on the floor of his private chapel, as well as wearing a sackcloth. The book said that John Paul II had left it up to the cardinals to decide whether he should abdicate if he was not able to make this decision due to some infirmity. The Holy Father comments that it was actually Paul VI who was the first to put in writing this kind of provision. Then, without any hesitation, he says, "I, too, have done so." While speaking of John Paul II, who loved to go skiing on the mountains, the Holy Father recalls a curious detail with a smile across his face. He had not been in the Vatican that long when he noticed a steep decline in the area of the mint. The then-cardinal Ratzinger, not being inclined in the least to sports, thought that the Polish pope could go there to ski and avoid going far away to do so. He adds, smiling, "I had not thought of the fact that it almost never snows in Rome!"

Speaking about snow, the Holy Father told us that when his mother went shopping during the winter months, she often used a slider sled. Being Maltese, I am no expert about snow. So I asked him if the sled had brakes. He told me, "But no, for that you simply use your feet!"

31 SUNDAY
JANUARY

The Holy Father informs us this morning that his eighty-six-year-old brother, Georg, despite his serious problems with sight, personally prepares breakfast on Sundays. He tells us, "He has a small machine and just pushes a button." Then he adds that when he was a cardinal and lived in the building in the piazza of the Leonine City, he, too, used a coffee maker on those days when his sister was away.

When it came to cooking, some time ago the pope told us of the one time, while still in Germany, he had a guest for whom he had to prepare something to eat. So he and his brother decided to do the one thing they knew: an over easy egg. But somehow, they managed to burn the egg! So they had to change the menu and offered the guest a fried egg instead!

I have a beautiful sensation while celebrating today's Holy Mass, feeling deeply immersed in the mystery being celebrated. I am also conscious of a strong closeness to my father, certain that he is already in Heaven. Something similar happened to me on Friday when, during the votive Mass of the Most Precious Blood of Jesus, I felt I was saved and redeemed by the blood of Jesus, which was mystically shed for me.

Today, as happens every year, a boy and a girl from Catholic Action, accompanied by the spiritual assistant and two officials, join us for the Angelus. At the end of the prayer, the girl delivers a short greeting in the name of her peers. Next, as a sign of peace, two white doves are released. One of the doves, perhaps somewhat frightened, flies back into the pope's study. Consequently, we have to release it outside once again. The Holy Father comments at lunch with a sigh, "Poor doves! Now they have to find food on their own!" After a while, he repeats the same thing, this time in a whisper.

4 THURSDAY
FEBRUARY

The president of the Italian Republic, Giorgio Napolitano, expressed his wish to visit the pope also this year. He wished to be accompanied by his wife and for the visit to be strictly private.

While on our usual walk after lunch, the Holy Father wishes to share his thoughts with us about the preparations for the meeting. Though there is certainly no need, I dare to mention some possible topics for discussion with the president — for example, his authoritative and sober inputs regarding Italian politics, the ongoing commitment to the unity of the Italian people, his visits across the country, and his appeal to values.

The President of the
Italian Republic, Giorgio
Napolitano, on a private
visit with Pope Benedict.

While we are having dinner, the Holy Father comments on
the security measures being taken for the president's visit. He
says, "We are prisoners!" He loved to go out walking around the
suburbs while he was still a cardinal. Now he misses those walks.
For my part, I have another reason to sacrifice a little bit more
of my freedom and keep the company of this special "prisoner."

11 THURSDAY
FEBRUARY

This day is dedicated to the Blessed Virgin of Lourdes. It is
also the day on which the Church celebrates the World Day
of the Sick, established by John Paul II in 1992. The pope is
scheduled to appear at the window of his study to bless the
sick who are assembled at St. Peter's Square for the recitation of the Rosary. I come up with an idea: the Holy Father
could hold a candle in his hand, one like those that the sick
will have in their hands, so as to highlight his closeness and
participation in their homage to Our Lady.

Once I enter the pope's study to set up the lectern and the
microphone, I am allowed to explain why I am carrying a lit

candle. The pope, however, gently observes, "It is impossible. I need both of my hands to bestow the blessing."

However, once the Ave Maria is intoned and the pope joins in its singing, I present myself once again with the candle. This time the pope takes it, with gentleness and without any sign of irritation at my insistence — another testimony to the humility of this man.

16 TUESDAY FEBRUARY

I look at the state of the weather before going out for the recitation of the Rosary in the Vatican Gardens. It is raining, but it is light rain. I think it is good for the pope to go out anyway. However, once we reach the Grotto of Our Lady of Lourdes, the rain increases to the point that the pope's brother decides to stay inside the car. "This is not a drizzle, but a persistent rain," observes the Holy Father with a hint that perhaps it would have been better to have stayed at home. I feel guilty for having convinced him to go out. However, upon noticing my embarrassment, he immediately adds, no doubt to make me feel at ease, "However, it was necessary to take a breath of fresh air, for it should do us well."

I have another little episode regarding the pope's generosity. I had to undergo surgery at Gemelli Hospital some months ago to take care of a hernia in my groin. When I returned from the hospital, the pope greeted me by saying, "This is wonderful. Fr. Alfred has returned!" Later, when we were in the sitting room at the end of the news program on TV, he noticed that I was struggling to stand up. He rushed toward me and said, "But you need assistance." Then he stretched out his hands to help me get out of the armchair. I was both embarrassed and edified by such attention. That evening, while speaking with my sister on the telephone, she asked how I was doing after the surgery. I told her, half joking, "I could not feel better! Think of it, instead of me helping the pope, it is the pope who is helping me!" I then told her what had happened. She remained very impressed with Benedict's sensitivity.

Since I am speaking about funny episodes, I might as well continue. This one relates to the fear — or better, the terror — the Holy Father has of mushrooms. It is autumn and we are at Castel Gandolfo. As we are taking our usual walk, I spot a beautiful wild mushroom, sprouting under a tree. I point this out to the pope. He asks if I like mushrooms. I reply, "Of course, especially with a great dish of fettucine!" to which the pope replies, "Then you will suffer, because I never eat them." I quickly retort, "But, Holy Father, do not worry. I eat them whenever I happen to be at a restaurant," thinking that I have closed our conversation. But the pope goes on to say, "You have to be very careful, for many of them are poisonous." I reply, "But I seldom read in the newspapers that people are poisoned in restaurants." Again, the pope comes back by saying, "Oh, but this is because they do not report it!" The two of us break out laughing, and I realize how much he truly dislikes mushrooms.

Some time later, the Holy Father told us of an episode involving mushrooms. It happened at his home when he was a small boy. He explained that his mother usually helped a needy neighbor with children. Not knowing how to repay his mother, one day the lady showed up with a basket full of mushrooms, which she gave to the Ratzingers and to another family. Georg and Joseph convinced their mother not to cook them, because some of them had a rather strange shape. They felt vindicated a few days later when they learned that the neighbors got very sick. Evidently, that childhood episode continues to trouble him throughout his life.

Continuing on the subject of mushrooms, there is another incident. It took place last February 8. A group of people from Genoa brought the Holy Father a carpet, woven in wool and silk, that depicted his coat of arms. It was made especially for him. It was a very beautiful and much-appreciated gift. Then, behold, after presenting the carpet, one of the Genoese got closer, carrying a package, and said, "There is another gift in here. It is a typical product from our region!" The pope asked what that would be, and the beaming gentleman exclaimed, "Dried mushrooms!" I have to say that the pope was very clever in hiding his discomfort.

21 SUNDAY FEBRUARY

Our annual spiritual exercises begin this evening. The preacher is a Salesian, Fr. Enrico dal Covolo. He chooses for his topic a theme that focuses on the vocation for the priesthood: "Lessons from God and the Church on priestly vocations." He has a very direct way of speaking, knows how to get people involved, and offers several ideas for reflection.

14 SUNDAY MARCH

The Holy Father pays a visit to the Evangelical Lutheran Church in Rome this evening. Pope John Paul II went there to meet with the Lutheran community on December 11, 1983.

The Holy Father is welcomed in Christ Church (Christuskirche) by the pastor, Rev. Jens-Martin Kruse, and Mrs. Doris Esch, the president of the Lutheran community. The pope speaks in German and says that although the current reality among Christians is marked with division, this should not lead to sadness but to solicit prayers to God that we may be one. He concludes by saying, "Let us give thanks for having been able to pray and sing together. Let us pray for each other, let us pray together that the Lord will grant us unity and help the world so that it may believe."

Today is a busy Sunday because we have guests for both breakfast and lunch. Completely out of the norm, a young German couple is in-

Pope Benedict meets the Lutheran community in Rome in the Christuskirche.

vited to Holy Mass. His name is Anton, and his mother is a first cousin of the Holy Father. Anton has recently been diagnosed with a malignant brain tumor, and he is due to report tomorrow to the hospital to begin treatment. While at lunch, Anton bursts into tears to the mortification of his wife, Barbara. The couple has two children; the firstborn, called Anton Jr., was baptized by Cardinal Ratzinger just a few months before his papal election. The second son carries the name of Benedickt Josef.

28 SUNDAY MARCH

Today the Holy Father's brother returns to Germany. We were very happy to have him among us. The main reason for his visit was to mark the pope's name day, the feast of St. Joseph, occurring on March 19. Finally, a day filled with serenity and peace!

During these days, the media has unleashed a factual and pointed smear campaign against the Catholic Church and, in particular, against the Magisterium of the pope. Without any doubt, the Holy Father's statements on very difficult issues, such as homosexual unions, the use of artificial contraception, and abortions, clash with the claims of some secularist groups who perceive every papal comment as a serious infringement on human rights and interference on the right of freedom of conscience. The devil uses every means to not let his kingdom be defeated and uses persons and groups in his war against the Good. However, all of us can attest on a daily basis that the pope remains absolutely serene and profoundly in peace. He never utters a word of discouragement or unease when we are at table or during our walks.

Now that the pope's brother has returned to Germany, I am left with some fond memories. The pope was so caring whenever he took his brother by the arm to assist him walking, or when alerting him to the presence of some obstacle, and on the occasion when he searched for his brother because he had not seen him arriving. The pope never showed any sign of irritation when his brother tried to learn some Italian words, or asked the meaning of some word, or when he repeatedly asked the pope to help him remember something he had forgotten.

29 MONDAY MARCH

Despite having so much on his mind, the Holy Father remembers that my mother is expected to arrive in Rome today for Holy Mass, and he asks me if she has arrived safely.

In the proximity of the fifth anniversary of the death of John Paul II, we have as a guest at luncheon Cardinal Stanisław Dziwisz, secretary of Pope Wojtyła and now archbishop of Cracow. The cardinal recalls the esteem and confidence John Paul II had toward him who has ended up being elected his successor. He says that, many times, Wojtyła, when he needed to make a difficult decision, asked those present if, first of all, they had learned Cardinal Ratzinger's opinion on the matter. The Holy Father is visibly embarrassed and comments, "It was due to the pope's kindness that he sought my opinion." When Benedict says "the pope," he always means John Paul II.

While speaking on the subject of humility, I recall that last Thursday, March 25, when a crowd of about forty thousand young people gathered in St. Peter's Square and cheered him by repeating "Benedetto, Benedetto," he made us understand by his gestures that they should be acclaiming not him but rather Jesus the Lord. He reaffirmed this later in one of his off-the-cuff replies.

1 THURSDAY
APRIL

There are practical jokes on the first day of April even in Germany. Today the pope told us what happened in 1972, when he was the archbishop of Munich. A well-known newspaper wrote that a tax was in the making for cat owners and that the readers could call a telephone number to express their comments and even their opposition. He, being a notorious cat lover, decided to call the number straight away. The person on the end of the line told him that he took note of it. Well, the following day, April 2, he opened the newspaper and discovered that it was all a practical joke. The pope remarked, "I was very naïve!"

8 THURSDAY
APRIL

I mention to the Holy Father promotional material is being prepared for his upcoming visit to Malta. The nuncio sent me a DVD and the pope, intrigued, wants to see it. After asking me, he seats himself in front of the computer in my office and watches the DVD. The archbishop of Malta and the president of the republic appear in two of these clips. Both urge the Maltese citizens to warmly welcome the successor of Peter. I think he is well pleased.

14 WEDNESDAY
APRIL

Today we go back to the Vatican from Castel Gandolfo, where we have stayed two extra days beyond the usual stay after the Solemnity of Easter.

While at table, I mention to the pope that last Sunday I was invited to celebrate Holy Mass at the Church of San Francesco a Ripa on the occasion of the departure from Rome of Sr. Chiara Pfister. She was the director of the Santa Marta Pediatric Dispensary at the Vatican, where she served for thirty years. The pope encourages me to assist all the volunteers who serve at that place during this difficult time of transition.

I recount to the Holy Father how, on my way to greet Sr. Chiara at her convent in the Vatican on the evening before her departure, I met a Salesian Sister, Sr. Enrica Rosanna, who told me a funny joke about a cat and mouse. Knowing that the pope loves stories about animals, and gaining permission to repeat it at table, I do so. There is a mouse that lives in a house and there is a cat that obviously chases it. Each time the mouse hears a meow, it knows it has to be on guard so as to avoid any kind of ambush. But one day, rather than a meow, it hears barking. Intrigued with the sound, it leaves its place of refuge and goes to see what this is all about. With no time for the mouse to comprehend what is happening, the cat instantly grabs it. The mouse says, "Hey, this is not fair. You cheated. Why did you bark?" The cat promptly replies, "Oh, my dear, if you do not know at least one foreign language these days, you should not venture to go anywhere!" The Holy Father has a good laugh. Later, during our walk on the terrace, he says that he is convinced there will be animals in Paradise — at least cats, for sure. What kind of Paradise would it be without cats? This could be a theological argument to elaborate on!

Pope Benedict XVI's love for cats is well known, and when I come across some episode about felines, I willingly share it with him. Just like that time I told him of the lady from Gozo, who has a summer house close to ours and is the owner of a particularly clever cat. At the end of the stay by the sea, the lady collected her cat and personal effects to return to the city. Anyhow, the cat disappeared after one day. She embarked on a search for it and feared the worst, thinking that it must have been run over by a car. Two days later, an acquaintance of hers contacted her and informed her that she had left her cat behind at the summer house, since the friend had seen it roaming around there. The lady did not take this seriously, because she was convinced that she had taken the cat with her. But, out of curiosity, she wanted to check out the report. She was greatly surprised when she discovered that her cat was in fact right there. The cat meowed happily upon seeing its owner. It remains a mystery as to how the cat walked five kilometers to the summer house. But for Pope Benedict the answer is simple: cats are animals with special qualities.

15 THURSDAY APRIL

We accompany the Holy Father this morning to celebrate Holy Mass at the Pauline Chapel for the Biblical Commission. He was one of its members for many years when he was a cardinal. He delivers a splendid homily on the primacy of obedience to God and on the true meaning of penance and pardon in the life of a Christian. It is reported in the evening news, but the pope is not pleased, because he considers it to be a private matter.

17 SATURDAY
APRIL

The pope is free from all audiences this morning. This enables him to leisurely reread all the speeches he will be delivering during his visit to Malta, his fourteenth apostolic journey. He calls me to his office toward midday, inviting me to sit down, as we go over his pronunciation of sentences in Maltese that will be inserted into his English-language speeches.

Palace of the Grand Master (Il-Palazz tal-Granmastru) in Valletta (Malta). Courtesy visit to the President of the Republic, Mr. George Abela, and to the members of the Maltese Parliament and Government.

On the left: S.|E. Msgr. Thomas Caputo, apostolic nuncio to Malta, accompanies Pope Benedict during the pastoral visit to the island.

Below: two Maltese girls await Pope Benedict's arrival.

We depart from Fiumicino Airport in the afternoon, arriving in Malta in less than two hours. Once the door of the aircraft is opened, the apostolic nuncio, Archbishop Tommaso Caputo, boards the plane to welcome the pope. On exiting the plane, I am overjoyed to see the warm welcome my people shower on the pope. I feel very proud when I hear the president of Malta reiterate the commitment of my country to the Magisterium of the Church.

After the welcoming ceremony, we travel to the presidential palace in Valletta, where we are greeted by, among others, the members of the Maltese Parliament. During a lull in the proceedings, the president seeks me out, greets me warmly, and thanks me for my contribution in making the visit possible.

With yesterday being Joseph Ratzinger's eighty-third birthday, five thousand children now gather under the balcony of the palace and sing best wishes in three languages.

We are transferred from Valletta, the capital city, to Rabat and Mdina, the old capital

A moment of silent prayer in the cave where the Apostle Paul was held prisoner following his shipwreck on the island.

of medieval Malta. A vast number of people line up along the road in a celebratory mood. At St. Paul's Cathedral, the pope meets with over two hundred religious men and women, who work overseas in the missions. This is followed by a moment of recollection in the grotto in which, according to tradition, St. Paul spent three months while on the island, after his providential shipwreck. The pope is immersed in prayer, savoring the presence of Paul, whom he knows so well through his letters.

18 SUNDAY APRIL

When we greet the Holy Father this morning, he informs us that he has not slept well. In fact, his face is pale, and he nods a few times during breakfast. An invisible sword pierces my heart, as I was the one who suggested to him to extend our stay in Malta by half a day so as to relieve the pressure generated by the packed program.

A number of text messages on my cell phone inform me that St. Publius Square, better known as the Granaries, where Holy Mass will be celebrated by the pope, is already packed with people in an atmosphere of great recollection.

I learn later that the Holy Father fell asleep during the celebration, and the master of ceremonies had to tap his fingers on the armrest a number of times to wake him up. The crowd of about fifty thousand participates with deep devotion in the eucharistic celebration. After Holy Mass, the pope meets with the parents of those Maltese priests who are serving at the Holy See, but so many other people join them that the encounter tires the pope out even further.

There is an important unscheduled event at the nunciature. The pope meets with victims of clergy sexual abuse. The Holy Father, though visibly exhausted, meets with each of

SAbove: from a catamaran, the Pope greets the young people gathered in Kalkara.

Below: a small group of youth representatives accompany the Pope on the catamaran.

them as a father would, putting the hands of each person into his own, an occasion that for me holds many similarities with Pentecost. This meeting means a lot to these individuals, who have suffered so much, and it appears that the encounter has helped them in no small way to turn the page, enabling them to move on in life. As the pope leaves the chapel, all of them ask us to thank him for this gesture.

We delay our departure from the nunciature by half an hour after lunch, hoping that the Holy Father recovers some energy. Nevertheless, the pope wants to greet everyone: the staff, the sisters, the benefactors, the heads of the various Maltese security services, and finally the seminarians. There is also time for a snapshot with the motorcycle police officers as we leave.

We board a catamaran in Kalkara to take us to an encounter with the Maltese youth. We are escorted by many boats and greeted with cannon salutes of welcome. It is very well choreographed, with Vatican flags all around making a spectacle in the Grand Harbour. There are many happy young people, especially those who, feeling almost incredulous, are on the catamaran next to the pope. They represent their peers.

Festive procession to the port of Valletta with various boats, including the Maltese dghajsa.

20 TUESDAY APRIL

Ever since our return from the apostolic journey to Malta, the pope has repeatedly praised the Church in Malta and has been full of compliments toward my people and the organizers of the visit. You can simply imagine the joy in my heart! I gather enough courage at a certain point to say, "Holy Father, we profoundly appreciate the great gift you have given us by choosing from the many invitations you receive to visit our land." He listens attentively and then says, "Thank you. But really, it is I who received the gift!"

I carry the conviction in my heart that something similar happened to St. Paul after surviving a furious storm. The Acts of the Apostles recount how he left Malta heartened by the rare sense of humanity of the residents, to whom he had offered the gift of the Christian faith. Something like this must have also happened to our beloved Pope Benedict XVI.

28 WEDNESDAY APRIL

I was contacted by *L'Osservatore Romano* a few days ago. At the request of its director, Giovanni Maria Vian, I was asked to give an interview regarding the pope's visit to Malta. I informed the Holy Father after we recited the Rosary, and he was in full agreement, saying, "Now that the event has taken place, it is a good idea to make some statement." So this morning, Gianluca Biccini, of the editorial staff, came over to carry out the interview.

I here share my answer to the question on how things went during the meeting between the Holy Father and the victims of clerical sexual abuse: "It was a very touching moment, filled with a special grace. It took place in the nunciature's chapel.

First of all, Msgr. Mario Grech, the bishop of Gozo, opened the meeting with a short prayer, within a climate of great recollection. It reminded me of the thought of what had gone on during Pentecost, when the Holy Spirit descended upon the apostles who were gathered together in the Upper Room with Mary. Above all else, the singular fatherly care of Benedict XVI emerged during the encounter. It suffices to say that the spokesperson for the victims used the following words when speaking with journalists: 'When I met the pope, I realized that I had in front of me a person who is very different from how he is described by the media.' He was deeply gratified by seeing the pope visibly moved and sincerely displeased for what had happened. On the other hand, Pope Benedict XVI deeply appreciated their courage to denounce those who had committed the abuses. Moreover, the victims were touched by the fact that the pope placed their hands between his own. That moment reminds me of the merciful gesture of the Lord who touched and healed. There was also a healing in this instance, perhaps not a physical one, but it was certainly a spiritual and psychological healing. This is so true that one of the victims stated, 'For me, this chapter is now closed. Now I can start anew with renewed confidence in the Church and in those members of the Church who are faithful in their priestly vocation.' The encounter lasted about half an hour. But there was the feeling, among those present, that if they had spoken for a longer time, the pope would have continued listening to them. And this took place despite the fact that he was very tired and much delayed in the scheduled program. When the meeting was over, those present asked us a number of times, and with great insistence, to extend to the pope their heartfelt thanks. One could read across their faces so much emotion. I must state that this meeting was very well prepared by the Maltese bishops and their collaborators. Archbishop Paul Cremona had already met the victims in his private residence. That meeting lasted for over two hours and in an atmosphere of great emotion."

29 THURSDAY APRIL

As in previous years — one might say it is by now a tradition — the president of the Italian Republic, Giorgio Napolitano, offered, in honor of the pope, a concert to mark the anniversary of his papal election. The Italian Youth Orchestra of Fiesole played in a crowded Paul VI Hall. The Holy Father has always appreciated this gesture of respect from the president.

14 FRIDAY MAY

We are back this evening from another demanding apostolic journey. This time the Holy Father visited Portugal. All of us retire to sleep very weary but also very pleased. This was a journey rich with ideas. Soon after our arrival in Portugal on Tuesday

The Pope re-reads the program of the apostolic journey during the flight to Portugal.

Greetings from Pope
Benedict to the crowd
gathered below the
balcony of the Apostolic
Nunciature in Lisbon.

morning, the pope paid a visit to the president of the republic
in Lisbon. The pope presided at Holy Mass in the afternoon. It
took place at the grounds of the old market and in the presence
of a huge crowd. The altar was placed directly on the banks of the
Tagus River, which we were able to admire during the celebration
because the back of the stage was made of transparent plastic.

I think that the speech the pope delivered to the world of
culture is one of the most important speeches of his pontificate. It took place at the Centro Cultural de Belém in Lisbon.
Once again, he placed as the centerpiece of his speech the
question about truth. He stated in very clear words, "Dear
friends, the Church considers that her most important mission in today's culture is to keep alive the search for truth,
and consequently for God; to bring people to look beyond
penultimate realities and to seek those that are ultimate."

We were taken by helicopter to Fatima on Wednesday
evening, where we immediately went to the renowned Marian
sanctuary. The pope paid homage to Nossa Senhora de Fátima by presenting her with a golden rose and praying in silence
in front of a huge crowd. It was personally comforting to me
to watch the pope with hands clasped in prayer, and with the
look of a son who was confident and grateful to her. I, too,

prayed at the feet of Our Lady, remembering many people dear to me, especially those who suffer.

The act of entrustment and consecration of all priests in the world to the Immaculate Heart of Mary was very moving. The pope, among other things, prayed, "Help us, through your powerful intercession, never to fall short of this sublime vocation, nor to give way to our selfishness, to the allurements of the world and to the wiles of the Evil One."

Thursday morning witnessed the celebration of the very impressive Holy Mass at the Square of the Apparitions in the presence of a crowd composed of about two hundred thousand people. Many concelebrating priests thanked the pope for the proclamation of the Year for Priests. As it had rained during the night, and the temperature dropped considerably, I was deeply moved by the faith of so many people who had slept outdoors on the grounds. The pope used words of tenderness to the sick, and I continue to reflect upon the sentence wherein he stated, "We would be mistaken to think that Fatima's prophetic mission is complete."

The meeting with the bishops of Portugal took place in the conference hall of the Casa de Nossa Senhora do Carmo de Fátima. Benedict began the meeting with an act of humility: "As you see, the Pope needs to open himself ever more fully to the mystery of the Cross, embracing it as the one hope and the supreme way to gain and to gather in the Crucified One all his brothers and sisters in humanity."

Then he spoke to the prelates with words of caution and encouragement: "In truth, the times in which we live demand a new missionary vigour on the part of Christians, who are called to form a mature laity, identified with the Church and sensitive to the complex transformations taking place in our world. Authentic witnesses to Jesus Christ are needed, above all in those human situations where the silence of the faith is most widely and deeply felt among politicians, intellectuals,

The Pope pays homage to
Our Lady of Fatima.

communications professionals who profess and who promote a monoculture ideal, with disdain for the religious and contemplative dimension of life."

We headed for the city of Porto on Friday. There the Holy Father presided at a Holy Mass in which many university students participated. They presented the pope with very interesting gifts at the end of the celebration. One gift consisted of a tracksuit equipped with sensors capable of performing clinical examinations. Another was an electric guitar made of a special lightweight material.

Earlier during the flight to Portugal, the Holy Father gave an interview to the journalists present. Among all of his answers, I was particularly struck by the one dealing with the Third Secret of Fatima. It was recalled by Vaticanists that in the year 2000 then-Cardinal Ratzinger was asked whether the message could be expanded to go beyond the assassination attempt on Pope John Paul II and include other sufferings on the part of popes: Was it therefore possible to include in that vision the sufferings in today's Church due to sins involving sexual abuse of minors? The Holy Father replied, "The Lord told us that the Church would constantly be suffering, in different ways, until the end of the world. The important thing is that the message, the response of Fatima, in substance is not directed to particular devotions, but precisely to the fundamental response, that is, to ongoing conversion, penance, prayer, and the three theological virtues: faith, hope and charity. Thus, we see here the true, fundamental response which the Church must give — which we, every one of us, must give in this situation. As for the new things which we can find in this message today, there is also the fact that attacks on the Pope and the Church come not only from without, but the sufferings of the Church come precisely from within the Church, from the sin existing within the Church. This too is something that we have always known, but today we are seeing it in a really terrifying way: that the greatest persecution of the Church comes not from her enemies without, but arises from sin within the Church, and that the Church thus has a deep need to relearn penance, to accept purification, to learn forgiveness on the one hand, but also the need for justice. Forgiveness does not replace justice. In a word, we need to relearn precisely this essential: conversion, prayer, penance and the theological virtues. This is our response, we are realists in expecting that evil always attacks, attacks from within and without, yet that the forces of good are also ever present and that, in the end, the Lord is more powerful than evil, and Our Lady is for us the visible, motherly guarantee of God's goodness, which is always the last word in history." He spoke off the cuff, and so his Italian was not perfect. However, the points he made are exceptionally important because they recall that persecution comes from within, from inside the Church, and that there is a call for repentance.

16 SUNDAY MAY

Waiting to appear from the window of his private studio in the Vatican for the recitation of the Angelus.

23 SUNDAY MAY

As I have already indicated, toward the end of the month of May the pope usually invites the sisters and priests of *Das Werk* to what is called in German *Maiandacht*. It is a moment of devotion filled with songs, the recitation of the Rosary, and litanies. A crown is brought to the event this time, one that, after the pope's blessing, is placed on a beautiful wooden statue of Our Lady. I know that the Holy Father really likes these acts of homage to the Blessed Virgin Mary.

3 THURSDAY JUNE

Today is a holiday at the Vatican: it is the feast of Corpus Christi. The Holy Father is unusually happy with similar occasions, such as the commemoration of some important saint. We go to the Basilica of St. John Lateran this afternoon. The program consists of the traditional celebration of Holy Mass in the square, followed by the procession with the Blessed Sacrament to the Basilica of St. Mary Major. However, due to heavy rain, the pope has to celebrate Holy Mass inside the basilica and the procession has to be canceled.

4 FRIDAY JUNE

Recently, the president of Malta, while traveling in China, was injured from a fall. I informed the pope, and he immediately sent a message through me, wherein he expressed his closeness and pledged prayers. After a few days, the pope asked me for an update and, taking advantage of the papal nuncio in Malta visiting the president in the hospital, he sent his blessing. The president was so moved that instead of kissing the nuncio's ring, he embraced the prelate, despite having orders to stay in bed.

I must say that whenever one of my countrymen seeks the pope's prayers through me, Benedict not only agrees to do so but after a while he also asks how things are going. Whenever he sees on the prayer list, which I prepare for him, the name of a Maltese person who is sick, he always asks me if I know that person. Then, after a few days, and at the end of the Rosary, he asks me if I have any news about the person.

6 SUNDAY JUNE

We are back this evening from the apostolic journey to Cyprus. Pope Benedict XVI's trip started last Friday and ended earlier today. He is the first pope to visit the island.

Soon after we landed on the island, we were taken to the Church of Agia Kyriaki Chrysopolitissa (St. Ciriaca Chrysopolitissa) for an ecumenical celebration. The church overlooks the archaeological site of a fourth-century paleo-Christian basilica that houses the column of St. Paul, an object of popular devotion. While in Nicosia, we were accommodated at the apostolic nunciature. The building is adjacent to Holy Cross Church, which is administered by the Franciscans. One is struck by the barbed wire wall close by, which separates the Cypriot side of the city from that part occupied by the Turks.

The pope, with his usual graciousness, conceded to answer some journalists' questions during the flight over. The first question was based on the assassination of Bishop Luigi Padovese, the vicar apostolic in Turkey who was killed by his driver three days ago. The Holy Father expressed his distress.

However, he promptly added, "This shadow has nothing to do with the themes and reality of our Journey since we must not attribute this event to Turkey or to the Turks. It is something about which we have little information. It was certainly not a political or religious assassination but a personal matter. We are still awaiting a full explanation, but do not let us now confuse this tragic situation with the dialogue with Islam and with all the problems of our Journey. It is a separate case that saddens us but must in no way cloud the dialogue that will be the theme and purpose of this Journey."

Another question is related to the difficult situation in the Middle East and the contribution that the Holy See could give in the search for a peaceful resolution. The pope replied, "I would say that we contribute mainly in a religious way. We can be of help by offering political and strategic

Pafos: ecumenical celebration in the archaeological site of the church of Agia Kyriaki (St Cyriaca) and Panagia Chrysopolitissa (Our Lady of the Golden City). In 1987 the Metropolitan Chrysostomos of the Cypriot Orthodox Church entrusted the church to the Latin Patriarchate of Jerusalem for the Roman Catholic community (Parish of St. Paul). The church is used by the various Christian communities: Anglican, German and Finnish Lutheran, and Maronite.

The barbed wire near the Franciscan convent which houses the Nunciature in Cyprus and in the buffer zone administered by the UN between the Greek Cypriot side and Turkish Cypriot side of the island.

advice, but the Vatican's work is always essentially religious, work that moves hearts. With all these episodes that we are experiencing we are always in danger of losing patience, of saying 'that's enough,' and of no longer desiring to seek peace. And here, in this Year for Priests, a beautiful story of the Curé d'Ars springs to my mind. To the people who said to him: 'It is pointless for me to go to confession and absolution because I am sure that the day after tomorrow I shall relapse into the same sins,' the Curé d'Ars answered: 'It doesn't matter, the Lord deliberately forgets that you will commit the same sins the day after tomorrow, he forgives you now, completely, he will be forbearing and will continue to help you and to reach out to you.' We should consequently imitate, as it were, God and his patience. After all the cases of violence, we must not lose patience, not lose courage, not

Column of St. Paul, archaeological site of the Early Christian basilica of the fourth century.

lose our forbearance in order to start again; we must create this readiness of heart to start ever anew, in the certainty that we can forge ahead, that we can achieve peace, that the solution is not violence but patience for the true good. Creating this attitude seems to me to be the principal task that the Vatican, its offices and the Pope can undertake."

The pope met with His Beatitude Chrysostomos II, archbishop of Cyprus, at the headquarters of the Orthodox archbishop. The latter is a person who wholeheartedly believes in the ecumenical dialogue and was Benedict's guest at the

Vatican three years ago. He greatly appreciated the fact that the pope began and finished his speech in Greek.

The celebration of Holy Mass by Pope Benedict in the Eleftheria Sports Center was very moving. It took place in the presence of the small Catholic community of Cyprus, comprised mostly of immigrants from the Philippines and Sri Lanka, whom the pope greeted warmly. The pope asked everyone to work for peace: "We are called to overcome our differences, to bring peace and reconciliation where there is conflict, to offer the world a message of hope. We are called to reach out to those in need, generously sharing our earthly goods with those less fortunate than ourselves. And we are called to proclaim unceasingly the death and resurrection of the Lord, until he comes. Through him, with him and in him, in the unity that is the Holy Spirit's gift to the Church, let us give honor and glory to God our heavenly Father in the company of all the angels and saints who sing his praises forever."

9 WEDNESDAY JUNE

German prelates known by the pope are frequently invited to lunch or dinner at the apartment whenever they come to Rome. Bishop Gerhard Müller of Regensburg comes today. He is preparing the publication of the opera omnia of the writings of Joseph Ratzinger. The Holy Father is interested not only in knowing what is happening in the diocese but also in the well-being of certain persons whom he has known for many years.

It goes without saying that the conversations of the visiting bishops cover many topics relating to the positive realities as well as the negative ones. The Holy Father states that the

Church in Germany is afflicted with an acute spirit of organization and bureaucracy, which threatens to weaken the spiritual and sacramental aspects of her mission. The pope already stated this during his visit to his homeland. I recall that it was during one of these lively meetings that Cardinal Archbishop Joachim Meisner of Cologne said, "I thank the Lord that during this period of strong upheaval in the Catholic Church, He has sent us Pope Benedict as our auspicious guide."

The attacks in recent times, especially those that take as their starting point the cases of pedophilia among the clergy, are clearly aimed at the pope and to silence the voice of the Church. The pope has stated several times that the sins that have stained some of the clergy are grave, but what the Church is undergoing is true aggression. It is profoundly unjust that they want to ascribe to Benedict sins that he did not commit. Indeed, if truth be told in an objective way about Pope Ratzinger, it was he who, from the time he was the prefect of the Congregation for the Doctrine of the Faith, resolutely fought the phenomenon by transferring the competence over these cases from the Congregation for the Clergy to the disciplinary section of his Congregation so as to individualize and appropriately punish those who were guilty and to provide assistance to their victims.

11 FRIDAY JUNE

This morning the Holy Father presided at Holy Mass, celebrated in the churchyard in front of St. Peter's Basilica, to conclude the Year for Priests. The year dedicated to priests was inaugurated last June on the occasion of the 150th anniversary of the death of the holy Curé d'Ars. The pope was deeply moved when he saw St. Peter's Square packed with fif-

teen thousand priests who have come from all over the world
to be close to the Vicar of Christ. As he passed by them, many
shouted a resounding thank-you for the Year for Priests.

The pope delivered a beautiful homily during which he
underlined the beauty and loftiness of priestly ministry. In
his comments on the Good Shepherd, the pope spoke of the
significance of the rod and the staff. It was a novelty for me
to discover that the rod serves against wild beasts who want
to attack the flock and against brigands who want to loot,
while the staff serves for support and help through passing
the "darkest valley" (Psalm 23). The pope said, "We have
let the Curé of Ars guide us to a renewed appreciation of
the grandeur and beauty of the priestly ministry. The priest
is not a mere office-holder, like those which every society
needs in order to carry out certain functions. Instead, he
does something which no human being can do of his own
power: in Christ's name he speaks the words which absolve
us of our sins and in this way, he changes, starting with God,
our entire life."

The pope shares a heartfelt prayer at the end: "Every
Christian and every priest should become, starting from
Christ, a wellspring which gives life to others. We ought to
be offering life-giving water to a parched and thirsty world.
Lord, we thank you because for our sake you opened your
heart; because in your death and in your resurrection you
became the source of life. Give us life, make us live from
you as our source, and grant that we too may be sources,
wellsprings capable of bestowing the water of life in our
time. We thank you for the grace of the priestly ministry.
Lord bless us, and bless all those who in our time are thirsty
and continue to seek."

There was a prayer vigil last night, also held in St. Peter's
Square. After some priests delivered their testimonies, the

Holy Father came down to confirm thousands of priests in their faith and ministry. The pope then remained to answer some questions posed by priests from all the continents. He stated that there are four things that must be priorities for every priest: the first is the Eucharist, the sacrament; the second is "the Proclamation of the Word in all its dimensions: from the personal dialogue to the homily"; the third is "caritas, the love of Christ: to be present for the suffering, for the little ones, for the children, for people in difficulty, for the marginalized; to make really present the love of the Good Shepherd." Lastly, "one's personal relationship with Christ." It seems to me that, in this regard, Benedict has outlined a portrait of himself.

The vigil concluded with Eucharistic Adoration and Benediction. Great joy and recollection were apparent in thanking the Lord for a year that was rich in grace and for a universal pastor so helpful in instilling confidence and courage.

Prayer vigil at the end of the Year for Priests, announced on the occasion of one hundred fiftieth anniversary of the death of the Curé of Ars.

20 SUNDAY JUNE

The heart of the Holy Father overflows with joy as he ordains fourteen priests for the Diocese of Rome. The pope recalls in his homily that a priest does not look for self-interest or personal glorification but must look at the face of Christ to always discover better his priestly mission, carried out in obedience to the great law of love.

26 SATURDAY JUNE

On our return from Cyprus, the Holy Father had asked me, at least on two different occasions, if I had taken a photo of Titica, the beautiful cat of the Franciscan friars, while we were their guests in Nicosia. Unfortunately, I had not taken one. So, seeing the pope's interest, I sent an e-mail to the Franciscans in Cyprus, and, low and behold, two beautiful photos of the cat arrived the next day! After obtaining prints from our photographer, we gave them to the pope. Seeing them, he was as happy as a child. One of the photos was framed and placed in Sr. Birgit's office, next to the statue of St. Joseph, the Holy Father noting that that was the proper place; thus, the Family of Nazareth has a cat in its home!

Titica, the cat of the friars' who hosted the Pope during his Apostolic Journey to Cyprus.

9 FRIDAY
JULY

A few days after arriving to stay at the Apostolic Palace of Castel Gandolfo for the summer, I accompany the Holy Father after breakfast to his apartment, taking the elevator. Today I am leaving for my summer vacation, and he asks me to convey his greetings to my mother, sister, the nuncio, and other relatives. I immediately notice that he has not mentioned my father. He remembers that my father is gone. Then he looks at me with his fatherly eyes and says, "She will get better." I spontaneously kneel before him and ask for his blessing. It is a beautiful moment that will stay with me forever. After he joins his hands, he raises the right one and bestows upon me his blessing with the Sign of the Cross. I feel truly privileged and deeply grateful for the pope's fatherly goodness.

10 TUESDAY
AUGUST

I return to Castel Gandolfo today, following a brief stop-over in Rome to take some things and also get my car out of the garage. The Holy Father, as always, gives me a very friendly welcome, and during lunch, the pope wants to know what I did

The Pope's desk in private office of the Apostolic Palace of Castel Gandolfo.

during my vacation, asking also for news about my family, the bishop of Malta, and the nuncio. I find him serene and in good form. Although he works a lot, writes, and reads, the quiet atmosphere of the summer residence refreshes him.

14 SATURDAY AUGUST

I am alone with the Holy Father these days because it is Msgr. Gänswein's turn to be on vacation. I am very blessed to experience special moments, especially during our walks. We have a great way of speaking with one another about many topics, like a son speaking with his father. I am aware that during these conversations, the pope fills my heart with a sense of a deep and gentle paternity, and I also have the impression that he, too, feels relaxed. I am greatly pleased, especially when he tells me that he is sleeping better these days. On a practical level, his face looks rested, and his soul seems serene.

The Pope walks in the Pontifical Villa Gardens.

15 SUNDAY AUGUST

It has become a tradition for the pope to go and celebrate Holy Mass at the Church of St. Thomas of Villanova on the Solemnity of the Assumption of Our Lady. It is located very close to the Apostolic Palace of Castel Gandolfo. Benedict is very happy today and is all smiles as he greets the many people standing behind the barricades, taking his time without any hurry. After the celebration of Holy Mass, he stops to speak with the new parish priest and invites him for tomorrow's breakfast.

Benedict recalls during his homily that this year is the sixtieth anniversary of when Venerable Pius XII, on November 1, 1950, solemnly defined the dogma that affirms that Mary, with Christ her Son, has already conquered death and is already victorious in the glory of Heaven in the totality of her being — that is, in "soul and body."

The Holy Father concludes his homily with these words: "Let us pray [to] the Lord that he will enable us to understand how precious in his eyes is the whole of our life; may he strengthen our faith in eternal life; make us people of hope who work to build a world open to God, people full of joy who can glimpse the beauty of the future world amidst the worries of daily life and in this certainty live, believe and hope."

24 WEDNESDAY AUGUST

The pope surprised all of us recently, at breakfast one morning, by informing us that he wished to take a short trip and visit some nearby places. It is a sign that he is feeling very well. So yesterday afternoon I went with the driver to the Church of Santa Maria al Tufo and then to Monte Cavo. We singled out a panoramic place from where one can admire the lakes of Albano and Nemi, as well as a spot suitable for a picnic in the woods. We also went to see the parish priest to ask him, at the Holy Father's request, to keep the whole event confidential.

The outing begins around 5:00 p.m. Apart from the pope, there is his brother, the four Memores, and Angelo Gugel, who was the butler of John Paul II for many years and then also for Benedict until 2006. Angelo gives a hand to the current butler, Paolo Gabriele, allowing the latter to take his vacation. We are also accompanied by two gendarmes and one of the doctors on call.

After the recitation of Vespers at the shrine, the Holy Father asks the parish priest, a Trinitarian, to tell us something about the history of Santa Maria al Tufo. The Holy Father is very intrigued when he is told that the current church building was constructed in 1927, the very year of his birth!

The church was closed so as to ensure our privacy. But, as we are departing, we are spotted by a young family who manage to approach us and ask the pope to bless their second child, who was born a few months ago. Seeing the gentleness and availability of Benedict, the couple request to have their picture taken

Picnic in the woods with the "papal family."

Panoramic site on Monte Cavo–Castelli Romani: group photo.

with him. The Holy Father agrees, and I take the photo. It does not take long for a small crowd to gather. The traffic comes to a standstill as people stop their cars to see what is going on.

After we arrive at the panoramic spot on Monte Cavo, we walk along part of the bluestone path of the Sacred Road of the ancient Romans, and taking the asphalt paved road, we descend as we recite the Rosary. The two gendarmes follow us along the path, but we also perceive others hidden in the woods.

I notice that, as the passing motorists come close, they turn off their engines as a sign of respect, so as not to disturb our prayer. A truck driver who came up the opposite way has also slowed down, and he makes the Sign of the Cross as we pass nearby.

But the best part is yet to come! When we arrive in the place that has been chosen for our picnic, we come out of the woods, and there we find a nicely covered table surrounded by some chairs for us, with the sun's rays filtering through the branches and flickering among the trees, playing a mesmerizing game. We sing a little, and then I tell a joke that is translated into German for the sake of the pope's brother. Afterward we have some sandwiches with ham, cheese, and salami. There is also orangeade — a favorite of the pope — beer, and water. Msgr. Georg Ratzinger joyfully exclaims, "I cannot remember the last time I ate in the woods!" All of us have a good time and arrive home in time for the evening television news.

29 SUNDAY AUGUST

The former students of Professor Joseph Ratzinger arrive at Castel Gandolfo for their annual meeting. The Swiss bishop Kurt Koch, recently appointed as the president of the Pontifical Council for Promoting Christian Unity, is among them. He is invited to lunch, and at a certain point he asks the Holy Father if he feels hurt by the recent attacks leveled against him. The pope makes no secret that he has felt aggrieved, but he immediately adds that during the course of this affair there have emerged many positive signs, indicating the vitality of the Church. The pope never loses his trust in Divine Providence and always sees the positive side of things.

Pope Benedict takes notes during the annual gathering with his former students.

3 FRIDAY SEPTEMBER

The Holy Father's schedule returned to full speed on September 1. However, the previous days of relaxation have proved very beneficial for his health and his spirit. As for me, I have the memory of the many interesting things he told me. For example, one time, when we were speaking about tobacco, he told us that during the war his father, who was a smoker, had planted about ten tobacco plants in the home garden to use their leaves. But the revenue officials showed up one day to collect the imposed tax! The pope commented, "At that point my father realized that it was not worth it!"

Another story regarded his mother. In accordance with the custom, every time she heard the cuckoo singing, she would beat her hand on the bag that contained money to ensure that it would never decrease.

He also told me about the day on which, while walking on the terrace, he leaned over to greet some Swiss Guards who were finishing their lunch in the courtyard below. A gust of wind arose and blew his white skullcap, which the good soldiers readily recovered.

And what about the theological correction, lighthearted but also firm, that I earned one day? I was narrating that I had baptized in Malta a child by the name of Jeremy and that the parish community welcomed the new member with great joy. The Holy Father gently told me that "it is more appropriate to say that the entire Catholic Church welcomed the newcomer rather than solely the parish community, since the latter forms part of the family that comprises the entire Church."

10 FRIDAY
SEPTEMBER

A newspaper today carries an article dedicated to mistakes, sometimes significant, that students make during exams. The pope was really amused when I recounted some of them, especially the one about a student who was obviously not well versed in geography and had written that the Babylonians lived next to a river full of tigers, wanting to refer to the Tigris River! Another one is about a theology student who, during the written exam, merited the following comment from the professor: "Your answer contains some grave theological errors, but do not worry. You have presented your answer in such a complicated way that no one will notice!" The pope laughed a lot at this too.

19 SUNDAY
SEPTEMBER

We have been on an apostolic journey in the United Kingdom since September 16, today included. We are now back in Rome with hearts full of gratitude and praise to the Lord for the way things have gone. Even the Holy Father was very satisfied. Extraordinary hospitality was shown. The streets and squares were full of people who wanted to see the pope. And to think that the news media had declared that the visit would be a disaster! There appeared in the newspapers, but not just there, all kinds of negative comments, sometimes going as far as threats against the pontiff. I believe that Benedict's meek and humble approach attracts people and makes his words and gestures more effective. Perhaps, in the end, even the journalists took notice: in fact, they reported that instead of meeting a rottweiler who bites, they encountered a gentle grandfather with a heart of gold. The Catholic bishop of Westminster, commenting at the end of the visit, stated, "Now the British know who the real pope is and how different he is from the one portrayed in the media!"

The journey began in Scotland, at Edinburgh, where Queen Elizabeth welcomed the pope inside Holyrood Palace. From a religious point of view, the majority of the population in Scotland is Presbyterian. But the British exhibited much warmth toward Benedict, and the comments became more favorable when the German pope, speaking to the royals, paid tribute to Great Britain for withstanding "a Nazi tyranny that wished to eradicate God from society and denied our common humanity to many, especially the Jews, who were thought unfit to live." Then the pope added, "I also recall the regime's attitude to Christian pastors and religious who spoke the truth in love, opposed the Nazis and paid for that opposition with their lives. As we reflect on the sobering lessons of the atheist extremism of the twentieth century, let us never forget how the exclusion of God, religion and virtue from public life leads ultimately to a truncated vision of man and of society and thus to a 'reductive vision of the person and his destiny.'"

After our stay at Glasgow, where Benedict celebrated Holy Mass at Bellahouston Park, we went to London. Here the pope delivered a memorable speech in Westminster Hall. Turning to the diplomatic corps, politicians, academics, and business leaders, Pope Benedict recalled the figure of St. Thomas More, that champion of freedom of conscience against the coercion of political power. He noted that "fundamental questions at stake in Thomas More's trial continue to present themselves in ever-changing terms as new social conditions emerge." In fact, "each generation, as it seeks to advance the common good, must ask anew:

Meeting with students, teachers, and parents in the sport's field of St. Mary's University College in Twickenham, London.

what are the requirements that governments may reasonably impose upon citizens, and how far do they extend? By appeal to what authority can moral dilemmas be resolved? These questions take us directly to the ethical foundations of civil discourse. If the moral principles underpinning the democratic process are themselves determined by nothing more solid than social consensus, then the fragility of the process becomes all too evident — herein lies the real challenge for democracy."

The pope's speech at Westminster merits being quoted in full because it addresses our current public debate on democracy. Equally memorable were the ideas Benedict proposed during the vigil prayer for the beatification of John Henry Newman at Hyde Park, and then during Holy Mass at Cofton Park of Rednal in Birmingham the following day. The

Holy Father paid tribute to the cardinal who had converted from Anglicanism, describing him as "a confessor, a son of this nation who, while not called to shed his blood for the Lord, nevertheless bore eloquent witness to him in the course of a long life devoted to the priestly ministry." This was truly a journey of great importance.

Birmingham: visit to John Henry Newman's room, where are kept some of his precious personal belongings.

22 WEDNESDAY
SEPTEMBER

The Holy Father loves recalling anecdotes from his time in Germany. During dinner, noticing that Emmental cheese is being served, he comments that only that type of cheese was served when he was a child in Germany. Next, when our conversation moves to some comments on an incident regarding a motorist entering the highway in the wrong direction and creating a panic, it is recalled that once even the notorious Swiss theologian Hans Küng was stopped by the police for driving his Alfa Romeo the wrong way. The judge, during the session in court, commented, "I have never come across this kind of exasperating person in my entire career!"

25 SATURDAY SEPTEMBER

The Holy Father is a little confused with time this evening. After receiving Cardinal Ouellet around 6:45 p.m., he goes to his quarters instead of joining us for the Rosary. I do not know what to do, so I place myself near the door and wait there. Minutes pass by, then I hear footsteps, but the pope does not come out. I am a little worried: Is something the matter with the pope? Finally, he comes out, with his hands covering his face in shame, totally mortified, and admits that he made a mistake with the daily routine. Since it is already 7:20 p.m., I suggest that we recite the Rosary indoors, walking along the halls adjacent to our offices. At my request, the pope gives me a moment to inform the driver that there is no need for him to wait for us. We are also a little late for dinner, and the pope, upon entering the dining room, asks everyone to excuse him, saying, "Were I in a monastery, I would have to do a suitable penance!" All of us laugh and try to put him at ease. But it does not stop there. In fact, the following day, when we have hardly gone out of the elevator at Villa Cybo to recite the Rosary, he immediately asks the driver to excuse him for having made him wait in vain the previous day.

There was another occasion when the pope expressed his sensitivity. It was during the journey in the United Kingdom. He noticed the photographer running to be in time to take some photos. After the greetings and photography, the pope turned toward me and commented, "Poor photographers. They are constantly running!" Indeed, they do not seem to have a peaceful moment!

Speaking of photos, one evening, while we were at Castel Gandolfo, the moon shone on Lake Albano and was reflected on the surface of the water. The pope suggested that I take a picture. A couple of days later he asked me if I had done it. When he discovered that I had printed some of the photos, he wanted us to see them together and then commented, "You have improved immensely in taking pictures!"

Benedict also always has a word of thanks and gratitude for the gendarmes. It is based on an authentic cordial attitude, marked with great simplicity.

11 MONDAY OCTOBER

The Holy Father for some time now has slowed in his walking during the recitation of the Rosary. He has also asked for the use of a cane to feel more secure. One reason for this might be inflammation in his left hip. When the pain intensifies to the point of giving him difficulties in going up the step leading to the altar, he asks for the application of an adhesive bandage specially made for such conditions.

One evening at Castel Gandolfo, after our usual walk and before bidding each other good night, he commented, "Now Fr. Alfred, as an experienced nurse, will come over to place the patch on me." He was referring to the year I had spent at Münster, in Raphael's Klinik. It was from 1980 to 1981. I felt flattered. I accompanied him to his quarters and did my duty as a "nurse."

Finally, today, after many delays, the pope asked that a second patch be put on. I had applied the last one some four or five days previously, the pope telling me every evening, "Tomorrow." While I was preparing the patch, the pope unbuttoned his entire cassock. Thinking to make a suggestion, I said, "I usually unbutton my cassock down to the middle and then step out of it." He told me that there was a time in the past when he did so, but one day he almost stumbled, and so he now prudently uses the other approach. We had a good laugh!

He made me laugh another time when he told me that he could not find two pairs of eyeglasses. He seemed worried and expected me to give him some good news each time I promised him to search for them. This I did on several occasions, looking for them in the sitting room or among his books — but two pairs of glasses together! He said, "I do not understand. It has never happened before that I needed so much time to find them!" But it was not all his fault. He had left them in the pockets of one of his cassocks, which had been put away in the wardrobe.

Speaking about eyeglasses, I told the pope an anecdote that takes me back many years, to the time when I was a child and used to go over to my grandparents. I told him that one day I saw my grandfather's eyeglasses resting on the dining room table. I was intrigued by the round shape of the lenses and picked them up. But my grandmother, fearing that my grandfather would chastise me, said to me, "It is better to leave those glasses alone. It would be far easier to handle the pope's glasses! Because if they break, you will never hear the end of it from your grandfather." Was this a prophecy?

13 WEDNESDAY OCTOBER

Whenever the pope's friends, who are bishops, visit Rome, they are invited for lunch or dinner at the Apostolic Palace. Cardinal Joachim Meisner, archbishop of Cologne, came today. At a certain point, wishing to thank the pope for his journey to the United Kingdom, he said, "That visit brought good results not only for the Church in the United Kingdom but also for our Church at Cologne and elsewhere. All those who talked to me were unanimous in stating that this is due to you, Holy Father." In response, the pope, raising his eyes toward Heaven, murmured, "In reality there was someone else who prepared the journey." Benedict is always this way: he attributes merit to God and not to himself.

14 THURSDAY OCTOBER

On the occasion of my birthday, the Holy Father wants to gift me a beautiful picture that was given to him when visiting Malta. It depicts St. Publius, whom the Maltese venerate. It has precious decorations in the form of little flowers, handmade with delicate, thin colored wires, which the Maltese call *ganutell*. I am informed that he personally chose this picture from the different objects that had been proposed. I should be accustomed by now to the gentleness of his soul and to the attention he has for others. Yet I always find myself emotionally moved.

It makes no difference for the pope what a person's occupation is. He was very concerned with the well-being of the ex-president Cossiga, who was ill. Once informed of his death, he celebrated Holy Mass for him as a friend rather than as the president. He was the friend who made him smile when he called him "the great German theologian," and who often sent him cakes and other kinds of gifts. One of the gifts from Cossiga was a black valise, which he gave to the Holy Father after he noticed that the satchel the pope used to send documents to the Secretariat of State was very shabby and, in his words, not worthy of the Supreme Pontiff. His comment that it was cracked all over became well known.

16 SATURDAY OCTOBER

Since the Holy Father loves a laugh, here is something funny. Recently, on the occasion of his pastoral visit to Carpineto Romano, a journalist wrote, among other things, that "a lock of the pope's white hair emerged from underneath the tiara." We had a great laugh. Obviously, the journalist

Pope Benedict his "sports version."

wanted to write miter, since the last time a pope used a tiara was back in 1963! Today, when we went to the terrace for the usual three-lap walk, I recommended that he put on the white cap with the sun visor as protection for his eyes. He exclaimed, "All right. I will put on the sporty tiara." In the end, when he took the cane to help himself walk better, he added, "And behold the sporty staff!" I suspect that these innovative definitions will enter our customary lexicon.

18 MONDAY OCTOBER

I wish to recount an incident that clearly indicates the Holy Father, despite having so much work to do, takes to heart the problems we, who are close to him, encounter. The problem concerns Maltese priests from Gozo who come to Rome and spend a period of time in some parishes for pastoral and study reasons. For some time now, the Italian Bishops' Conference has not recognized them as parochial vicars, meaning that these young priests, who perform wonderful work and complete their doctorates in Rome, receive not a salary but rather a small contribution that is insufficient for them to make ends meet. Meanwhile, the small diocese, subordinate to the Archdiocese of Malta, is not able to pay for their studies. Thus, they have to look after themselves with what they manage to earn from their pastoral service in a parish. I explained the problem to the pope. He commented that even in Germany there are not as many diligent priests. He said that when the first opportunity presents itself, he will bring their plight to the attention of the president of the CEI, Cardinal Bagnasco. I thought that due to his many commitments and the apostolic journey to Great Britain, it would be impossible for him to remember the priests from Gozo doing service or studying in Rome. However, to my great surprise, on the day of the scheduled meeting with the president of the CEI, he told me, "Today we meet with Cardinal Bagnasco." I immediately understood what he meant. He wanted to know if I had left him a memo precisely about this issue. In fact, I had prepared it. The pope, immediately after his meeting with the cardinal, told me, "I explained to him that he can follow the model being used for the Polish priests." The fact is that Polish priests residing in Rome for pastoral service and studies are, by way of exception, recognized as parochial vicars, even if they are enrolled in one of the pontifical universities. Later, as I was conveying the heartfelt thanks from the bishop of Gozo for his concern, the pope replied, "It is clear that a small diocese of twenty-seven thousand people does not have the necessary economic means!"

27 WEDNESDAY OCTOBER

The Holy Father does not fail to update us on what happens in the course of his activities. We are grateful because this makes us feel like a family. Today, for instance, he informs us of a bishop who, immediately following the Wednesday general audience and at the moment called the *baciamano* — that is, an opportunity to kiss the pope's ring and greet him — spoke to him about the difficulties and sufferings in his diocese. The pope replied that "difficulties and sufferings are necessary." It was a fatherly reminder to look at everything always in light of the Lord's plans.

28 THURSDAY OCTOBER

The pope carries a special relationship with the saints. They are never far from him and form part of his daily life. There are times when I think that he is already living in Paradise! He gives special attention to honor the saints through the liturgy. Today, for example, the Church commemorates Sts. Simon and Jude. The pope forgot to sing the "Holy, Holy, Holy" during Holy Mass and instead recited it. He realized this once he was in the sacristy and commented, "But Simon and Jude will forgive us."

29 FRIDAY OCTOBER

By now the pope regularly uses a cane, even when his hip does not bother him. Someone suggests that he should not use it, because it tends to make one walk lopsidedly. He adds lightheartedly, "Truthfully, noble people have always walked with canes even when they had no problems with walking." I am sure the Holy Father does not compare himself to nobility. Rather, he wants to point out that a cane did not cause serious problems to noble persons, and so the same applies to him!

10 WEDNESDAY NOVEMBER

As noted before, the pope never hesitates to recount for us episodes that took place when he was in Germany, especially those tied to tradition. For example, one day we heard thunder during lunch, and he told us that in Bavaria, during thunderstorms, they used to light a black candle to protect themselves from the lightning.

In the afternoon, we go to the terrace for our usual three-lap walk. He talks about the upcoming consecration of a new church and tells us that, in his younger days on such occasions, the bishop, after scattering ashes across part of the floor of the rectory, wrote the Greek and Latin alphabets with the end of his pastoral staff. When I ask him the reason for this custom, he replies, "Oh, I think it was to indicate the universality of the Church."

Today, after we recite the Rosary, I inform the Holy Father that tomorrow, November 11, is the wedding anniversary of my parents. "Really?" he asks. "Yesterday would have been my parents' ninetieth anniversary!" Then he goes on to say that, in the past, November 11 marked the beginning of Advent in the Ambrosian Rite and that it was customary to cook a duck to underline the final day before the start of the fast that would last until Christmas.

It is so nice to listen to the pope who shares such memories: we live next to a wise and pleasant old man.

18 THURSDAY NOVEMBER

I return from Malta in the evening, where I participated in the funeral of Bishop Emeritus Msgr. Nikol Ġużeppi Cauchi of Gozo. His family was very moved when I conveyed to them the pope's condolences, and they asked me to thank him on their behalf.

I last saw the bishop about a month ago, on the occasion of the presentation of a book on the pope's visit to Malta. On that occasion, Bishop Cauchi had profusely apologized for being unable to participate in the papal ceremonies during the apostolic visit to Malta, an absence due to his ailments. I had immediately reassured the bishop that the pope fully understood his condition, but, nonetheless, I promised that I would reiterate his apologies. I did, and I also told the pope that the old bishop, in his customary way, had also told me a joke during our meeting. Soon after breakfast, Benedict, while folding his napkin, looked at me and said, "So ..." He wanted me to tell him the joke. I asked him to give me a moment to recollect myself because I was not yet ready to repeat it. He waited patiently.

20 SATURDAY NOVEMBER

We are on the terrace for our usual walk after dinner, with the Holy Father wearing the white cap with the visor. Noticing a full moon, he comments jokingly, "The cap will protect me from the moon!" I then confess that I never understood the exact meaning of the words of Psalm 121, which states, "The sun shall not smite you by day, nor the moon by night." I think that he will have an explanation. Instead, he candidly states, "I, too, do not know the exact meaning of those words." I am always struck by the humility of the theologian pope who recognizes his own limitations.

We witness this modesty on a daily basis, such as when he asks us the correct pronunciation of words in English or Italian, as well as the name of some bishop or cardinal when he realizes that he has confused him with another. He is not perfect, he knows it, and, what's more, he admits it.

4 SATURDAY DECEMBER

Today, during lunch, the pope talks about one of his priest friends who suffered from insomnia. He went to the doctor to ask for advice and was told, "Read some theology book, and you will surely go to sleep!" Our conversation then moves to the strange letters we frequently receive from some eccentric persons. We agree that it appears that normal people reveal their true nature when they write. The pope recalls that once, while he was still a cardinal, he received a letter from a gentleman who had proclaimed himself emperor of the world and had decided to appoint Cardinal Ratzinger as the king of Germany. However, a few lines later he wrote that since Cardinal Ratzinger did not govern well, he was making him abdicate. Thank goodness!

Cardinal Ratzinger in the archive of the Congregation for the Doctrine of the Faith, portrayed by Gianni Giansanti, on October 21, 1993.

8 WEDNESDAY DECEMBER

Today is the Solemnity of the Immaculate Conception of Our Lady. We sing the "Lord, Have Mercy," the "Glory to God," the "Holy, Holy, Holy," and the "Lamb of God," as well as the Our Father, along with the usual processional and recessional hymns at Holy Mass. However, I wish to quote the words the Holy

Father said at the beginning of the celebration: "Our joy grows during this Advent Season for today we have the Solemnity that honours Mary, called the all beautiful because, in her, everything reflects God. The fact that she is without sin, does not distance her from us who are sinners, but rather draws us all together to become like her. For this reason, Mary opens her arms to welcome and to transform us. She is full of the love of God, and she loves us and does not distance herself from us, but rather comes close to us. By coming closer to us, Mary makes us closer to God."

I am always struck by Benedict's Marian devotion. It is simultaneously profound and inconspicuous. It goes hand in hand with his care for the liturgy. The pope sees in all of this a reference to the Faith and Scripture. For example, a few days ago, right before the morning Holy Mass, he came across his secretaries with their albs on but not yet wearing the liturgical vestments, and he said, "You look like two angels!" He was referring to the Gospel account that refers to the empty tomb of Jesus and speaks of the presence of two angels.

14 TUESDAY DECEMBER

Some cardinals are guests for today's lunch. The pope comments in their presence that he regrets that the days of the month are no longer referred to by the day's saint, as used to be in the past. For example, there was a time when instead of saying, "August 28," one said, "St. Augustine," or instead of saying, "July 16," one said, "Our Lady of Mount Carmel."

While at dinner, we mention the snowfalls in northern Italy, and the pope recalls an advertisement of the German railways. It said, "Everyone speaks about the weather, but not us!" This was their way of saying that bad weather was not a problem for them and that their trains were always on time. The pope then says in a playful tone, "But there was one time during a train ride in Bonn when we were asked to disembark thirty kilometers before our arrival because of snow!" When all is said and done, even the Germans are not perfect!

15 WEDNESDAY DECEMBER

I have already stated that the pope does not like mushrooms and shellfish. It appears that even the statues that adorn the Apostolic Palace inside the Vatican know this. It seems that particularly shrimp with their protruding antennas are anathema to him. Benedict narrates a funny incident about this. One day he went to a restaurant and the waiter asked him, "Reverend, we have fruits from the forest and those from the sea. Which would you prefer?" Thinking of shellfish and shrimp, Ratzinger replied without hesitation, "From the forest, please." And so they served him mushrooms freshly picked from the forest!

16 THURSDAY DECEMBER

As usually happens with people of a certain age, the pope frequently recalls persons who are no longer with us, especially family members and friends. There are times when he speaks about them, and there are also times when we realize he is thinking about them when he either touches or pauses in silence by an object he had received from someone, such as, for example, a nativity crib statuette.

Today, during dinner, he recalls the anniversary of his mother's death forty-six years ago. He says of her, "She died at my brother's home, during the Council." He was in Rome at the time and returned home to offer support.

18 SATURDAY DECEMBER

Every evening, before the Holy Father goes to the chapel for Vespers, I usually switch on the light for him in advance. This time I also lit the candles of the Advent wreath. However, I had some trouble lighting the candles this evening because the wick was buried into the hardened wax. And so, when the pope arrived at the chapel, one of the candles went out on its own. The conversation at dinner moved toward this little problem. I, in a critical tone, noted that the candles were being blown out the wrong way. The Holy Father, in a submissive and apologizing tone, said, "It was I who extinguished them that way." When I heard this, I wanted the ground to swallow me. After dinner, still feeling mortified, the pope came to my office and asked me if I could blow out the candles. He said, "You know, I am not that practical." His humility is disarming.

20 MONDAY DECEMBER

Sala Clementina,
Apostolic Palace: speech
by the Holy Father to
cardinals, archbishops,
bishops, and the Roman
Curia on the occasion of
Christmas greetings.

26 SUNDAY DECEMBER

This evening we mentioned the subject of Christmas carols and the fact that some children do not understand all their words. For example, the pope said that his brother, Georg, since he was small, was convinced that "the little sheep" in the crib that were mentioned in a carol were sisters and not real sheep!

This afternoon we gathered in the sitting room around the Christmas tree, which was decorated with stars made out of straw and beeswax candles. After we finished singing, the pope told us about one Christmas during the war. The minor seminary was taken over to accommodate wounded Polish soldiers and the students were asked to go to the rooms of the wounded to cheer them up with some carols. But it was not easy, because many of the poor soldiers, almost all of them quite young, had very serious injuries, including limb amputations. Toward the end of the war the students were given permission to go home for Christmas. "This was wonderful, because every year my brother, Georg, composed a music piece for us to play together. He played the violin, our sister played the piano, and I played the harmonium." He explained that this last instrument was in almost every house at that time, just like the kneeler. Truly, those were different times!

27 MONDAY DECEMBER

Today at dinner, the pope told us that when he was a child the family cat, looking for some warm place, always went into the kitchen, and his mother, every evening before she went to bed, had to put it inside the barn. But the cat did not like leaving the warm place, and so it always held on to the wood logs in an attempt to remain there. When his father opened the barn door every morning, the cat was always ready to jump out. I asked him, "What was its name?" He replied, "Honestly, we had more than one cat, and they were all called Mitzi — that is, pussycat."

30 THURSDAY DECEMBER

After the Holy Father has heard so much about a particular cat, finally, today, he has had the pleasure of meeting that cat: the cat of the commander of the Vatican Gendarmerie. The two siblings of Mr. Domenico bring the cat, called Leo, to the gardens after we recite the Rosary. It is a very large cat, and the pope pets it for a long time. We joke about the event at table. I say, "Perhaps we shall read on tomorrow's *L'Osservatore Romano* that the pope received in a special audience His Highness Prince Leo, elevating him at the same time to the position of arch-cat!" The pope bursts out laughing and says, "Thus, apart from the pontifical arch-physician, we will also have the pontifical arch-cat!"

My Days with
BENEDICT XVI
2011

6 THURSDAY JANUARY

The Holy Father likes to keep himself informed on the weather conditions. With this in mind, we have put a barometer on the terrace. The pope, just after going up there, asks us what it says. Then, today, he tells me, after we finish the Rosary, that it is said in Bavaria that from December 13 until Christmas, the day becomes longer at the pace of a rooster; from Christmas Day to the Epiphany, at the pace of a deer; and from the Epiphany to Candlemas the day stretches by a whole hour.

10 MONDAY JANUARY

There is another anecdote that I pleasingly recall. It relates to an afternoon when we were going out to recite the Rosary. Before we entered the elevator, we put on our coats and scarves over our cassocks to protect ourselves from the cold. But since it was warm inside the house, I put them on right at the sound of the pope closing his door. This way there was just enough time for me to get ready before he arrived at the elevator. But today I did not pay attention and found the pope right in front of me. In order not to make him wait, I help him put on the white jacket and then enter the elevator hurriedly with my coat across my arms and my cap in my hands. Seeing that I am in some difficulty when trying to put on the coat inside the elevator, he takes my cap in his hands. Then he grabs the collar of my coat so as to help me put it on. I feel very embarrassed with the whole thing, and not knowing exactly how to make him stop, I say, "If my mother comes to know that the pope is helping me dress, she would scold me." But he candidly replies, "But this is something normal. We must help one another." Benedict is truly a humble and uncomplicated man. We can always imitate him!

11 TUESDAY JANUARY

Right before our walk in the Vatican Gardens for the recitation of the Rosary, the Holy Father tells me of a dream he has had this afternoon during his short siesta. He had to go to the pope for an audience — for him, "the pope" is always John Paul II. And he was late! He looked for the papers he was supposed to show the Holy Father but could not find them, and it was already time for the audience to commence. Trying to be kind while listening to his story, I say, "Then even the pope, like the rest of us, has dreams in which he feels unprepared." He nods and smiles.

15 SATURDAY JANUARY

As noted above, we always put on something to protect us from the cold when we go out for the recitation of the Rosary. Once the day begins to get longer, the pope switches from wearing the Basque beret to wearing a cap with a visor to protect his eyes from the sun. In the past, the pope used to carry sunglasses, but once he discovered the usefulness of the visor, he did not wear them any longer. Today I make a mistake, and instead of the cap I hand him the beret. I feel mortified, but he says, "I will make a small penance and walk with my head lowered."

We are invited to dinner this evening by Ingrid Stampa, who for many years was a faithful collaborator of Joseph Ratzinger. I share a joke at the pope's recommendation. So, we are in Scotland in the convent of very poor nuns who have been forced to sell everything to simply survive. The mother superior is very sick, almost at death's door. The other nuns take her a cup of hot milk, but she turns it down. The condition of the superior worsens. Then the youngest nun goes to the kitchen and adds a fair bit of whiskey to the milk. She goes back to the superior and ... surprise! The reverend mother first takes a sip, then another, then a third, and finally pulls herself up and exclaims, "Please, sell everything we have but not the cow from which you have gotten this milk!" The pope laughs heartily.

At 9:00 p.m. sharp he looks at the clock, excuses himself, leaves the table, and goes to call his brother, who celebrates eighty-seven years today. When he returns, he says, "We have never imagined that we would live so long!"

Can I add something about the jokes? The pope told us that among the many newspapers he receives, there is one that prints stories that make one laugh. I confided, "Honestly speaking, I read that newspaper just for its jokes!"

The dove of peace, just launched from window of the papal study, returns to Pope Benedict.

29 THURSDAY JANUARY

The Holy Father asks us during breakfast about upcoming meetings. Today I remind him that next Sunday we will be joined for the Angelus from the window of the Apostolic Palace by some children from the Catholic Action in Rome. They will be accompanied by their teachers for the traditional launch of two doves. Recalling that last year, one of the doves turned around and immediately entered the pope's study, I jokingly volunteer to dress up as a wolf to scare off another possibly frightened dove and force it to fly into the open air. The pope says, "Well, instead of a wolf you might be better off as a seagull." He is referring to the fact that nowadays seagulls have taken over the Roman skies and scare off all the other birds.

3 THURSDAY FEBRUARY

Since I know that the Holy Father loves anecdotes, especially about animals, I tell him of the scene I witnessed from my study window. There was a black cat while workers were dismantling the manger in St. Peter's Square. The cat wanted to run away toward Borgo Pio, but the line of people waiting to enter St. Peter's Basilica was so dense that it could not do so. The cat made its first unsuccessful attempt, then failed at the second attempt, but went back again. Finally, the cat sprinted like an arrow and succeeded in vanishing. A stubborn cat! The pope has a good laugh.

4 FRIDAY FEBRUARY

While at dinner, we allude to tomorrow's episcopal consecration the Holy Father will preside at in St. Peter's Basilica. He tells us that in the past, the bishop to be consecrated fasted on the eve as an adequate sign of an internal preparation. I ask him if this rule of fasting was applied only for an episcopal consecration. He tells me that there was a time when one fasted for all ordinations, including that of priests and deacons. He seems somewhat nostalgic for those times.

6 SUNDAY
FEBRUARY

There are always many commitments, but the pope does his best to respect Sunday as a day of rest, and to dedicate the day completely to the Lord. Since today is a Sunday that promises to be a quiet day, we recall the racket that took place last Sunday when one of the doves of peace decided to change course and fly into the papal study rather than into the open air. It forced us to chase it with a certain amount of anxiety. The pope retorts with a smile, "Ah well, today we have a Sunday of peace without the doves of peace!"

10 THURSDAY
FEBRUARY

The Holy Father wants to give me a big surprise! I ask the pope to be excused from dinner so as to participate in the celebration of Holy Mass with the Maltese community in Rome because today we celebrate the feast of the shipwreck of St. Paul on the shores of the island. The pope not only grants me permission but presents me with a picture wherein he is depicted during his apostolic visit to Malta. The background portrays the picturesque dock where Benedict XVI held his meeting with the youth. I tell the pope, "Holy Father, thank you for this precious gift and thoughtful gesture." One can see that he is pleased.

12 SATURDAY
FEBRUARY

During our short walk following the Rosary, we speak about the upcoming consistory, at which time some cardinals will receive a higher rank. Those cardinals who reside in Rome enjoy the title of cardinal deacon or cardinal priest or cardinal bishop. After a few years, the pope might raise a cardinal to a higher rank, depending on what is available. In regard to this stepping up, the pope recalls with a smile a witty remark made by an elderly cardinal, at the time still a cardinal deacon while he served as the archpriest of St. Peter's Basilica. He played on the word *priest*. He said, "I am an archpriest, but still a cardinal deacon!" Curia headaches!

19 SATURDAY
FEBRUARY

I told the Holy Father during this evening's supper that I could hear a choir singing from my room last evening. It was from a choir that had gathered by the piazza fountain below the Apostolic Palace. The pope then told us that in his time there was a custom that when a priest celebrated his first Holy Mass, people went to his home in the evening to sing in his honor. It even happened to him, and the following day his mother found her flower beds all in a mess!

23 WEDNESDAY
FEBRUARY

We alert the Holy Father to the fact that he might hear gunfire these days and that he should not be alarmed. It is not war but a means to chase away the seagulls that assemble in the evening in the churchyard in front of the Vatican Basilica. It seems that blank shots might do the trick. But the pope is skeptical. He says that the same thing was tried with the starlings, but after a few days the birds realized there was no real danger and came back. However, the problem of the seagulls is serious. They are aggressive and intrusive. One day we watched with horror two seagulls on the terrace that were determined to eat the small red fish in the pond. The birds fled when we got there, leaving two fish gutted.

The pope today met Cardinal Angelo Comastri, the archpriest of St. Peter's Basilica and the president of the Fabric of St. Peter. The first thing the pope asked was, "And the seagulls?" The pope said, "The cardinal told me that they got rid of them. I smiled sadly, thinking of those poor fish and the seagulls that, nonetheless, still fly stubbornly over our heads."

24 THURSDAY FEBRUARY

The pope always has a ready retort. Today I told him that Munich's soccer team, Bayern, won an important match. I said, "Holy Father, you must be happy that the team close to your heart has won!" He immediately replied, "Well, when it comes to a soccer team, it cannot go deep down into my heart!" On another matter, I noticed yesterday that the pope only nibbled at his lunch. I say, "Holy Father, but this bite of a meal is practically invisible!" The pope replied, "Fr. Alfred, you need a ew pair of eyeglasses!"

25 FRIDAY FEBRUARY

There are occasions when the pope shares funny episodes from the time of his long academic life. For example, he tells us today of a professor who was stingy. Thus, in order to save on paper, he used the back of a letter to write his replies. "One day he learned that paper cost less at a nearby place. He did all kinds of calculations to see how much he would save, even taking into account the cost of gasoline! Then he asked his assistant to take him with his car, even promising him a snack. He convinced him! The assistant took him, and the professor gave him a sandwich and a drink instead of paying him for the gasoline. He established that this cost less!"

3 THURSDAY MARCH

During breakfast we discussed today's lunch that the Holy Father is putting on for those who were involved in translating into various languages the second volume in his *Jesus of Nazareth* series. There will be eleven guests, and they will enjoy a nice spread.

The pope tells us that Pope John Paul II used to have frequent guests, among whom was the less than quiet, lively prelate monsignor, who brightened the atmosphere with many stories. The pope says with a smile, "There were times when he prevented others from talking." He adds that there was an occasion, soon after the movie *The Jeweler's Shop* had been released, that this friendly prelate proceeded to declare in front of everyone, including John Paul II, that he had heard that the movie was a bit boring, forgetting that it was based on a book written by Karol Wojtyła himself bearing the same title. I smile, recalling that there are times when I am guilty of similar gaffes.

4 FRIDAY
MARCH

Our affection toward the Holy Father grows more and more. This is largely due to his way of being so simple and open, sometimes even disarming. Yesterday we waited by the elevator for about ten minutes before going down for the Rosary. Now, the pope is never late; rather he arrives a few minutes in advance. Thus, when he arrived, he immediately apologized and admitted, "I nodded off!" We had to reassure him that it was not a big deal. But the delay of about ten minutes is repeated today. The pope apologizes again and assures us that this time he had not slept but had some problem with his cassock. He says, "You know that unbuttoning and buttoning all those buttons requires a certain amount of time."

19 SATURDAY
MARCH

The Lenten spiritual exercises finish today, which is the Solemnity of St. Joseph, the chaste spouse of the Blessed Virgin Mary. It happens to be my turn to express before breakfast the best wishes for the Holy Father's name day. Following a short song in German, I say more or less the following greetings: "Beloved Holy Father, we were a bit hesitant to determine if it would be appropriate to immediately give you this morning our best wishes on the feast of your patron saint, being still within the silence of the spiritual exercises. But we were emboldened by today's liturgy, which celebrates St. Joseph without interrupting our

Lenten journey. After all, St. Joseph is a man of eloquent silence and also the person who always says yes to God and to the designs of Divine Providence. Moreover, Lent urges us to listen to the Word so as to renew our own yes to God. Holy Father, our best wishes form a prayer. All of us pray for you every day, but we do so today in a special way and with particular joy. We are grateful to the Lord for being at your service in such a close way. On behalf of all of us, I extend our warmest best wishes, proposing to follow your many good examples, which we not only want to admire but also to emulate. A heartfelt thanks, Holy Father." I am very enthralled with the gentle gaze of the pope as he listens with pleasure to my poor words!

20 SUNDAY MARCH

Today we accompany the Holy Father on his visit to consecrate a new parish in the boundaries of Infernetto. The pope is very happy because the church is dedicated to St. Corbinian, the first bishop of Munich-Freising, of whom he himself was a successor.

His face is illuminated during the ceremony, especially when hearing the children's choir. He adds in his homily a few historical notes on the saint that were not included in the booklet. St. Corbinian — we are talking about thirteen hundred years ago — was a French priest who founded a monastery near Paris. Though he was held in high esteem as a spiritual counselor, he was attracted to the contemplative life. So he came to Rome to pray near the tombs of the apostles Peter and Paul. But Pope Gregory II, who admired him, ordained him a bishop and commissioned him to go as a missionary in Bavaria, where there was a lack of priests to proclaim the gospel. The saint commissioned the construction of a cathedral on a hill in Freising, the city of the duke. The seat of the diocese remained there for over a thousand years — that is, until it was transferred to Munich after the Napoleonic era. The diocese is still called the Diocese of Munich-Freising, and the majestic Romanesque cathedral remains the heart of the diocese. The pope says, "So we see that saints uphold the Church's unity and universality. Universality: St. Corbinian connects France, Germany and Rome. Unity: St. Corbinian tells us that the Church is founded on Peter and guarantees to us that the Church founded on the rock will endure forever. One thousand years ago she was the same Church that she is today, because the Lord is always the same. He is always Truth, ever old and ever new, very up to date, present, and the key opening the future."

24 THURSDAY MARCH

Pope Paul VI appointed Joseph Ratzinger bishop of Munich thirty-four years ago today, March 24, 1977. The Holy Father remembers distinctly that the notification arrived when one of his students was preparing to defend his doctoral thesis at Regensburg University.

The anniversary also made him recall his predecessor in Munich, Cardinal Julius August Döpfner, and one particular incident. A lover of mountains, he requested, when he was appointed bishop, to rearrange the dining room at the bishop's palace to make it look like an Alpine hut. But his request was never followed through on!

27 SUNDAY MARCH

Evening prayer in the private chapel. In the kneeler's shelf are kept cards with prayer requests.

The Holy Father delivers a beautiful introduction at the beginning of the celebration of Holy Mass. I'll try to recall it. He says, "Today's Gospel excerpt presents Jesus as the source of living water that satisfies the thirst of the Samaritan woman and of those who draw it from him. Jesus, the Son of God, is the only source of eternal life and he calls us to himself to quench our thirst. He does so every time we approach with faith the Banquet of his Body and Most Precious Blood. The new life which he gives us not only quenches our thirst for the divine but, despite our limitations, also transforms us into small springs of living waters for those we approach with evangelical joy." Benedict urges us with this very clear image to seek peace of the heart in Christ, making us His collaborators to dispense heavenly peace to others.

3 SUNDAY APRIL

The pope states at the Angelus that yesterday was the sixth anniversary of the death of John Paul II. He says, "I remembered him with affection in prayer, as I am sure you did too. During the Lenten journey we prepare for Easter, we joy-

Breakfast after the Holy
Mass in the courtyard of
the Swiss Guards.

fully approach the day on which we will venerate as Blessed
this great Pontiff, a witness to Christ, and rely even more
on his intercession."

I do not celebrate Holy Mass with the Holy Father this
morning, because I have been asked to preside over the one
for the Pontifical Swiss Guards in their chapel. The Holy
Father asks me during luncheon how things went. He was
very pleased with the warm welcome they gave me after Holy
Mass. There was breakfast in the yard, where their musical
band was also present.

4 MONDAY APRIL

Today the pope spoke of Cardinal Marc Ouellet at lunch.
Benedict XVI has called him to head the Congregation for
Bishops. It was also stated that recently the cardinal had
presented in the Vatican Press Office the pope's second
volume of *Jesus of Nazareth*. At a certain point I built up
enough courage to ask the pope the specific reason for
choosing Ouellet. After a moment of silence, the Holy

Father replied, "Because he is a person who has many good qualities." I must admit that I was intrusive. In any case, I realized that the pope greatly appreciates the Canadian cardinal, and thought he is perhaps a cardinal whom Benedict sees as his possible successor.

14 THURSDAY
APRIL

The Holy Father shows a mixture of reluctance and resignation when it comes to taking medicine. When, at the end of the meal, he realizes that there is some tablet to take, he exclaims, "Ah! This is still the poison!" In fact, the Italian term for "drug" (farmaco) comes from the Greek word *phàrmakon*, meaning poison! Then he tells us that when he was younger, or less elderly, he did not follow medical prescriptions with great concern. He said, "Once my doctor, finding me better, congratulated me. He told me that I was great in taking all the medication. Little did he know that I did not take even half of it!"

16 SATURDAY
APRIL

The pope turns eighty-four today. We gather together before breakfast to welcome him with a beautiful song. Of course, there is a cake at lunch. Greetings are arriving from all over the world, a sign of great affection. The pope, being his usual serene and amusing self, tells us that the mother of Cardinal Schönborn, archbishop of Vienna, still drives despite being almost one hundred years old!

21 HOLY THURSDAY
APRIL

I notice that on this special day dedicated to the ministerial priesthood and the Holy Eucharist, the Holy Father is visibly happy. During our usual walk on the terrace this evening, we speak of today's two beautiful celebrations: this morning's chrism Mass at St. Peter's, and this evening another intense Holy Eucharist, the Holy Mass of the Lord's Supper at the Basilica of St. John Lateran. I point out some concelebrants at the basilica, including Fr. Mario Pangallo, a dear professor at the Lateran University. I describe him as "very intelligent and altogether humble." The pope comments, "It is not easy to find a professor who is both intelligent and humble at the same time." He knows this from experience.

Chrism Mass in St. Peter's.

25 MONDAY APRIL

I reminded Pope Benedict at the end of breakfast that he was scheduled to meet the Schilgen family from Münster after the Regina Coeli prayer. I had heard him mention them before. The pope, smiling, said, "I know ... and I am very curious."

While Joseph Ratzinger was a student at the Georgianum Seminary in Munich between 1947 and 1950, he had Professor Joseph Pascher as his director and one of his teachers. As a seminarian, he received from him a human and priestly formation that left a deep impression on his spiritual journey.

After the National Socialists closed the theology faculty of the University of Munich in 1939, Pascher relocated to northern Germany, where he taught pastoral theology and pedagogy at the University of Münster. His dwelling was completely destroyed during one of the raids of World War II. Consequently, Carl and Margarethe Schilgen extended him hospitality in their home. It was precisely in the home of his gracious hosts that he wrote the famous volume entitled *The Eucharist*. The friendship continued after Pascher

Pope Benedict welcomes with emotion the reminiscences of Prof. Joseph Pascher. On receiving the copy of the dedication made to Signora Margarethe he exclaims: "You brought me such a precious gift of the Prof. Pascher!"

The dedication of Prof. Joseph Pascher to Messrs. Schilgen: "Es ist Zeit, daß wir uns alle an der Stelle, an die uns Gott gestellt hat, in die große Sendung einordnen. Münster März 1950 Joseph Pascher" (It's time that we all — where God has placed us — we submit to great mission. Munster March 1950 Joseph Pascher).

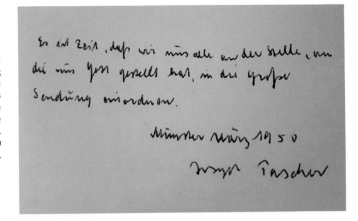

The thank you note with which Pope Benedict thanks Mrs. Schilgen for the gift of the copy of the Prof. Pascher's dedication t: "Liebe Frau Schilgen, herzlichen Dank für Ihren Ostergruß und besonders für die Erinnerungen an Prof. Pascher wie auch an Bogenhausen. Mit österlichen Segensgrüßen Ihr Benedictus PP XVI" (Dear Mrs. Schilgen, Thank you very much for the Easter greetings and above all for the memories of Prof. Pascher and also of Bogenhausen. With the Easter blessing His Benedictus PP XVI).

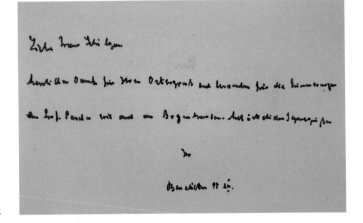

returned to Bavaria, and in March 1950 he presented a complimentary copy of the book to Margarethe with an autographed dedication.

Thus, after so many years, the day has arrived when the granddaughter of the Schilgens will bring many memories of the beloved professor to Benedict. Among them is a gift that is a beautiful framed copy of the dedication to her grandmother. The meeting is very emotional as Christina, the granddaughter, tells Pope Benedict of the bond between Professor Pascher and her family.

1 SUNDAY MAY

Today is a very memorable day! The Holy Father has beatified his direct predecessor, John Paul II. From early morning hundreds of thousands have converged on St. Peter's Square and the Via della Conciliazione for the occasion, while millions follow the ceremony by television and radio. The pope says in his very touching and beautiful homily, "Six years ago we gathered in this Square to celebrate the funeral of Pope John Paul II. Our grief at his loss was deep, but even greater was our sense of an immense grace which embraced Rome and the whole world: a grace which was in some way the fruit of my beloved predecessor's entire life, and especially of his witness in suffering. Even then we perceived the fragrance of his sanctity, and in any number of ways God's People showed their veneration for him. For this reason, with all due respect for the Church's canonical norms, I wanted his cause of beatification to move forward with reasonable haste. And now

The image of the blessed John Paul II hanging at the central Loggia of the Vatican Basilica.

the longed-for day has come; it came quickly because this is what was pleasing to the Lord: John Paul II is blessed!" The pope raises his voice while pronouncing these last words. One can sense his emotions.

Next, Benedict recalls that this Sunday is the Second Sunday of Easter, which Blessed John Paul II wanted to dedicate to Divine Mercy. Hence the reason for choosing it as the day for today's celebration: "Today is also the first day of May, Mary's month, and the liturgical memorial of Saint Joseph the Worker. All these elements serve to enrich our prayer, they help us in our pilgrimage through time and space; but in heaven a very different celebration is taking place among the angels and saints! Even so, God is but one, and one too is Christ the Lord, who like a bridge joins earth to heaven. At this moment we feel closer than ever, sharing as it were in the liturgy of heaven."

We have Cardinal Stanisław Dziwisz and Archbishop Mietek as guests for lunch. They were the private secretaries of the new Blessed. Don

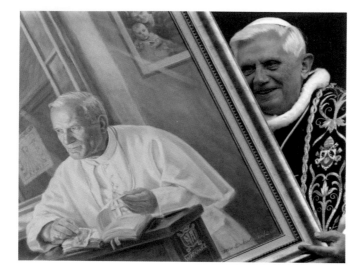

Pope Benedict admires a portrait of John Paul II received as a gift.

Stanisław expresses his deep serenity and speaks of the many graces that John Paul II is pouring down from Heaven, especially to couples who have difficulties having children and for cancer patients. At this point I would like to share a story that I have just heard from a couple from Gozo, our neighbors.

Some time ago, the wife had an annoying ringing in her ears. She had gone to the ear, nose, and throat specialist who explained to her the syndrome and that it was very difficult to treat. After a few days of suffering, when she could not even sleep well, she asked her husband to fetch the holy card of John Paul II, which I had sent them and which had a tiny attached relic. She put it on her ear and laid down her head to sleep, and the annoying hum simply went away. At first she said nothing to anyone about it, but after a few days, noting that the syndrome had completely disappeared, she decided to be present in Rome precisely for the beatification.

It is clear that the Holy Father is very impressed by these stories, for he tells me so during our walk on the terrace. I tell him about other instances of miraculous healing of other people I know. He enjoys listening to these accounts.

9 MONDAY
MAY

This past Saturday and Sunday, May 7 and 8, the pope went on a pastoral visit to Aquileia and Venice. I was not with him. I only accompany him when he journeys beyond Italy. So I went to Bergamo for these two days to catch up with friends who told me of an extraordinary experience of a family they knew. A young woman of about twenty years of age had a successful heart operation. However, a few days later she suddenly fainted and went into a coma as a nurse was giving her medication at home. The situation was extremely serious, and an air ambulance was called. By now she was given up for dead, so much so that the pilot had radioed the emergency hall that they were bringing in a dead girl, since her lips had turned purple and her heart had stopped. Her parents, however, began organizing a prayer vigil and also sought prayers

A short transfer in a gondola during the pastoral visit in Venice.

from Pope Benedict. A couple of hours before the vigil, the young woman woke up, and the prayer vigil was turned from a petition to a joyful thanksgiving to God. I reported to the Holy Father the gratitude of the young woman, Valeria, and of all of her family and friends. All of them saw a supernatural intervention in this awakening.

11 WEDNESDAY
MAY

Yesterday afternoon, before we went to the Vatican Gardens for the recitation of the Rosary the Holy Father asked us for a rosary. He told us that his rosary had broken into two pieces. So I retrieved two rosaries and left them in his office. I made a big mistake! I did not know that usually white rosaries are given to ladies, and the black ones are reserved for men. But the pope, instead of chiding me, simply commented that it is the custom in Bavaria that men use black rosaries and ladies use white ones. Once again, I appreciated how refined he was.

12 THURSDAY
MAY

There has been all kinds of chatter in these last few weeks on the Internet and other means of communication regarding the "alleged" prophecy according to which yesterday, May 11, there was supposed to be an earthquake. Many citizens were alarmed, and the National Institute of Geophysics and Volcanology at Frascati was inundated by phone calls. Some parents from various parts of Italy went so far as to prohibit their children from going on a school trip to Rome. At table we comment about the tendency to readily believe certain announcements. Unfortunately, while we ignore the gospel warnings to avoid falling into eternal perdition, we readily believe in strange prophecies. The Holy Father says thought-fully, "It almost seems that people have a need to live in fear." But he does not say anything else besides this.

17 TUESDAY
MAY

The pope really knows the saints. This morning, when I state that according to my little calendar today is the feast day of St. Pascal Baylon, the pope immediately adds, "He is the patron saint of eucharistic congresses because he was in love with the Eucharist." Then he speaks about the tradition according to which, during his funeral Mass, Fr. Pascal opened his eyes at the moment of Consecration. This is the reason why, I suddenly realize, when we were small and had to rise at a certain hour, we were told to pray to St. Pascal!

18 WEDNESDAY
MAY

On our way toward the Grotto of Lourdes for the customary recitation of the Rosary, we notice an old train motionless on the tracks in front of the railway station. Normally there are only cars of some merchant train, but this time it's a passenger train. We are told that it formed part of a convoy from 1930 and that it will be used next Saturday by the participants of a symposium that is being organized to commemorate the sixtieth anniversary of the establishment of Caritas Internationalis. It is scheduled to depart from Vatican City and travel to Orvieto. It is a steam train.

At this point the Holy Father confides in me something of a surprise: "I would love to go to one of the train stations, purchase a ticket, and take the train." I ask him if, when he was teaching, he used to go by train to university. He tells me that he took it whenever he returned home to his brother for the holidays. The Holy Father moves me tenderly. It is something normal for us to go to a station, purchase a ticket, and board a train. But for the pope, this is an impossible dream.

4 SATURDAY JUNE

We are accustomed to having a lit candle on the table during meals in the papal apartment. This is also done in Germany and many other countries. The candle at our table today is consuming much of its center and very little of its sides, to the point that the flame is barely visible. After concluding the prayer before lunch, the Holy Father, thinking that the candle is out, exclaims, "Ah, I see that you follow the ancient liturgical tradition of leaving the candle unlit after the feast of the Ascension as a sign that the Lord has ascended into Heaven!" I find this study of symbols to be very interesting. He finds a spiritual and liturgical reference for every aspect of life.

6 MONDAY JUNE

Today I give to one of the Memores a poster that carries the list of all the popes of the Church over the centuries, beginning with Peter, all the way down to Benedict XVI. She will give it as a gift to a boy she knows, who had expressed a wish to have it. Thus, we speak about popes during dinner. When I state that we must be grateful to the Lord because now a long time has passed since that of the decadent popes, and now we have popes who are saints and blesseds, Benedict nods and adds that the Catholic Church is the longest surviving monarchy in history. Then the pope tells us of an incredible theory of which I was unaware. Years ago a legend spread that claimed Pope Paul VI was kidnapped and imprisoned in the Vatican dungeons and replaced by a double who was controlled by the Masons. He exclaims, "Highly unlikely!"

7 TUESDAY JUNE

We speak at breakfast about the penitential pilgrimages that are undertaken at this time. The pope tells us that his father, as a sign of gratitude that the Ratzinger family remained largely unscathed during the war, went on foot from Regensburg to the Shrine of Our Lady of Altötting, some one hundred kilometers away. At the time, Mr. Ratzinger was already sixty-seven years old!

16 THURSDAY JUNE

The Holy Father tells me of a dream he had. He was at the house of the politician Massimo D'Alema, discussing theological topics. In the dream, the pope was surprised that D'Alema, who was once a proponent of the Communist Party, was so prepared on the subject matter. Then, at a certain point, D'Alema's cat entered the room and approached the pope. Benedict caressed the cat and the cat purred. But the dream ended at this point because the pope woke up. I said to him, "It is true that dreams end at the most beautiful moment!" It turns out that D'Alema does not have a cat, but we know for sure he has a dog.

While on the subject of animals, the Vatican City does not allow the keeping of pet animals. There are a few exceptions, one of which is granted to Archbishop Domenico Calcagno, secretary of the Administration of the Patrimony of the Holy See. He keeps a very affable dog called Diana, known for her intelligence and good behavior. "Just think," the archbishop once said to us, "when I go to the office, Diana remains alone, listening to classical music. One time I forgot the sausages in the kitchen. She remained there looking at them with a watering mouth. But she never touched them." The pope commented, "This Diana deserves to be canonized!" I retorted, "Perhaps, Holy Father, she even deserves the Pro Ecclesia et Pontifice award because she has demonstrated heroic virtues and generous service to a man of the Church!" The pope, smiling, replied that he was in agreement.

17 FRIDAY JUNE

Some time ago, the pope asked me if the loud chimes of the bells of the clock of the Basilica of St. Peter could be heard from my bedroom, which faces the square and is right above the pope's study. I told him that I could hear them, but that by now I was accustomed to putting plugs in my ears since the windows are not sufficiently soundproof. He told me, "I am going to speak with the archpriest of the basilica, Cardinal Comastri." He did so at the earliest opportunity. Today, in fact, the pope tells me with a satisfied look that the cardinal has agreed to turn off the chimes during night hours. Later I learn that the pope has made the request as if it was his need rather than mine! I marvel at so much concern.

In the meantime, Benedict is preparing for the visit to the Republic of San Marino. It is scheduled to take place the day after tomorrow, Sunday. He will spend the day there on the Solemnity of the Blessed Trinity and will celebrate Holy Mass at the stadium in Serravalle.

23 THURSDAY JUNE

Today, the feast of Corpus Christi, Benedict celebrates Holy Mass on the square of the Basilica of St. John Lateran and then participates in the procession to the Basilica of St. Mary Major, followed by thousands of people. He explains during the homily that "the Feast of *Corpus Christi* is inseparable from Holy Thursday, from the Mass *in Coena Domini*, in which the Institution of the Eucharist is solemnly celebrated. Whereas on the evening of Holy Thursday we relive the mystery of Christ who offers himself to us in the bread

During the traditional Corpus Domini Procession along via Merulana in Rome.

broken and the wine poured out, today, on the day of *Corpus Christi*, this same mystery is proposed for the adoration and meditation of the People of God, and the Blessed Sacrament is carried in procession through the streets of the cities and villages, to show that the Risen Christ walks in our midst and guides us toward the Kingdom of Heaven." The pope concludes his homily with these beautiful words: "Let us walk with no illusions, with no utopian ideologies, on the highways of the world bearing within us the Body of the Lord, like the Virgin Mary in the mystery of the Visitation. With the humility of knowing that we are merely grains of wheat, let us preserve the firm certainty that the love of God, incarnate in Christ, is stronger than evil, violence and death."

The Holy See is one of the few countries that wanted to maintain the traditional celebration of the Solemnity of Corpus Christi on a Thursday. The pope asks me if it was also this way in Malta. I tell him that unfortunately today is a normal working day for the Maltese and that the feast of the Body and Blood of Christ is celebrated the following Sunday, along with the procession with the Blessed Sacrament, which is preceded by the so-called Forty Hours Devotion, which recalls the amount of time Jesus remained in the tomb.

29 WEDNESDAY JUNE

After an absence of about six months, the Holy Father's brother is back today to spend a few days at the Vatican. He has undergone knee surgery and has stayed in Regensburg for a long time for rehabilitation. But this time the reason for Msgr. Georg Ratzinger's visit carries with it something very special. He has come to celebrate the sixtieth anniversary of

Precious photograph the Ratzinger brothers' day of priestly ordination.

his priestly ordination. It coincides with the pope's anniversary because the two brothers were ordained priests together on the same day.

When the pope arrives at the dining room for breakfast, we greet him with a song. The pope accepts it with great emotion and also, I would venture to say, with modesty, for he did not wish to give the anniversary much importance. We give the pope as a gift one of the original holy cards printed for his ordination. It is placed inside a beautiful laced silver frame. Meanwhile, we give his brother, Georg, a bench for his piano, which is now in the apartment he stays in when he comes to visit us. He says, having tried out the piano recently acquired, "It is an instrument that is a bit old, but then, after all, my hands are also old!"

8 FRIDAY JULY

We came for some rest to the summer residence of Castel Gandolfo yesterday. This morning we celebrated Holy Mass on the actual sixtieth anniversary of the first Holy Mass of Fr. Joseph Ratzinger, celebrated in St. Oswald Church at Traunstein. The pope recalled this very special day while we were having breakfast. The sky was blue, there was joy in the air, and the local band accompanied the two brother-priests from their home to the parish church, with women and men dressed in traditional costumes. When

Holy Mass was over, guests filled the garden at their house, celebrating the occasion with the brothers' family. The Holy Father had no tears in his eyes as he recalled the event. Rather, there was a serene gaze full of gratitude to the Lord.

As per tradition, the new priests Ratzinger impart the blessing to family and faithful.

14 THURSDAY JULY

When I am alone with the Holy Father, I would say that there emerges an understanding similar to the one between a father and his son. Today I feel the urge to thank him for the abounding kindness he has shown me during these years I have been in service to him. While I apologize for my possible shortcomings, I feel the need to tell him also of my appreciation of the homily he delivered on June 29 on the occasion of his sixtieth anniversary of priesthood. I tell him that I was impressed even with what he shared in front of the Grotto of Our Lady of Lourdes on the evening of June 28. He was speaking to some young people who were discussing their vocation, of the beautiful as well as difficult moments he experienced as a priest. When I confide in him that I cannot imagine that he, too, has lived through some difficult times, he responds, "It would be naïve to think that there is a priesthood devoid of sacrifices and sufferings." We share this while sitting on our usual bench next to Our Lady of the red fish, having already recited the Rosary.

11 THURSDAY AUGUST

Left photo: Private visit in the church of Santa Maria in Valle Porclaneta in Magliano of the Marsi.

Right photo: Songs are sung before the picnic under the trees.

18 THURSDAY AUGUST

At lunch with a representation of young people who participated in Would Youth Day Madrid.

21 SUNDAY AUGUST

The papal procession toward the Cuatro Vientos esplanade for the celebration of the Holy Mass, which closed the XXVI World Youth Day.

The Pope together with a WYD volunteer in the pavilion of the new Feria de Madrid, before returning to the Vatican.

5 MONDAY SEPTEMBER

I returned rather late yesterday evening from a short holiday at home. This morning, while I am reciting my Lauds at the back of the chapel, I hear the Holy Father's room door opening. His room is situated opposite the chapel. As usual, I stand up so as to leave him alone to pray before Holy Mass. But raising my eyes, I notice that he is approaching to greet me. He asks if I have rested well and seeks news about my mother and relatives.

22 THURSDAY SEPTEMBER

Leaving for the apostolic
journey to Germany,
September 22–25, 2011.

14 FRIDAY OCTOBER

My mother decided that to mark my birthday, she would
make a surprise visit to Rome with one of her friends so that
we can celebrate it together. She decided the timing of the
visit without consulting me, and we found ourselves at a time
when the Holy Father had no public ceremonies. Consequently, her friend would not have the opportunity to receive
Holy Communion from the pope, something she wished very
much to do. When I explained the situation to the Holy
Father, he immediately replied, "But, if they wish, they can
always come for our Holy Mass in the private chapel!" You
can imagine the joy of my mother and her friend Caterina.
The pope also wished to greet them at the end of Holy Mass,
as well as to give each a rosary.

When I met the Holy Father before lunch, I told him, "My mother and her friend wish to thank you again. They are super happy with this privilege." The pope replied, "But it was only right to do so!"

I also remember another visit of my mother to Rome. She and her friend rented an apartment close to St. Anne's Gate. When Benedict heard that she was here, he wanted to invite her for lunch. In thanking him for the invitation, my mother said she would prefer meeting him at breakfast. The pope made her sit next to him, and in order to put her at ease, he inquired about her daily life, in particular regarding the cats and the chickens that she tends in the garden. The pope willingly posed for some photos of the occasion before taking his leave. I received an envelope late that afternoon from the Photographic Service of the *L'Osservatore Romano*. It contained the photos that were taken earlier in the morning. To my great surprise, one of them showed the pope holding my mother's hand. This was the way he wanted to express his gratitude for my loyal service to him.

23 SUNDAY OCTOBER

The pope presents us with an edifying witness even in the way he celebrates Holy Mass. First and foremost is his preparation in the sacristy. We notice these days that he is spending a longer time in recollecting himself before he comes out. Perhaps he has some special intentions to pray for!

I have noticed on a number of occasions that while I am preparing the chalice with wine for the Offertory, and he realizes that I am reciting the brief prayer as the water is joined to the wine, he remains silent. However, if I recite the prayer silently in my heart, he recites it in a low voice. Even in these small details he shows respect to the person who assists him.

There are some small holy cards that portray him during some of his international journeys. Some are used as bookmarks in our hymn book. I have noticed that when he comes across one of these, he turns it over so that it is what is written on the back rather than his photo that is visible. I take this gesture as a sign of humility: he wants to avoid any risk of self-exaltation.

31 MONDAY OCTOBER

There is a colony of parrots at the Vatican Gardens. This afternoon, when the recitation of the Rosary is hardly over, they fly over our heads, chirping away, which almost scares us. This reminds the Holy Father of a German priest who produced syrup from a plum tree in his garden and had to fight off the birds that pecked the fruit. In order to ward them off, he tied a rope around the branches and extended it to his study so that every time the birds got near, he pulled the rope to move the branches and scare off the birds. The birds responded with a menacing cry, as if to say, "We will make you pay." The priest managed to collect a lot of juice in a barrel, but during the preparation process he must have made some kind of a mistake, as one terrible day the barrel exploded. The pope commented that in the end the birds had their revenge!

5 SATURDAY NOVEMBER

The evening news carries a segment that portrays a competition on the beauty of cats, showing many felines all coiffed up in a laughable and ridiculous way. While watching, the pope makes no comment. But afterward, as we are going up in the elevator for our usual walk on the terrace, he says somewhat sarcastically, "They think that cats all dolled up that way are more beautiful. In fact, it is the opposite." He adds, "But the November issue in the Maltese calendar of the cats carries a very beautiful picture of one that is looking up with a sweet expression." While he is saying this, he imitates the gesture of the cat so that I will understand better what he means. This pleases me because I gave the calendar as a gift.

10 THURSDAY NOVEMBER

The pope is in deep silent prayer before he enters the chapel for Holy Mass. It has now been for a number of days that he stays there for a longer time and prays with great intensity. The pope is currently having therapy to help improve the functioning of the muscles in his legs. I am asked to help during some of the exercises. At a certain point, during these exercises, when he has to raise his arms as high as he can and hold them so for a while, he says, "This is like the end of the war!" We laugh. At the end of the session, he goes on to say, "Just as I had to do in front of the American soldiers at the end of the war."

20 SUNDAY NOVEMBER

Today we have returned from a very demanding three days' journey to Benin, Africa, where Benedict went for the signature and delivery to the bishops of the Post-Synodal Apostolic Exhortation *Africae munus*. There were many meetings, and the local people were filled with great joy. However, it was an exacting test of the health of the pope.

Pope Benedict surrounded by the children of the Don Bosco Center in Benin.

During the outbound flight on November 18, the pope met with the accompanying journalists, always showing his gentleness and availability. While replying to various questions, he recalled the figure of his great friend, the cardinal of Benin, Bernardin Gantin, who died in 2008. He described him as an intelligent man, practical, profound, down to earth, and with a sense of humor.

This morning's Holy Mass at Amitié Stadium in Cotonou stands out among the events during the visit. The pope recalled during Holy Mass that 150 years have passed since the Cross of Christ was first planted in the land of Benin. He said, "Today, we give thanks to God for the work accomplished by the missionaries, by the 'apostolic workers' who first came from among you or from distant lands, bishops, priests, men and women religious, catechists, all those who, both yesterday and today, enabled the growth of the faith in Jesus Christ

Festive reception and group photos in Cotonou.

on the African continent. I honour here the memory of the venerable cardinal Bernardin Gantin, an example of faith and of wisdom for Benin and for the entire African continent."

2 THURSDAY DECEMBER

The Holy Father is particularly excited during the days that lead up to Christmas. Today he comments on a phrase in yesterday's Midmorning Prayer in the breviary. It stated that we should welcome salvation as people jumping for joy like little lambs for the awaited Messiah who is almost at the gates. Next, he speaks about the beautiful Bavarian Christmas traditions that were recently depicted for us in a movie in Clementine Hall.

During dinner he tells us that when he was very small, he memorized the verses of the hymn "Rorate Coeli" because the family sang it in preparation for Christmas. It seems that in those days there were not many hymns available for the Advent season. But then a book was published that contained many beautiful hymns. The pope said, "And I was very happy."

30 FRIDAY DECEMBER

This evening we speak about those notices, which at times are carried in newspapers, that declare the death of someone who in fact results in being still alive and well. I tell the pope that in Malta my mother had on more than one occasion informed my father of the death of someone who afterward, when he went shopping, he encountered on the street. At that point, the pope tells us that something similar had happened to him many years ago. The parish priest called him and told him that his father had died. One can imagine the anguish of the young Joseph. He immediately informed his brother and sister, and together they went to look for their mother at the station and told her the terrible news. Then they rushed home, and there was their father, tranquil, intent on shining his shoes. It is impossible to know how to silence such rumors.

31 SATURDAY DECEMBER

Today, the last day of the civil year, the pope celebrated First Vespers of the Solemnity of Mary, Mother of God, and led the Te Deum inside the Vatican Basilica. Addressing the faithful, he said, "Another year is drawing to a close, as we await the start of a new one: with some trepidation, with our perennial desires and expectations. Reflecting on our life experience, we are continually astonished by how ultimately short and ephemeral life is. So we often find ourselves asking: what meaning can we give to our days? What meaning, in particular, can we give to the days of toil and grief? This is a question that permeates history; indeed it runs through the heart of every generation and every individual. But there is an answer: it is written on the face of a Child who was born in Bethlehem two thousand years ago, and is today the Living One, risen for ever from the dead. From within the fabric of humanity, rent asunder by so much injustice, wickedness and violence, there bursts forth in an unforeseen way the joyful and liberating novelty of Christ our Savior, who leads us to contemplate the goodness and tenderness of God through the mystery of his Incarnation and Birth. The everlasting God has entered our history and he remains present in a unique way in the person of Jesus, his incarnate Son, our Savior, who came down to earth to renew humanity radically and to free us from sin and death, to raise us to the dignity of God's children. Christmas not only recalls the historical fulfillment of this truth that concerns us directly, but in a mysterious and real way, gives it to us afresh."

There is a festive climate in the apartment, and at the end of dinner we toast the New Year.

My Days with

BENEDICT XVI

2012

7 SATURDAY
JANUARY

Yesterday was the feast of the Epiphany. The Holy Father announced the names of twenty-two new cardinals, among whom is the Maltese Augustinian friar Prospero Grech. He is well known by the Holy Father, who has always appreciated his academic credentials and his great sense of humor. Fr. Grech called me this morning and asked me if I was willing to give to the Holy Father a letter of thanks. I told him I would be more than happy to do so. Later on he came over to give me the letter and, smiling, said, "You should tell him that I have always been convinced of the infallibility of the pope, but I began to have some doubts once he appointed me a cardinal." The pope had a good laugh when I told him, and so did the rest of us.

29 SUNDAY
JANUARY

After the Angelus prayer, the launch of the dove of peace with the children of Catholic Action of Rome.

6 MONDAY FEBRUARY

I ask permission to leave the office for about an hour to go to a nearby bookstore, named Benedict XVI, located at Pius XII Square. This new bookstore, dedicated to the works of Joseph Ratzinger, has the coat of arms of the pope engraved in limestone from Malta. It is a copy of the one that stands at the entrance of the apostolic nunciature on the island. The president and director of the Libreria Editrice Vaticana asked me to inaugurate the bookstore, given the fact that the carved stone is from my homeland. When I return, the Holy Father asks me how the ceremony went and who was present.

Unveiling of Benedict XVI's coat of arms in the library of the same name in Piazza Pius XII.

13 MONDAY FEBRUARY

I have just returned from a short visit to Nichelino, a municipality near Turin. The local parish priest invited me to celebrate Holy Mass to mark the fifth anniversary of the death of a priest, a friend and conational of mine, who ministered there for about twenty-six years. As I imagined, the Holy Father asks me to give him details about my visit. He is pleased to know that more than two hundred young people had come to listen to me talk on the mission of the Supreme Pontiff. I also tell him of visiting the sports center that the Maltese priest constructed, and that today it is frequented by thousands of young people and children, serving as a great deterrent against drugs and other problems present in that periphery. The pope asks me, "Did you give a good homily?" I reply, "Holy Father, I think so. I only hope that it was not too long!"

14 WEDNESDAY MARCH

Today, among the different groups participating in the general audience, there is a returning delegation from Malta with a Benedictine torch of peace. There are also people from Alba Fucens and Mercogliano who have come to the Vatican for the blessing of the statute of St. William, patron saint of Irpinia. They are accompanied by the bishop of Avellino and the abbot of Montevergine. Since the saint is depicted with a dog at his feet, I comment to the pope during lunch, "Saints become more amiable when they have an animal next to them." Benedict replies, "They also become more human," in the sense that we feel closer to them in our daily life.

29 THURSDAY MARCH

Today we returned from the important apostolic journey to Mexico and Cuba, initiated on March 23. The Holy Father faced this demanding trip with faith and courage. Thus, he reiterated his desire to give himself completely to the Church and to the Lord. However, I noticed on several occasions that he was very tired. The time zone difference of seven hours from Rome and the very heavy program took their toll. But Benedict never complained, and, in fact, he repeatedly apologized for his fatigue.

Benedict replied to the numerous questions posed by the journalists during our flight to León, the first leg of the visit. First of all, he recalled the historic apostolic travels to Mexico and Cuba by John Paul II, and with great humility he stated, "I try to go in his footsteps and continue that which he has begun."

The pope did not avoid any topic. He spoke about the scourge of drug trafficking, he touched on the theme of social

The Holy Father welcomed
by children on his arrival
in Mexico.

justice and liberation theology, he stressed that the Church is always on the side of the freedom of conscience and of religion (having on his mind the situation in Cuba), and finally, he spoke about the new evangelization. He said, "There is a common situation in the world: there is secularization, the absence of God, the difficulty of approaching him, of seeing him as a reality that is relevant to one's life." From here arises the necessity of presenting the Christian faith as a rational option, a "core" Christianity, without forgetting that other than rationality there is also the heart. He concluded, "We must be of good courage and connect heart and reason so that they may cooperate, for only in this way is man complete and really able to help build, and to work for, a better future."

I must say that even though I should be accustomed by now to these "lessons" of Professor Ratzinger, I always remain in awe. His clarity is without equal, but there is never the pride of an expert in him. He is a father who puts his wisdom at our disposal.

Once we arrived in Mexico, one appointment followed another at a fast pace: the welcome ceremony at Guanajuato

International Airport, the greeting to the children at the Plaza de la Paz, the celebration of Holy Mass at the Guanajuato Bicentenario Park, the recitation of the Angelus, the celebration of Vespers with the Mexican and Latin American bishops inside the Cathedral of the Most Holy Mother of Light, dinner on the patio of the cathedral, and lastly, and outside the program, the improvised greetings to the crowd that had gathered in front of Miraflores College.

I was honestly worried about the Holy Father's well-being because, during the fourteen-hour flight to Mexico, he did not have a moment of rest, not even to recharge his energy. After the welcome ceremony, we headed toward our residence, but the pope stood up in the popemobile for more than an hour, greeting and blessing the thousands of people who had lined up along the route. However, despite his fatigue, the pope never held back. That evening he would have liked to have had a light dinner and then to retire to his room to rest. But when he was informed that some Mexican bishops had been invited, he remained with them until dinner was over.

The following evening, when a crowd gathered by the college, asking him to come out to greet them, he willingly did so and gave them his blessing. Next, a traditional mariachi band improvised a concert, and a girl gave him a sombrero. He immediately put it on and said, "Now I know why Pope John Paul II said that he felt like a Mexican pope!" These joyful people, who suffer from

Pope Benedict with the sombrero gifted by a folk group, the mariachi, which improvises a concert in front of the Miraflores residence.

the arrogance and violence of the drug cartels, find in the pope a refuge and a father who loves and defends them.

Having saluted Mexico, the pope went to Cuba next, another delicate and demanding visit. There were numerous celebrations and meetings. Following the welcome ceremony at Antonio Maceo Airport, we went to the main square of the city to celebrate Holy Mass in commemoration of the 400th anniversary of the discovery of the statue of Our Lady of Charity of El Cobre. The next day we visited the shrine. Finally, we reached the capital, Havana, on March 28. Holy Mass was celebrated in the Plaza de la Revolución. The pope said, "The truth is a desire of the human person, the search for which always supposes the exercise of authentic freedom." Then came the heartfelt invitation to all the Cubans: "Dear friends, do not hesitate to follow Jesus Christ. In him we find the truth about God and about mankind. He helps us to overcome our selfishness, to rise above our vain struggles and to conquer all that oppresses us. The one who does evil, who sins, becomes its slave and will never attain freedom (cf. John 8:34). Only by renouncing hatred and our hard and blind hearts will we be free and a new life will well up in us."

From his pope mobile, Pope Benedict greets the crowd gathered for Holy Mass in the historic Plaza of the Revolution.

Fidel Castro came in private to the nunciature before we departed the country. The pope was surprised when he expressed his wish to read some of the pope's publications. Thus, once we were back in Rome, the first thing that the Holy Father did was to send the elderly leader three texts on the social doctrine of the Church. These were accompanied with a personal letter to Fidel. Once again, we can say mission accomplished! But how much effort on the part of Benedict!

Private meeting with Fidel Castro in Apostolic Nunciature in Havana, Cuba.

2 MONDAY APRIL

There is a teddy bear among the many gifts the pope received while he was visiting Mexico and Cuba. It came from a young family from León. The pope took the teddy bear in his hands and kissed it when it was given to him. Now it is here with us on a small table in the dining room, waiting for Benedict to decide where to put it. One of his rooms, which contains many books, already has two teddy bears sitting on a small sofa. He thinks that perhaps this one should join them. However, he has asked for our opinion and for a few suggestions for names, one of which will be given to the newcomer.

He tells us that one day, when they were still children, he and his sister, Maria, had a quarrel because both of them wanted to play with a teddy bear. His sister was pulling it from its head, and he was pulling it from its feet. The teddy bear ripped in two. Their mother very patiently sewed it up.

8 SUNDAY APRIL

The Holy Father presented us with splendid homilies during Holy Week and the Easter Triduum. Each was in the form of a meditation that helps us to penetrate better the salvific mystery of Our Lord with faith and with our life. The pope prepares these meditations during the week of spiritual exercises and polishes them up afterward — that is, during the brief spare time allowed by his many commitments.

On Holy Thursday, during the celebration of the chrism Mass, Benedict wanted to refer to a group of Austrian priests, without mentioning the name, that is harshly challenging his magisterial teaching. He said, "Recently a group of priests from a European country issued a summons

Churchyard of the St. Peter Basilica: Solemnity of Holy Easter.

to disobedience, and at the same time gave concrete examples of the forms this disobedience might take, even to the point of disregarding definitive decisions of the Church's Magisterium, such as the question of women's ordination, for which Blessed Pope John Paul II stated irrevocably that the Church has received no authority from the Lord. Is disobedience a path of renewal for the Church? We would like to believe that the authors of this summons are motivated by concern for the Church, that they are convinced that the slow pace of institutions has to be overcome by drastic measures, in order to open up new paths and to bring the Church up to date. But is disobedience really a way to do this? Do we sense here anything of that configuration to Christ, which is the precondition for all true renewal, or do we merely sense a desperate push to do something to change the Church in accordance with one's own preferences and ideas?" Benedict, gentle and without any criticism, invited the protesting priests to imitate Jesus, especially in humility and obedience. It was all said in a fatherly tone, which even impressed the spokesman of the group.

16 MONDAY
APRIL

Today is a very special day. It is Pope Benedict XVI's eighty-fifth birthday. The day begins with the celebration of Holy Mass in the majestic Pauline Chapel of the Apostolic Palace. A small German delegation is present. Even more majestic, if I may say so, is the unscripted homily the Holy Father delivers in German. He has traveled along God's plan for him, and he expresses his gratitude to the Lord and to all of those who have helped him along the way. He says, "On the day of my birth and of my Baptism, 16 April, the Church's liturgy has set three signposts which show me where the road leads

Pope Benedict receives
congratulations on his 85th
birthday from a couple
of children in traditional
Bavarian costume.

and help me to find it. In the first place, it is the Memorial of
St. Bernadette Soubirous, the seer of Lourdes; then there is
one of the most unusual Saints in the Church's history, Benedict Joseph Labre; and then, above all, this day is immersed
in the Paschal Mystery, in the Mystery of the Cross and the
Resurrection. In the year of my birth this was expressed in a
special way: it was Holy Saturday, the day of the silence of
God, of his apparent absence, of God's death, but also the day
on which the Resurrection was proclaimed."

Benedict recalls that on that Holy Saturday of eighty-
five years ago, the celebration of the Easter Vigil, according
to custom, was anticipated in the morning and was followed
with the darkness of Holy Saturday, without the Alleluia.
He notes, "It seems to me that this singular paradox, this
singular anticipation of light in a day of darkness, could
almost be an image of the history of our times. On the one
hand, there is still the silence of God and his absence, but in
the Resurrection of Christ there is already the anticipation
of the 'yes' of God, and on the basis of this anticipation we
live and, through the silence of God, we hear him speak, and

through the darkness of his absence we glimpse his light. The anticipation of the Resurrection in the middle of an evolving history is the power that points out the way to us and helps us to go forward. Let us thank the good Lord for he has given us this light and let us pray to him so that it might endure forever. And on this day, I have special cause to thank him and all those who have ever anew made me perceive the presence of the Lord, who have accompanied me so that I might never lose the light." And these are his concluding words: "I am now facing the last chapter of my life and I do not know what awaits me. I know, however, that the light of God exists, that he is Risen, that his light is stronger than any darkness, that the goodness of God is stronger than any evil in this world. And this helps me to go forward with certainty. May this help *us* to go forward, and at this moment I wholeheartedly thank all those who have continually helped me to perceive the 'yes' of God through their faith."

20 FRIDAY APRIL

The symphonic orchestra of Leipzig wished to mark the pope's birthday by offering a wonderful concert in honor of their illustrious countryman. The pope told me a few weeks ago after we recited the Rosary that the orchestra made the request of playing for him three years ago. Then he said, "I agreed to it because at the time I thought that I would be already dead in three years. And yet here I am!" We had a great laugh. But this is the second time that Benedict has mentioned to me the end of his life.

30 MONDAY
APRIL

There are times at the Vatican when one has to save face. The pope, smiling, tells us what happened this morning. The Holy Father had a scheduled audience with a new ambassador to the Holy See, during which the ambassador was to present his credential letters from his government. But it just so happened that, when the ambassador arrived at the Apostolic Palace, he realized that he did not have the letters with him. So, what was he supposed to do? The audience was about to start and there wasn't adequate time for him to retrieve the letters. The best thing to do was to present the pope with an empty envelope! Thus face was saved, mainly for the benefit of the photographers. The letters arrived at a later date.

The pope tells us of another funny episode. It has to do with the senior executives of a printing house who presented him with a precious volume, assuring him this was the only prepublication copy available. In fact, he had received a copy a few days before. But he did not want to disappoint these gentlemen, and so he acted as if he was seeing the book for the first time. But what remains a classic is the one when the pope, who dislikes mushrooms, was given a package of mushrooms. However, he gave a heartfelt thanks to the donor and told him that he accepted the gift most willingly.

4 FRIDAY
MAY

The television news this evening depicted photos of a child sitting in front of a huge glass wall. On the other side was a real lion raising one of its paws in an attempt to nab him. This made the pope recall that when he was a child, they had cats at his home that stood at the window and behaved like the lion and that child. Only, with these cats, they lifted up their paws in an attempt to catch the birds in their garden.

7 MONDAY MAY

It is known that the Holy Father is not a great soccer fan. However, when there are soccer matches of a favorite team of one of us, he always asks us about the results. Yesterday the television news spoke of a match being held that evening between Milan and Juventus. The pope looked at me this morning during breakfast and said, "I cannot decipher from your looks what has happened at the soccer match. How did Juve do yesterday?" I replied, "Well, I will try to make my face more decipherable." Then, using my fingers, I pulled up my lips toward my ears to form a big smile. He said, "Now I understand. Juve won!" And speaking of my favorite soccer team, after I proudly went over its many victories and glorious history, the pope sighed in irony and said, "Phew! And to think that until recently I did not even know that there was a team called Juventus!"

12 TUESDAY JUNE

We have lived through moments of great suffering during these past few days, and we feel stunned. After repeated articles in the Italian newspapers regarding confidential letters sent to the Holy Father, suspicion fell on Paolo Gabriele, the pope's butler, whom we see as a son and a brother. Unfortunately, the search carried out by the Vatican Gendarmes in the Gabriele residence yielded many strictly confidential documents that were stolen from the papal apartment and photocopied. Needless to say, the whole affair greatly sad-

Milan — Family Day
2012: the Pope's Angelus
at the San Siro Stadium
with the confirmands.

dened both the pope and the rest of us. Joined to this sadness is that of Paolo being confined to a security room at the gendarmerie. The anxiety and agitation emanating from these events have robbed us of our sleep. Benedict does not show it, but he is affected by this affair, for it involves him directly. Displeasure is mixed with uneasiness.

Divine Providence wanted the scheduling of the Holy Father's pastoral visit to Milan to be from June 1 to June 3. The visit was to mark the World Meeting of Families. This enabled the pope to enjoy for a couple of days the affection of thousands of people who welcomed him, greeted him, and strengthened him during various gatherings. He has truly received a very enthusiastic welcome in Milan. On the other hand, the testimonies from families across the world were simply beautiful!

285

It was a shot in the arm for Benedict, filling him with assurance and hope during this very sensitive moment.

I do not have the duty of accompanying the pope when he travels within Italy. So I took the opportunity to spend these few days with my cousins in the United States. There, in a setting of love and friendship, I officiated at a marriage, gave First Holy Communion, and conducted three Baptisms. I received much comfort in exchange.

Today, having returned from our respective travels, we go for our usual walk on the terrace. I do not want to bring up the topic regarding the recent events that directly concern the apartment. It is the pope himself who spontaneously brings up the subject concerning the Paolo Gabriele affair. He never voices words of blame or condemnation. Rather, he speaks like a father who cannot understand his son. He whispers, "But did he ever think of his family and the pain he would bring to his wife and children?" Then he becomes pensive. I can only imagine the turmoil that might be within the soul of the Holy Father during these days. I am doing everything to remain close to him and to support him with discretion. I hope that he remains mindful of the family climate around him, though this has been violated in such a terrible manner.

15 FRIDAY JUNE

The Church continues to appear on the pages of the newspapers, which report almost exclusively negative news and ways to accuse her. The sensationalism of the media is unleashed in such instances. The Vatican is often painted as a place full of conspiracies. All of us have a sense of grief because our Holy Father is a victim of many injustices.

It has been some time now that Benedict prefers to use the aid of a cane even at home. He always uses it when coming out of his room and heading toward the dining room. I am always ready to put it away right before he sits at table. This has become almost automatic for me. But he always smiles, showing his appreciation of my assistance: "Oh! Thank you very much! You are here!"

But today I am absent-minded when he comes out of his room, and so, before entering the dining room, he places the cane against a console in the corridor. I immediately apologize, to which he replies, "Usually an angel appears to take away the cane. But he failed to show up this time." I respond, "An angel without wings!" He retorts, "An angel with internal wings!" This was for me a great gift on the feast of the Sacred Heart. Will the pope overcome this unsettling moment? One can tackle physical ailments, but certain internal wounds are more insidious. Pope Benedict occupies the first place in my prayers.

16 SATURDAY JUNE

When I approach the Holy Father this morning to give him his cane, he says, "Behold! There is a splendid epiphany today!" *Epiphany* means "manifestation," and the pope, in using this term, wants to highlight that I was "revealed" at the right time. These seem to be funny phrases, but to me they are important words of appreciation. They provide me with the courage to overcome the difficult moments of the assignment that has been entrusted to me, and that is currently undergoing some very delicate moments. I see the pope as being tired and pensive.

26 TUESDAY JUNE

During these days, so as to slightly distract as well as cheer up the pope, we try to shift our conversation toward soccer matches that are being played in Poland and Ukraine for the European Championship. We bring up the subject of the colors of the national flags. The pope explains to me that the yellow in the Vatican flag stands for the gold of one key of Peter, while the white stands for the silver of the other key. Benedict always finds a way to teach us something new, even when we try to be a bit lighthearted!

29 FRIDAY JUNE

Today after lunch, motivated by the pope's homily on the occasion of the Solemnity of the Patron Saints of Rome, Peter and Paul, we speak about brotherhood. The pope had said, "The Bible tells us that the story of brotherhood began in a very dramatic way, that is with the killing of Abel by his brother Cain, but that Jesus Christ, who made us true brothers with forgiveness and mutual mercy, has redeemed it forever. What would brotherhood be without Jesus Christ who restored to it its authentic meaning?" The pope might also have had in mind the present situation of the pontifical family, on the heels of the recent grievous events.

I took a cue from today's first reading, which narrates how an angel appeared to Peter and led him out of prison, guiding him up to the entrance that led to the city, and then disappeared. The pope commented in a low voice, "A beautiful story, indeed!" With a heavy heart I felt that perhaps the Lord wants me to accompany Benedict, like the angel who guided Peter, and then disappear.

7 SATURDAY JULY

We arrived at Castel Gandolfo a few days ago. I see the pope more relaxed. Things have been very difficult recently. I believe the pope was right in leaving the environment of the apartment, with all that it now represents regarding the sad events linked to the Gabriele case and the publication of strictly confidential documents.

While on our usual walk, he asks me about the schedule for my summer vacation. I respond, "Holiness, I would have chosen these days, but rest assured that I can come back any time if need be." He tells me, "Let us hope that no such need arises!" I would not say that he seemed worried, because Benedict never shows it, but absorbed in thought.

12 THURSDAY JULY

We talk during breakfast about the beautiful concert that took place yesterday evening in the large courtyard of the Apostolic Palace. The concert included the Fifth and Sixth Symphonies of Beethoven. It was performed by the West-Eastern Divan Orchestra under the direction of Maestro Daniel Barenboim. It is currently on a summer tour. The concert was a gift to the Holy Father to mark St. Benedict's feast day. Giorgio Napolitano and his wife were present, and afterward the two joined us for dinner at the invitation of the pope.

The West-Eastern Divan Orchestra was founded in 1999 by the Argentine-Israeli Maestro Barenboim and Edward Saïd, a writer of Palestinian origin. They bring together professional young musicians from different religions (Jews, Christians, and Muslims) living in areas of conflict, such as Israel, Egypt, Jordan, Syria, Lebanon, and Palestine.

The orchestra, whose name is in homage to the poetry collection *West-östlicher Divan* by Goethe, wishes to bring to the entire world a message of peace through the universal language of music.

The pope used beautiful words in his address: "You can imagine how glad I am to welcome an orchestra like this one that was born from the conviction, indeed, from the experience that music unites people over and above any division; for music is a harmonization of differences, as occurs at the beginning of every concert with the 'rite' of tuning up. A symphony can emerge from the tones of the different instruments. However, this does not happen by magic or automatically! It is only achieved with the hard work of the conductor and of every individual musician. It is a patient, demanding commitment that requires time and sacrifices in the effort to hear each other, avoiding excessive protagonism and giving due priority to the successful performance." The pope went on to explain that the Fifth

The Pope and the President of the Italian Republic, Giorgio Napolitano, at the West-Eastern Divan Orchestra concert.

and Sixth Symphonies of Beethoven express two aspects of life: drama and peace, man's struggle against adverse fate and the idyllic environment that bestows serenity. He said, "The message I would like to draw from this today is the following: to achieve peace it is necessary to be engaged, putting violence and weapons aside, to commit oneself with personal and community conversion, through dialogue and the patient search for possible agreement."

I accompanied the Holy Father from the dining room after dinner, taking the elevator up to his room. He walked very slowly, with the help of his cane. We greeted one another, and I went on my knees and asked for his blessing, as I do every time I go on vacation. The pope reminded me to greet my mother, my sister, and the rest of the family in his name.

11 SUNDAY AUGUST

Castel Gandolfo, courtyard of the Apostolic Palace: concert given by Caritas of Regensburg.

13 MONDAY AUGUST

I am back in the office after my summer vacation. I am taken aback seeing the pope pale and his face more hollow. He has certainly not slowed down. He made a pastoral visit to Frascati, and, of more importance, he used the summertime to complete his third volume of *Jesus of Nazareth* and also work on a new encyclical that is scheduled to be published on the occasion of the Year of Faith. He also polished up the talks he will deliver during the very challenging upcoming journey to Lebanon, as well as other presentations intended for those bishops who will be coming soon for their *ad limina* visit. Finally, he also caught up with his personal correspondence. How can a man at his age work so much? The explanation may only be that he is receiving supernatural assistance.

15 WEDNESDAY AUGUST

Following the tradition for the celebration of the Solemnity of the Assumption, this morning the pope celebrates Holy Mass at the parish church of Castel Gandolfo. He delivers a beautiful homily, especially when he speaks off the cuff, explaining that today's feast recalls that there is space for God in the world, just as there is space for man in God. He says, "Today there is much discussion on a better world to be awaited: it would be our hope. If and when this better world comes, we do not know, I do not know. What is certain is that a world which distances itself from God does not become better but worse. Only God's presence can guarantee a good world. Let us leave it at that. One thing, one hope is certain: God expects us, waits for us, we do not go out into a void, and we are expected. God is expecting us and going [on] to that other

Greetings in the principal languages at the end of the Angelus prayer.

world we find the goodness of the Mother, we find our loved ones, we find eternal Love. God is waiting for us: this is our great joy and the great hope that is born from this Feast. Mary visits us, and she is the joy of our life and joy is hope."

The Holy Father tells us during lunch that there was once a time in the south of Germany that it was customary to bless vegetables and fruit on Assumption Day. The reason for this was that apparently when Mary's tomb was opened, the air took on the scent of fresh vegetables and fruit, a sign of hope and fertility.

18 SATURDAY AUGUST

We talk about names during today's lunch, particularly about those, at times really strange, that sisters have to choose on the day of their religious profession, replacing those given to them at Baptism. The pope tells us that when he was in kindergarten one of the sisters was called Corbiniana, a name the children could never pronounce well.

Speaking of kindergarten, when I was small, I used to cry because I wanted to go to school with my brother, older than me by a year, and did not want to stay home. The pope told me that it was just the opposite with him! He did not go willingly, so much so that one day he stated that those children who help their mothers should be exempt from going to school. At the time he was just four years old!

19 SUNDAY
AUGUST

The Holy Father comments on today's Gospel (see John 6:51–58) during the Angelus. This excerpt is at the end and forms the apex of the discourse given by Jesus at the synagogue of Capernaum, having provided food with five loaves and two fish to thousands of people the day before. Benedict explains, "Jesus reveals the meaning of this miracle, namely that the promised time had come; God the Father, who had fed the Israelites in the desert with manna, now sent him, the Son, as the true Bread of life; and this bread is his flesh, his life, offered in sacrifice for us. It is therefore a question of welcoming him with faith, not of being shocked by his humanity, and it is about eating his flesh and drinking his blood (cf. John 6:54) in order to obtain for us the fullness of life." He goes on to say that it is clear that this speech was not aimed at procuring an approval: "Jesus knew this and gave this speech intentionally. In fact, it was a critical moment, a turning point in his public mission. The people, and the disciples themselves, were enthusiastic when he performed miraculous signs; the multiplication of the loaves and fishes was a clear revelation that he was the Messiah, so that the crowd would have liked to carry Jesus in triumph and proclaim him King of Israel. But this was not what Jesus wanted. With his long address he dampens the enthusiasm and incites much dissent. In explaining the image of the bread, he affirms that he has been sent to offer his own life and he who wants to follow him must join him in a deep and personal way, participating in his sacrifice of love. Thus, Jesus was to institute the Sacrament of the Eucharist at the Last Supper, so that his disciples themselves might share in his love — this was crucial — and, as one body united with him, might extend

Castel Gandolfo,
Angelus, Sunday
August 19.

his mystery of salvation in the world." I always admire the ability of Benedict: how, even in a few lines, he manages to express himself with very clear comments, never superficial, yet understandable to all.

Today I thought that perhaps the pope, when speaking of Jesus, could have in mind also his own experience. He never seeks approval. Also, he himself breaks the Bread of Life for thousands, for millions, of people. He does so not to evoke some triumphant acclaim but, rather, to always reaffirm the sacrifice of the Cross, in which Jesus becomes the Bread, the Body and the Blood to be offered in atonement.

During our customary walk after lunch, we speak of the crowds who participate in the Sunday Angelus both in Rome and here at Castel Gandolfo. I say, "It is a unique phenomenon in the world that is certainly due to the devotion people have toward the Holy Father." Benedict immediately observes, "No. It is the strength of the faith that makes this happen."

29 WEDNESDAY
AUGUST

Castel Gandolfo: a
greeting to the French altar
servers on the occasion
of their pilgrimage to
Rome under the motto:
"To serve the Lord, joy
of man, joy of God."

2 SUNDAY
SEPTEMBER

Today the pope presides at Holy Mass celebrated at the Mariapolis Center at Castel Gandolfo. It marks the conclusion of
the annual meeting of the *Ratzinger Schülerkreis*, the group
of his former students who gather every summer to discuss
a specific theme. The homily Professor Ratzinger delivers
during the celebration is fascinating, and to give it justice, it

should be presented in full. He speaks about the diligence, works, and human customs that, with the passage of time, multiply to the point that they end up hiding the wisdom given by God. It is a phenomenon that also occurs within the Church, where "human elements are added and they lead either to presumptuousness, the so-called triumphalism of praising oneself rather than God, or to bondage, which needs to be removed, broken and smashed." Therefore, "what must we do? What must we say?" The pope supplies the answer: "I think that we are precisely at that impasse in which we see in the Church only what we ourselves have made, and our joy in the faith is marred; that we no longer believe and no longer dare to say: he has shown us who the truth is, what the truth is; he has shown us what man is; he has given us the law for an upright life. We are concerned only with praising ourselves and we fear being bound by rules that hinder our freedom and the newness of life."

Next, the Holy Father reflects on the notion of truth, which is always at the center of his teaching. He says, "If we read today, for example, in the Letter of James: 'You were made in the word and in the truth,' who of us would dare to rejoice in the truth that we have been given? The question immediately arises: but how can one have the truth? This is intolerance! Today the idea of truth and that of intolerance are almost completely fused, and so we no longer dare to believe in the truth or to speak of the truth. It seems to be far away; it seems something better not to refer to. No one can say: I have the truth — this is the objection raised — and, rightly so, no one can have the truth. It is the truth that possesses us, it is a living thing! We do not possess it but are held by it. Only if we allow ourselves to be guided and moved by the truth, do we remain in it. Only if we are, with it and in it, pilgrims of truth, then it is in us and for us. I think that we need to learn anew about 'not-having-the-truth.' Just as no one can say: I have children — they are not

297

our possession, they are a gift, and as a gift from God, they are given to us as a responsibility — so we cannot say: I have the truth, but the truth came to us and impels us. We must learn to be moved and led by it. And then it will shine again: if the truth itself leads us and penetrates us."

Finally, the pope addresses his audience composed of scholars and intellectuals, and gives them a warning against what he calls "the intellectualization of the faith and of theology" — that is, the tendency to reduce even the faith to a game of the intellect in which "'we pass each other the ball,' in which everything is an intellectual sphere that does not penetrate and form our lives, and, thus, does not lead us to the truth.... Let us ask the Lord forgiveness for our indifference, for our misery that makes us think only of ourselves, for our selfishness that does not seek the truth but follows habit, and that perhaps often makes Christianity resemble a mere system of habits. Let us ask that he come with power into our souls, that he be present in us and through us — and that in this way joy may be born in us again: God is here, and loves me. He is our salvation! Amen."

4 TUESDAY
SEPTEMBER

Today, during lunch, we speak about the Maltese altar boys who served at St. Peter's during this past summer. They were filling in for those who went on vacation. This service was begun fifty years ago. He asks me, "But have you ever served as an altar boy?" I reply that, apart from occasionally serving Holy Mass at Don Bosco Oratory, I was never an official altar boy, but only one in reserve. This was the reason why I never came to serve at the Vatican when I was a boy. I add that, on the other hand, I now have the honor of being the altar boy every morning for the Holy Father in person when, during Holy Mass, I assist at the washing of hands. He nods and smiles.

11 TUESDAY
SEPTEMBER

An invitation has arrived from Bavaria. It is an invite to participate in the inauguration of the rehabilitation of the building that used to be the home for the Ratzinger family at Pentling. It has been meticulously restored and transformed into a museum with a conference room. The pope tells us that in order to make it similar to the one of his time, they even went so far as to cut down some trees. He is pleased that he has been invited, but thinking of the many scheduled commitments he already has, as well as his limited energy, he immediately adds, "I think it will be a little difficult to go." He continues by telling us that the house was rebuilt in record time. They began in May and the work was finished by Christmas. He says that the expenses were paid from the royalties of his book *Introduction to Christianity*, the result of the lectures by Professor Ratzinger at Tübingen in 1967. It is a fundamental text. I notice that in his eyes, as he recalls those times, there is nostalgia for all those significant events lived in that house.

13 THURSDAY
SEPTEMBER

We have notice that the pope's walking has become more laborious, showing signs of uncertainty in his balance. As a result, for some time now, he allows me to put my arm gently under his, to offer him support, especially when going down the stairs. He always thanks me. His difficulties, however, do not affect in any way his memory.

Speaking of steps, he told me that when Archbishop Frings of Cologne became old and was not able to walk steadily, his secretary always put him on guard by exclaiming, "*Stüfchen, Eminenz!* A step, Eminence!" However, with me, I simply limit myself to offer him support without saying anything. It seems to me that he appreciates this.

14 FRIDAY SEPTEMBER

Beginning today, and for the next three days, the pope is visiting Lebanon to mark the signing and publication of the Post-Synodal Apostolic Exhortation of the Special Assembly for the Middle East of the Synod of Bishops. Before land-

Benedict XVI in Lebanon during what will prove to be the last Apostolic Journey from Italy of his pontificate.

ing at Beirut International Airport, Benedict met with the journalists who were accompanying him.

21 FRIDAY SEPTEMBER

Since the Holy Father knows that I am a fan of the Juventus soccer team, he never fails to ask me news about the results of their games. Soccer does not interest him in the least, and perhaps he has never seen a soccer match in his life, but he keeps himself updated to make me happy.

We speak today about the results of an important soccer match. The Juve played in London against Chelsea, a strong team. My team was losing two to zero but then managed to tie the score — a significant feat. He asks me, "So, are you happy?" I say, "Certainly!" He replies, "I thought that since you were quiet, they might have lost." I reply with a mischievous look, "I thought the Holy Father might have watched the game on television and he already knows the result." He gives a pleasant smile and then exclaims, "You have a very active imagination!"

29 SATURDAY
SEPTEMBER

Castel Gandolfo,
September 29. Employee
leave of the Papal Villas
and their families, followed
by a charity raffle.

4 THURSDAY
OCTOBER

The Pope visiting Loreto.

11 THURSDAY OCTOBER

These days are very intense for Benedict. He was in Loreto on Sunday, October 4, where he celebrated Holy Mass in the square. He celebrated Holy Mass in St. Peter's Square last Sunday for the opening of the Synod of Bishops and the proclamation of St. John of Avila and St. Hildegard of Bingen as Doctors of the Church. And today, also in the churchyard of the Vatican Basilica, he presided over Holy Mass to mark the fiftieth anniversary of the opening of Vatican II. The young Joseph Ratzinger participated in it as the theological expert of Cardinal Frings, archbishop of Cologne. The Holy Father also initiated the Year of Faith, which, he explained, "is linked harmoniously with the Church's whole path over the last fifty years: from the Council, through the Magisterium of the Servant of God Paul VI, who proclaimed a Year of Faith in 1967, up to the Great Jubilee of the year 2000, with which Blessed John Paul II re-proposed to all humanity Jesus Christ as the one Savior, yesterday, today and forever. Between these two Popes, Paul VI and John Paul II, there was a deep and complete convergence, precisely upon Christ as the center of the cosmos and of history, and upon the apostolic eagerness to announce him to the world. Jesus is the center of the Christian faith. The Christian believes in God whose face was revealed by Jesus Christ. He is the fulfillment of the Scriptures and their definitive interpreter. Jesus Christ is not only the object of the faith but, as it says in the *Letter to the Hebrews*, he is 'the pioneer and the perfecter of our faith.'" Therefore, Jesus is the center of this important Year of Faith, which was desired by the Holy Father. It is a perfect setting, made all the more significant with the presence of Patriarch Bartholomew I of Constantinople and Archbishop Rowan Williams of Canterbury, as well as that of the patriarchs and major archbishops of the Oriental Catholic Churches.

The fraternal kiss shared with Bartholomew I, Ecumenical Patriarch of Constantinople, and with Rowan Williams, Archbishop of Canterbury.

Today's celebration, to recall the Council, is marked with specific signs that refer precisely to the actual opening of that great assembly: the initial procession recalls the memorable one of the Council Fathers when they solemnly processed to enter the basilica; the enthronement of the book of the Gospels, which is a copy of the one used during the Council; and the consignment by the pope of the seven final messages of the Council and of the *Catechism of the Catholic Church*.

Then, this evening, in recalling the famous "Speech to the Moon" of John XXIII, there is a torchlight procession from Castel Sant'Angelo to St. Peter's Square, just as it was done half a century ago. Pope Benedict XVI addresses the crowd from his study window at the Apostolic Palace. It is emotionally exciting to see the crowd gathered below, waiting in anticipation. The pope does not want to wear a stole and speaks off the cuff as a good father.

14 SUNDAY OCTOBER

We notice that the pope's voice is a little hoarse, but he, as usual, tells us not to worry. Then, to diffuse the situation, he tells us that when he was young, during his years in the seminary, if the rector had his voice a little low and uncertain, the students used to nudge each other with their elbows and speculate how many times the rector had emptied his glass of wine! But one cannot think such of Benedict, because he does not touch any alcohol.

30 TUESDAY OCTOBER

For today's lunch, the Italian pasta dish of *penne all'arrabiata* (pasta with a hot chili sauce, literally translated as "angry penne") was on the menu. However, my sauce was only tomato sauce, devoid of hot chili peppers, because these days I have to keep away from anything spicy. The Holy Father commented, "I see you prefer not to get angry." I responded, "Indeed, I prefer serenity in life!" He immediately added, "Anyway, you never get angry. It is not in your temperament." I am pleased with this observation, however, not only because of his compliment but because some of Benedict's meekness has rubbed off on me!

6 TUESDAY NOVEMBER

The driver, after we finish our short walk following the recitation of the Rosary, brings to the pope one of the three cats that were discovered in the Vatican Gardens. It is the only one that survived, as we suspect that the other two have fallen victim to a fox that wanders around those parts. The pope speaks to the cat, calling it *Mitzi*, which in German means "pussycat" or "kitten." They always used to gain the attention of the pope whenever the three kittens were together. One day they stretched out over the cushion of the kneeler that is at the Grotto of Our Lady of Lourdes. The pope said his prayers standing up so that he would not disturb them.

11 SUNDAY NOVEMBER

We have sad news this morning at breakfast. The Holy Father informs us of the demise of the cat Chico. It was his brother who broke the news to him. You might recall that the cat became famous when Cardinal Joseph Ratzinger was elected pope. The cat belonged to a neighbor in Bavaria, and every time the cardinal went there to spend a couple of days of rest, Chico happily kept him company. Benedict told us, "When I arrived and put the key in the keyhole to open the door, Chico was already by the door and the first to sneak in." Apparently, the cat had such a restless and teasing character that the cardinal took him to his neighbors at night, for he never knew how it would behave. The Holy Father murmurs, "I think he will spend a lot of time in Purgatory." I rise to the defense of Chico and say, "Maybe he asked for forgiveness at the last moment, like the good thief did!" The pope looks at me and smiles.

19 MONDAY NOVEMBER

Today our conversation centers around the pope's coat of arms. It carries the bear of St. Corbinian. I point out that it is paradoxical that many coats of arms, not only Benedict XVI's but also those of Bern and Berlin, depict the bear but never the saint. He explains, "When one looks at the bear, one is reminded of the saint. In any case, the bear depicted in those of Berlin and Bern have nothing to do with St. Corbinian. They are

Pope Benedict's papal coat of arms.

depicted for the simple reason that once upon a time those areas had forests that also had bears." This was a lesson in cultural heraldry!

20 TUESDAY NOVEMBER

There is today the official presentation of the third and final book by the Holy Father on Jesus. The new volume is on the childhood of the Lord. It is presented during a press conference in one of the rooms of the Pontifical Council for Promoting the New Evangelization. While at table we told the pope that, during the press conference, someone inquired if he foresees projects for other books. He exclaimed in a peremptory tone, "No projects!" It was as if he wanted to say, "I have finished what the Lord asked of me, and now is the time to think of the final goal."

29 THURSDAY NOVEMBER

We tell the Holy Father during this morning's breakfast that his next audience will be with the circus and carnival people. The event is being put on by the Pontifical Council for the Pastoral Care of Migrants and Itinerant People. They will be bringing a lion cub for him to caress. While I recall that already some years back such an animal was brought to him, I want to reassure him by saying, "Holiness, I assure you that it will not be the same lion!" We have a good laugh. Then the pope tells us that many years ago in Germany, one of his professor colleagues, for whatever reason, got it into his head to buy a lion cub. But when he discovered how much meat was needed for the cub's nourishment, he happily settled for a cat!

1 SATURDAY DECEMBER

Today, as scheduled, the pope receives in audience the circus people. A small group of jugglers, clowns, and trapeze artists perform in front of the Holy Father. Benedict XVI, at the end of the audience, does not hesitate to approach and caress a lion cub, named Simba. Being carried in the arms of his trainer, Simba is immortalized by innumerable camera flashes while the pope, looking content, caresses its head. The pope will not let go. He says, "He is great, and calm."

The "City of Rome" circus gave a second cub the name of Benedict, in honor of the pope.

His great love for cats overcomes Pope Benedict's fear of caressing the little lion, Simba.

5 WEDNESDAY DECEMBER

This afternoon, on our arrival at the Grotto of Our Lady of Lourdes for the recitation of the Rosary, a hailstorm broke out. Since we were unable to take our usual walk in the Vatican Gardens, we recited the mysteries of the Rosary as we walked around the altar inside the cave. We felt protected in all aspects by Our Lady.

These are intense working days for the pope. He is just back from delivering speeches to the Plenary Assembly of the Pontifical Council for Justice and Peace and the community at the Venerable English College in Rome. Next, he has to speak to the International Theological Commission, followed, on December 8, by the traditional act of homage to the Virgin on the day of the Immaculate Conception at Piazza di Spagna. In addition, almost every day, there are audiences, and finally, on December 21, he will deliver a major message to the Roman Curia on the occasion of the exchange of best wishes for Christmas. This is an incredible pace, almost merciless for a man of his age. Yet he made time to write an article for the *Financial Times*, which started with the famous words of Jesus: "Render unto Caesar what belongs to Caesar and to God what belongs to God." He writes that "the birth of Christ challenges us to reassess our priorities, our values, our very way of life. While Christmas is undoubtedly a time of great joy, it is also an occasion for deep reflection, even an examination of conscience."

31 MONDAY DECEMBER

Benedict, in St. Peter's Square, welcomed the young participants at the thirty-fifth international meeting of young adults two nights ago. It was organized by the Taizé Community. He recalled that God does not ever leave us alone and isolated. Rather, God gives us the comfort of the communion of the Church. This evening, at the celebration of the First Vespers of the Solemnity of Mary, Mother of God, and the singing of the Te Deum, he recommended praising the Lord and expressing our sorrow for our failings. He said, "In particular, let us thank him for the grace and truth that have come to us through Jesus Christ. In him lies the fullness of all human time. In him lies the future of every human being. In him will be brought about the fulfillment of the hopes of the Church and of the world."

Back home, the Holy Father tells us that on the last day of the year at Regensburg, the dean of the cathedral

Praying in front to the Crucifix of the Taizé Community during the prayer vigil in the churchyard of the Basilica of St. Peter.

chapter usually delivered a long sermon. But during the years of Nazism, since it was known that there were spies among the faithful who would inform their bosses of any criticism of the regime — criticisms that in fact were never absent — the dean decided to conduct the Way of the Cross instead of delivering his homily. Thus, the spies, in order not to be discovered, had to kneel fourteen times, one time for each station! Continuing still on the subject of the last day of the year, the pope tells us that during his time in Regensburg, the bishop used to invite for the evening Fr. Joseph Ratzinger and other priests to share a glass of sparkling wine and some Christmas pastries called *Plätzchen*. Next, on New Year's Day, all of them went together for lunch at a restaurant managed by a Croatian. Lunch was free because, due to his work, the latter could not go to Holy Mass, and the restaurateur explained to them that this was his way to make up for it!

Today brings to an end another challenging year at the service of the Holy Father. Every minute of every hour, every day spent next to him is a grace. We look forward with confidence, in the certainty that the Lord is with us!

My Days with
BENEDICT XVI
2013

1 TUESDAY JANUARY

"May God bless us and make his face to shine upon us." This is how Pope Benedict, using the words of Psalm 66, opens his homily at Holy Mass this morning, the first day of the New Year, which celebrates the Solemnity of Mary, Mother of God, and the World Day of Peace. The Holy Father comments that "it is especially significant that at the start of every New Year God sheds upon us, his people, the light of his Holy Name, the Name pronounced three times in the solemn form of biblical blessing. Nor is it less significant that to the Word of God — who 'became flesh and dwelt among us' (John 1:14) as 'the true light that enlightens every man' (1:9) — is given, as today's Gospel tells us, the Name of Jesus eight days after his birth (cf. Luke 2:21)."

The pope asks what the foundation is for a true peace. He gives the answer: it is "the certainty of contemplating in Jesus Christ the splendor of the face of God the Father, of being sons in the Son, and thus of having, on life's journey, the same security that a child feels in the arms of a loving and all-powerful Father. The splendor of the face of God, shining upon us and granting us peace, is the manifestation of his fatherhood: the Lord turns his face to us, he reveals himself as our Father and grants us peace. Here is the principle of that profound peace — 'peace with God' — which is firmly linked to faith and grace, as Saint Paul tells the Christians of Rome (cf. Rom. 5:2). Nothing can take this peace from believers, not even the difficulties and sufferings of life. Indeed, sufferings, trials and darkness do not undermine but build up our hope, a hope which does not deceive because 'God's love has been poured into our hearts through the Holy Spirit which has been given to us' (5:5)."

Msgr. Georg, the Holy Father's brother, is once again in our midst for a few days. He brings us happiness because, despite his old age and his ailments, he has a sunny disposition and a good dose of healthy irony.

3 THURSDAY JANUARY

It has become a custom that the Sistine Chapel Choir offers a concert in honor of Msgr. Georg Ratzinger. He is the chapel maestro emeritus of the renowned Regensburger Domspatzen, the choir of boys and young men at the Regensburg Cathedral. The concert is performed privately in the chapel that carries the same name. It is the same chapel that is famous throughout the world for its frescoes by Michelangelo and other renowned painters.

Private chapel of the Apostolic Palace in the Vatican: Pope Benedict reads aloud Breviary prayers to his brother with poor eyesight.

At the end of the concert, which also included a performance of some parts from the Mass composed by the same Maestro Georg Ratzinger, there is an exchange of greetings. Photos are also taken. The papal ushers approach the pope to bring him to the movable platform. But the first thing he asks is, "And my brother?" He did not want to be there alone. He feels reassured once he sees that there is already someone who is looking after him.

Msgr. Ratzinger has problems with his knees. He recently underwent surgery, and he uses an electric wheelchair when he is with us.

5 SATURDAY JANUARY

I am surprised as well as honored this morning when the Holy Father gives me two letters, asking me to read them and then give him my opinion. I see in his gesture a further confirmation of his esteem and confidence in me.

8 TUESDAY JANUARY

Today, talking about the transfer of a bishop who has a problem relocating his books reminded the pope of his own transfer from one university to another. His father went to give him a hand and was amazed by the great number of books owned by his son. "And to think that at the time they were still few in number! Who knows what he would say if he were to see the loads of books I now have on my bookshelves!" the pope concludes.

27 SUNDAY JANUARY

Today the Holy Father relates to us another anecdote concerning his family's relationship with animals. During the first years of his parents' marriage, his father often left his wife alone in the house, with baby Maria, due to his work. So, one day, his father decided to buy a dog so that his wife would have some protection. Unfortunately, every time someone passed the house, the dog would bark menacingly. This alarmed the mother, for she could not understand why it did so. In short, the dog, which was called Asso, made her more anxious instead of putting her at ease!

5 TUESDAY FEBRUARY

Today's date will remain imprinted in my memory and in my heart for the rest of my life. The Holy Father calls me to his office this morning. He asks me to make myself comfortable and says he has something important to tell me. Immediately afterward, in fact straightaway, he tells me the shocking news: he has decided to abdicate the papacy! His last day of governance as pope will be February 28. He calmly explains to me, "I am going to take up residence at the former cloistered monastery in the Vatican Gardens, which is currently under renovation. But you, monsignor, will remain with the new pope." Understandably surprised and shocked, I ask him if I will have the possibility of seeing him. He replies, "I will remain withdrawn from the world, but it will be possible for friends to visit." I comment, "If the new pope wishes, I will be at his service." Immediately the pope explains, "Your presence will be necessary, especially during the transition phase." I am rendered speechless, but I

Bird's eye view of the Monastery Mater Ecclesiae in the Vatican Gardens.

understand that Benedict has already thought of everything. His decision is very painful to me, and now I understand the precise reason why he has spent such a long time in prayer. The pope reflects for a long time and relies fully on the Lord. When he makes a decision, he certainly does not go back on it.

6 WEDNESDAY FEBRUARY

During today's general audience in Paul VI Hall, the Holy Father continues with his reflection on the Creed. He does so with his usual lucidity. However, I must confess that I cannot follow him as I usually do. I also think of all the people who are listening to him, of all the faithful across the world, all of them in the dark as to what will happen shortly. Now, with my mind more clear, yesterday's news is tearing my soul apart. Little by little, as Benedict's decision begins to sink in deeper, I am moved to tears. While the pope was speaking with me, I thought for a moment to tell him to reconsider, but then I held myself back because I had seen that the pope was very serene, and I realized he had thoroughly gone over this decision while praying. Furthermore, I did not want to revive the turmoil he certainly must have lived through in days and weeks past.

At lunch, as a way to diffuse the tension, we joke among ourselves. As earlier, at the general audience, at the time of the *baciamano*, an elderly cardinal came to the pope, sweating profusely, the Holy Father comments with full sympathy: "There were two reasons for this: he was fat and old!" And knowing that the Holy Father never liked sports, I think of a joke: "I would like to add another reason why he was sweating so much. It is because he never practiced any sport!" The pope immediately retorts, "If he did any sport, he would be already dead!" We have a good laugh. We try to behave as we have always done, but my heart is heavy.

11 MONDAY FEBRUARY

The Holy Father wants to announce his resignation from the papacy in a public setting. For this reason, the pope pre-empts today the ordinary consistory for the canonization of three new saints. And so it happens that in the presence of the cardinals, he reads in Latin the act of abdication. How can such words be forgotten? "*Decisionem magni momenti pro Ecclesiae vitae*. A decision of great importance for the life of the Church." These were the words chosen by Benedict to

Pope Benedict reads the act of resignation from the pontificate, a memorable, historic moment.

introduce this historical announcement. The Holy Father, as always, does not play with words.

"*Conscientia mea iterum atque iterum coram Deo explorata* … After having repeatedly examined my conscience before God, I have come to the certainty that my strengths, due to an advanced age, are no longer suited to an adequate exercise of the Petrine ministry. I am well aware that this ministry, due to its essential spiritual nature, must be carried out not only with words and deeds, but no less with prayer and suffering."

The Holy Father readily admits his limitations and explains why he feels inadequate: "However, in today's world, subject to so many rapid changes and shaken by questions of deep relevance for the life of faith, in order to govern the barque of Saint Peter and proclaim the Gospel, both strength of mind and body are necessary, strength which in the last few months, has deteriorated in me to the extent that I have had to recognize my incapacity to adequately fulfil the ministry entrusted to me." He goes on to explain that "for this reason, and well aware of the seriousness of this act, with full freedom I declare that I renounce the ministry of Bishop of Rome, Successor of Saint Peter, entrusted to me by the cardinals on 19 April 2005, in such a way, that as from 28 February 2013, at 20:00 hours, the See of Rome, the See of Saint Peter, will be vacant and a Conclave to elect the new Supreme Pontiff will have to be convoked by those whose competence it is." Everything is real and I am not dreaming. But, humanly speaking, it is still difficult to believe what is happening.

Following the act of resignation, Pope Benedict ever keeps his serene face.

Then the pope expresses words of gratitude to the cardinals who have been around him and supported him during these years. He proceeds to say, "Dear Brothers, I thank you most sincerely for all the love and work with which you have supported me in my ministry, and I ask pardon for all my defects. And now, let us entrust the Holy Church to the care of Our Supreme Pastor, Our Lord Jesus Christ, and implore his holy Mother Mary, so that she may assist the Cardinal Fathers with her maternal solicitude, in electing a new Supreme Pontiff. With regard to myself, I wish to also devotedly serve the Holy Church of God in the future through a life dedicated to prayer." I break down crying.

As the realization of what is happening gradually sinks in, there is initially an expression of surprise across the faces of the cardinals, followed by that of awe and admiration. The pope has read with a secure and serene voice, but some cardinals, perhaps because they are standing a bit away from the papal chair or because they are not comfortable with Latin, do not understand immediately and are constrained to seek information from their confreres.

The dean of the College of Cardinals, Cardinal Angelo Sodano, has some words to say after Pope Benedict finishes speaking: "Holiness, venerated and beloved successor of Peter, your very moving message resounded in this Hall as a bolt of lightning from the skies. We listened with a sense of loss and almost disbelief. In your words we see the great affection that you have always had for God's Holy Church, for this Church that you love so much. Now, let me tell you on behalf of this Apostolic Cenacle, the College of Cardinals, and on behalf of your beloved collaborators that we are closer than ever to you as we have been during these almost eight luminous years of your pontificate. On 19 April 2005, if I remember correctly, at the end of the conclave, I asked you with an anxious voice, 'Do you accept your canonical election as Supreme Pontiff?' And you, although moved with trepidation, did not hesitate to answer that you accepted, trusting in the Lord's grace and the maternal intercession of Mary, Mother of the Church. Like Mary on that day, she gave her 'yes,' your luminous pontificate began, keeping that continuity, in that continuity with your 265 predecessors in the Chair of Peter, which cover two thousand years of history. It began with the Apostle Peter, the humble Galilean fisherman, down through the great popes of the last century from St. Pius X to Blessed John Paul II. Holy Father, before 28 February, the day that, as you have said, you wish to place the word 'end' to your pontifical ministry, one carried out with so much love and with humility, before 28

February, we will be able to better express our feelings. So, too, will the many pastors and faithful throughout the world, as well as all those of good will, together with the authorities of many countries. Also, still this month, we will have the joy of listening to your voice as Pastor: on Ash Wednesday, on the Thursday meeting with the clergy of Rome, during the Sunday Angelus, and at the Wednesday general audiences. Therefore, we still have many occasions to hear your fatherly voice. Your mission, however, will continue. You have said that you will always be near us with your witness and your prayer. Just as certainly as the stars always continue to shine, so will the star of your pontificate always shine among us. We are near to you, Holy Father, and we ask you to bless us." How can one describe those moments? It is impossible to find the right words.

At lunch, still visibly emotional and not knowing exactly what to say, I blurt out an observation: "Holy Father, you appeared very tranquil while you were pronouncing your act of abdication." "Yes," a determined Benedict replies. He does not utter one more word. I understand that there is no need for further comments.

13 WEDNESDAY FEBRUARY

"Dear brothers and sisters, as you know, I have decided ..." Pope Benedict is unable to finish the sentence because immediately the crowd breaks out into great applause. This occasion is his final address before the last general audience, and the first after the announcement of his abdication. This cannot be like any other. In fact, the applause seems to go on forever. The faithful are expressing their affection and closeness with their clapping. It is a real and actual hug.

Benedict says before he resumes his speech, "Thank you for your kindness," and then continues, "To renounce the ministry which the Lord entrusted to me on 19 April 2005. I have done this in full freedom for the good of the Church, after much prayer and having examined my conscience before God, knowing full well the seriousness of this act, but also realizing that I am no longer able to carry out the Petrine ministry with the strength which it demands. I am strengthened and reassured by the certainty that the Church is Christ's, who will never leave her without His guidance and care. I thank all of you for the love and for the prayers with which you have accompanied me." There is again an outburst of applause and Benedict stops speaking. Every member of the faithful is living this moment in diverse ways. I can see eyes watering, but also smiles and serene faces.

It is Benedict himself who does not give in to emotions, who manages even today to benefit everyone with his usual clear catechesis. He speaks of temptations and says that we should be careful not to impose our conditions on the Lord. He says, "What is the essence of the three temptations to which Jesus is subjected? It is the proposal to exploit God, to use him for one's own interests, for one's own glory and for one's own success. And therefore, essentially to put oneself in God's place, removing him from one's own existence and making him seem superfluous. Each one of us must therefore ask himself or herself: what place does God have in my life? Is he the Lord, or am I?" He goes on to say that no one is immune from the temptation to put God "in a corner," especially today, in an epoch that is dominated by "the eclipse of the sense of the sacred." He says, "Today it is no longer possible to

Pope Benedict's fatherly embrace in thanksgiving of the filial affection of the participants at the general audience.

324

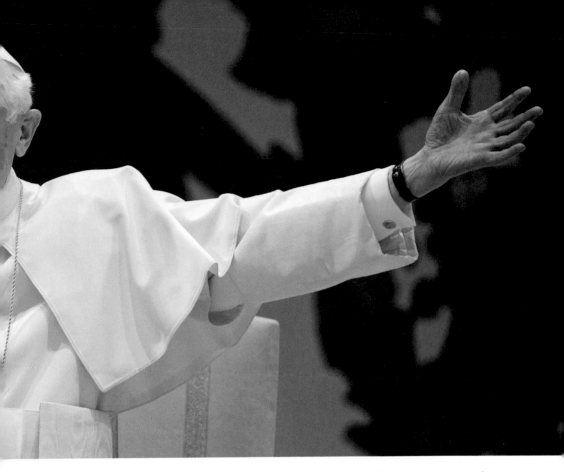

be Christian as a mere consequence of living in a society that has Christian roots: even those who are born into a Christian family and receive a religious education must every day renew their decision to be Christian, that is, to give God first place in the face of the temptations that a secularized culture constantly suggests to them and in the face of the critical opinion of many of their contemporaries." He continues, "The trials to which society today subjects Christians are indeed numerous and affect their personal and social life. It is far from easy to be faithful to Christian marriage, to practice mercy in daily life, to make room for prayer and inner silence; it is far from easy to oppose publicly the decisions that many take for granted, such as abortion in the case of unwanted pregnancy, euthanasia in the case of serious illness and embryo selection in order to prevent hereditary diseases. The temptation to set faith

NIHIL AMORI CHRISTI PRAEPONERE

GRAZIE SANTITÀ
CL UNIVERSITARI ROME

aside is always present and conversion becomes a response to God that must be strengthened several times in life."

Benedict XVI recalls during this penultimate general audience that in our own times there are many conversions of people who return to God, even after many years of distancing themselves from the faith. He cites the case of Etty Hillesum, a young Dutch Jew who discovered God in the hell of Auschwitz, where she would die. He also refers to the American Dorothy Day, a Marxist militant who discovered that one may be revolutionary and effective, much more than any slogans and demonstrations, by going to church and bowing one's head in prayer. He said, "The alternative between being closed into our own egotism and openness to the love of God and of others, we might say, corresponds to the alternative of the temptations of Jesus: an alternative, that is, between human power and love of the Cross, between redemption seen in material wellbeing alone, and redemption as a work of God to which we should give primacy in life. Being converted means not shutting ourselves into the quest

Banners expressing gratitude held aloft by an excited crowd.

for our own success, our own prestige, our own status, but rather ensuring that every day, in the small things, truth, faith in God and love become the most important things of all."

The pope greets people in nine different languages at the end of the audience. Then he says in Italian, "I have felt almost physically during these not-so-easy days for me, the power of prayer which the love of the Church, your prayer, brings to me. Continue to pray for me, for the Church, for the future Pope. The Lord will guide us."

I make an effort not to betray my sadness. I try to speak about cheerful things at lunch. I say, "Holy Father, I have noticed that during the audience the Portuguese monsignor, in his turn, has said, 'At the end of the audience, we will recite the Our Father in *Latin*.' However, the speaker from Brazil, using the native accent, usually says 'in *lacin*.'" The pope smiles, but it seems to me that his mind is very far away.

26 TUESDAY
FEBRUARY

We begin to receive many requests since the Holy Father announced his resignation from the papacy. Everyone wants to meet the pope or to participate at the morning Holy Mass in his private chapel. But our response can only be but one: we are very sorry, but this is not possible. I say to the Holy Father, "I feel privileged even for this: to be able to kiss the Fisherman's Ring every day and to be able to concelebrate Holy Mass with you." The pope replies, "But you are my family." I add, "I also feel privileged because I am the Holy Father's altar boy every day!" Benedict asks, "Then, you also consider yourself an altar boy?" I reply, "Most certainly, Holy Father! He who carries out the liturgical service of washing the hands of him who presides may consider himself an altar boy." I notice that he is holding himself back from laughing.

27 WEDNESDAY FEBRUARY

Today is the last and final general audience, the last meeting between Benedict and the people of God. Benedict says, "I thank all of you for having come in such great numbers to this last General Audience. Heartfelt thanks! I am truly moved, and I see the Church alive! And I think we should also say thanks to the Creator for the fine weather which he gives us even on this winter day. Like the Apostle Paul in the biblical text which we have heard, I too feel a deep need first and foremost to thank God, who gives guidance and growth to the Church, who sows his word and thus nourishes faith in his people. At this moment my heart expands and embraces the whole Church throughout the world; and I thank God for all that I have 'heard' in these years of the Petrine ministry about the faith in the Lord Jesus Christ and the love which truly circulates in the Body of the Church and makes it live in love, and about the hope which opens and directs us towards the fullness of life, towards our heavenly homeland."

The Holy Father states what will now be his mission: "I feel that I bear everyone in prayer, in a present, God's present, in which I gather together every one of my meetings, journeys and pastoral visits. In prayer I gather each and all, in order to entrust them to the Lord: that we might be filled with the knowledge of his will, with all spiritual wisdom and understanding, and that we might lead a life worthy of him and of his love, bearing fruit in every good work." Benedict goes on to say that "at this moment I feel great confidence, because I know, we all know, that the Gospel word of truth is the Church's strength, it is her life. The Gospel purifies and renews, it bears fruit, wherever the community of believers hears it and receives God's grace in truth and charity. This is my confidence; this is my joy."

The pope recalls the memory of April 19, almost eight years ago, when he accepted his election to the Petrine ministry, and says, "At that moment, as I have often said, the words which echoed in my heart were: Lord, why are you asking this of me, and what is it that you are asking of me? It is a heavy burden which you are laying on my shoulders, but if you ask it of me, at your word I will cast the net, sure that you will lead me even with all my weaknesses. And eight years later I can say that the Lord has truly led me, he has been close to me, and I have been able to perceive his presence daily. It has been a portion of the Church's journey which has had its moments of joy and light, but also moments which were not easy; I have felt like Saint Peter with the Apostles in the boat on the Sea of Galilee: the Lord has given us so many days of sun and of light winds, days when the catch was abundant; there were also moments when the waters were rough and the winds against us, as throughout the Church's history, and the Lord seemed to be sleeping. But I have always known that the Lord is in that boat, and I have always known that the barque of the Church is not mine but his. Nor does the Lord let it sink; it is he who guides it, surely also through those whom he has chosen, because he so wished. This has been, and is, a certainty which nothing can shake. For this reason, my heart today overflows with gratitude to God, for he has never let his Church, or me personally, lack his consolation, his light, his love." He goes on to reveal that "in these last months I have felt my energies declining, and I have asked God insistently in prayer to grant me his light and to help me make the right decision, not for my own good, but for the good of the Church. I have taken this step with full awareness of its gravity and even its novelty, but with profound interior serenity. Loving the Church means also having the courage to make difficult, painful decisions, always looking to the good of the Church and not of oneself."

All of us are very busy these days due to the relocation. When I asked the Holy Father what will happen to the two little teddy bears that have accompanied him as he relocated from one city to another, he said, "They are already packed away." Then he remembered a transfer that took place many years ago. When the mover arrived, he took the suitcase and, feeling it to be very light, he said, "But this is empty!" It was not true. It contained the two teddy bears!

28 THURSDAY FEBRUARY

This is a date that will remain in history. Today, at precisely 8:00 p.m., the pontificate of Pope Benedict XVI comes to an end and the Holy See will be vacant, *sede vacante*.

The entire world follows on live television the transfer of the pope from Vatican City to the Apostolic Palace of Castel Gandolfo. All of us are deeply moved as the pope exits the apartment for the last time, but the Holy Father does not show any particular emotion. Down below, at San Damaso Courtyard, we find many employees from various offices, in addition to the superiors at the Secretariat of State. Deep emotions are everywhere. The Pontifical Swiss Guards line up along the arches, with their commander in full uniform. The pope, smiling, greets all of them by waving his hand. I notice many with tears in their eyes.

We are taken by car to the heliport in the Vatican Gardens. Here the pope greets other prelates before we embark. As we fly up, our hearts heavy, we see people waving their hands and handkerchiefs. The Holy Father, in turn, greets them from the window. Before heading toward the Castelli Romani, the white helicopter makes an extensive round over St. Peter's Square, where many people are gathered. Joseph Ratzinger will return here as pope emeritus once the

The helicopter of the Italian Air Force ready for take-off from the Vatican heliport to the Apostolic Palace of Castel Gandolfo.

renovations of the former monastery are completed. He will never return to the apartment, our home, and henceforth he will lead a retired life.

During our flight across the skies of Rome, the bells of the churches in the city run in full peal in salute. On our arrival at the pontifical villas, the Holy Father is welcomed by the city authorities before we are transferred to the residence. Soon thereafter, the pope goes to the balcony, which overlooks the square in front of it. There are people everywhere. The pope delivers a few words of gratitude for their affection, their closeness, and their support. He describes himself as being a "pilgrim who has arrived at the last stage of the earthly journey." Then he goes inside. On November 12 of last year, when Pope Benedict was visiting the home for the elderly of the Community of Sant'Egidio, he exclaimed, "It is beautiful to be old! At every phase of life, it is necessary to be able to discover the presence and blessing of the Lord and the riches they bring. We must never let ourselves be imprisoned by sorrow! We have received the gift of longevity. Living is beautiful even at our age, despite some 'aches and pains' and a few limitations. In our faces may there always be the joy of feeling loved by God and not sadness."

The atmosphere during dinner is normal as much as possible, in that none of us behave differently from our usual selves. After the regular evening walk, I bid the pope good night and kiss his ring. As is my habit, I address him by calling him "Holy Father." This night, however, is anything but tranquil for me.

Below: the last words addressed from the balcony of the Apostolic Palace of Castel Gandolfo to the crowd gathered in the square.

Opposite page: Pope Benedict retires moments before 8 p.m., the end of his pontificate.

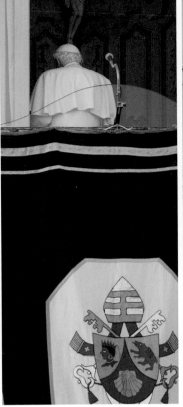

2 SATURDAY
MARCH

There is a distinct contrast between the frenzy of the media, which is still here and looking around to take some photos and get some news, and the tranquility that reigns within the Apostolic Palace.

Many might be under the impression that we have nothing to do or have plenty of free time on our hands. In fact, there is no lack of work. Letters arriving from every part of the world keep us busy. Many people wish to express to the pope emeritus their affection and gratitude for what he did during the years of his pontificate as well as for his courageous choice of abdicating, which only a deeply humble man can do. It is worth noting that much of the correspondence contains something that is dear to those who have written. People attach calendars, holy pictures, a CD of sacred music, poems, sketches, and musical compositions, as well as books or articles that they had written, as if every one of them wants to donate something of himself or herself to the pope! Above all else, they promise him their prayers. The bookshelf I normally use to place the correspondence is loaded to capacity.

Those persons who write seem to do so as if they have lost a father. If before they did not dare to write certain things, now they express the true feelings that were hidden in their heart. The pope comments, "These are beautiful letters!"

If I ever needed any confirmation of the Holy Father's peace of mind, I am given it this morning when he shows me where he placed the "historic" teddy bears. He tells me that one of them dates back to 1928. It was a Christmas gift to him by his mother when they were living in Marktl am Inn. It was the teddy bear that he liked most in the toy store as he passed it on the way to school, and he wept profusely when it disappeared from the store's shop window. He wasn't aware that his mother had purchased it as a surprise gift. Meanwhile, the other teddy bear was bought in 1939 at Aschau. On its sailor's cap was written the name *Ximbu*. The pope tells me, "See, it is not called Xuereb, but Ximbu sounds like it!" Next, he tells me about the troubles with the teddy bears over the years. Ximbu lost an eye one day, and the child Joseph, in an attempt to replace it with hot wax, instead ended up causing burns on its face.

4 MONDAY
MARCH

The Holy Father remains tranquil as he awaits the day when the conclave begins. In the meantime, the cardinals meet today for the first so-called general congregation.

Benedict confides in me during our walk that he has come to know that the miracle for the canonization of John Paul II has been recognized. He reveals that what struck him was the coincidence of the timing of the approval with that of the announcement of his resignation of the papacy. It happened toward 12:30 on Monday, February 11.

5 TUESDAY MARCH

This morning the Holy Father hands over the Fisherman's Ring, which, in times past, was destroyed when a pope died. Instead, now it is only scratched across as a sign that the pope who wore it is no longer the reigning pontiff. Yesterday, when he brought it to the office to turn it over, I asked him if I could kiss it for the last time. He consented, and I noticed that my request pleased him.

The Fisherman's Ring of Benedict XVI's Pontificate.

13 WEDNESDAY MARCH

Benedict looks forward with great anticipation to the conclave and the election of the new pope. He is eager to know
who will succeed him. Our prayers are intense, knowing that
we are united with the whole Church in invoking the assistance of the Holy Spirit. We watch on television the moment
of the proclamation, "*Annuntio vobis gaudium magnum:
habemus papam.*" Impressed by the words and gestures of the
elected pontiff, we go down to the dining room for dinner in
a joyous atmosphere.

The phone rings during the meal to inform us that Pope
Francis has been trying to speak with Pope Benedict on the
phone. They ask in amazement, "But where were you? We
have called several times, and no one answers." Pope Francis
had wanted to greet Pope Benedict before he went to the
central balcony of the Vatican Basilica to salute the crowd
waiting in the square. But we, like the rest of the majority of
people around the world, had been watching television, and
the phone in that room is always kept muted. They assure us,
"However, the pope will call later."

It is very moving to be present for the phone call that the
new pontiff eventually makes to Benedict. Just to hear Benedict XVI saying, "Thank you, Holy Father" stirs admiration.
"Thank you for thinking immediately of me, and I promise
you my obedience and my prayers beginning this very moment." I am most edified hearing him saying this.

15 FRIDAY MARCH

Today I experience many emotions as well as many lasting
memories. They are special moments that I am sure will

remain historical. From February 28, the last day of the pontificate of Benedict and the day we left the Apostolic Palace for good, up to today, March 15 — that is, two days after the election of the new pope — I have continued to stay with the pope emeritus at Castel Gandolfo. The purpose was to keep him company and to assist him in secretarial matters.

The moment of my separation from Pope Benedict was a heart-wrenching moment for me. I had the fortune of living five and a half years with him, and now, suddenly, I had to leave him. Things were rushed as I was unaware that today was the day I had to pack and leave Castel Gandolfo. It obviously also meant leaving Pope Benedict for good, and separating myself from him, especially at such short notice, was a very difficult moment. The reason I had been requested by the Vatican to pack in a hurry and go to Santa Marta was because Pope Francis was opening his mail on his own without a secretary to help him. I went to the chapel several times this morning, asking for guidance, for I felt a little confused. However, the way things were happening so rapidly, I had the sensation that something extraordinary was happening, even regarding my life. After chapel, I went crying to the study of Pope Benedict, and with a lump in my throat, I tried to tell him how sad I was and how difficult it is for me to leave him behind. I thanked him for being such a benevolent father to me. I assured him that all my experiences, both privately and professionally, while living in such close proximity with him in the Apostolic Palace, have greatly helped me to have a clearer look at "the things of Heaven." Then I knelt to kiss his ring, which was no longer that of the Fisherman, and he, with a fatherly gaze of tenderness so particular to him, stood up and gave me his blessing.

Heliport of the Pontifical
Villas of Castel Gandolfo.
The first meeting
between Pope Francis
and Benedict XVI.

AFTERWORD

BAVARIAN, RATHER THAN GERMAN

After being in the secretariat of Pope Francis for a few days, Vatican Radio asked me to respond to the following questions, 2013.

You spent every day for almost six years next to Pope Benedict. You were there in joyful moments as well as in difficult ones. You were there during official occasions and ceremonies, but also in the intimacy of family life. Fr. Alfred, you propose in your diary an unpublished portrait of Joseph Ratzinger, one that is surprising in many aspects. But what has remained more branded in your heart?

The first image that comes to mind goes back to the last moments I spent with Benedict XVI at Castel Gandolfo. Before I said my goodbye, I told him, "Holiness, thank you for your great paternity. All of the experiences I had while living here with you have helped me to seek better the things of Heaven." It was truly so. It was truly a human and spiritual journey. Certainly, I no longer had a private life during the years I was at his service, but this detachment from the world was healthy for the spirit. Looking back, I am full of gratitude. Some might think that in accepting to put myself at the service of the pope, I renounced everything, and in a certain sense this was true, but I received much in exchange. I am convinced that if, instead of responding to the call of the Lord, I had taken it upon myself to organize my life, I would never have been able to imagine it to be as beautiful, as rich, and as full as it has really been.

Pope Benedict inevitably will be remembered foremost in history books for his resignation of the Petrine office and his decision to retire. But his pontificate deserves to be remembered for much more than that. His Magisterium was of the highest level, full of ideas that are still valid today. What will remain in remembrance of him? What is the foremost contribution Benedict XVI has given to the Church and to humanity?

I feel we should thank him for his crystal clarity on the theological and liturgical levels. But I would not mind if he were to be remembered as the pope of renunciation. It was given totally and with great courage. The final act, that of his abdication, from this point of view was not the last ring of the chain that was constructed from the outset. It was carried out day after day, entirely dedicated to self-denial, generosity, and commitment to God's plan. Pope Benedict XVI was never concerned about the applause from the world, for he never sought it. Instead, he placed himself at God's disposal and that of the Church as a "humble worker in the vineyard of the Lord," to quote the words he spoke on the day of his papal election. Even his abdication from the papacy is also borne of this availability, from this altruism. For him, God came first, the Church came first. I would also like to see him remembered as a man who has taught us how to live the spirit of brotherhood. He has done so with his teachings, but also with the direct experience in relating to his brother, Georg, toward whom he has always shown much affection and solicitude.

But according to you, Fr. Alfred, would Professor Ratzinger have preferred to spend his old age in the company of his beloved books, studying and writing? In other words, did he not perceive the pontificate as a burden from the very beginning?

On two occasions Cardinal Ratzinger, having reached the age of seventy-five, asked John Paul II to allow him to retire so as to be able to devote himself to his studies and to finish those books he cared so much about. He was not granted his wish, and then came his election as pontiff. Humanly speaking, a pontificate is always a burden, and it was surely so for Joseph Ratzinger. But the pope totally accepted the will of God and went along with it. The fear of failing, even due to age, was certainly real in him, so much so that it led to his abdication. But this act of Benedict was not one of rebellion, not an affirmation of self, but an adherence to the plan God had for him.

Without doubt, there were difficult moments during Benedict's pontificate. How did he deal with them?

The Holy Father suffered. He suffered a lot, especially for unjustifiable attacks that at some point, I think in 2010, occurred on a daily basis. Since he is a sensitive man, he endured pain. But he is also a man of great faith, and so, through his conversations with the Lord, he was able to garner that energy that is necessary to confront all problems and all attacks. Moreover, he never fell into victimization. One never heard him utter a word of disdain or a complaint regarding the treatment he was subjected to. As I state in the diary, it is significant that when the actions of his butler, who was guilty of sneaking out very confidential documents from the papal apartment, came to light, the pope was not concerned for himself but for that young father of a family and for his future

343

and that of his family. And when Benedict was subjected to a barrage of unjust criticism regarding the pedophilia cases, he never uttered a single negative word against the press, which had orchestrated a defamation campaign. Instead, he forcefully denounced what he called the "internal persecution" against the Church, which was caused by the infidelity of some of her sons. This, too, was a great teaching.

And you, Fr. Alfred, being Maltese, and therefore a man who comes from the Mediterranean, how did you live with a German pope?

Listen, I think it is better to refer to Ratzinger with the adjective Bavarian, which is different than being German. He is the son of a land, that is, Bavaria, whose religiosity is much more similar to that of Malta than to other parts of Germany, especially in the north. This is the reason why there was always harmony between us. I felt that we stood on common ground. And then he was a man who was extremely attentive to the needs of other people. He was really fatherly, in the fullest sense of the word. He was interested in me, not by being inquisitive but because he was part of my life.

If you, Fr. Alfred, were to speak about the pontificate of Benedict XVI to young people who did not know him, or who heard about him in a superficial way, what would you say to them? Who really was Benedict XVI?

I know that some of them will be amazed. The first word that comes to my mind is *affability*. Benedict was a man full of tenderness. I can say this for it is based on my personal experience. This is why I feel very hurt when, regarding Joseph Ratzinger, I hear of judgments that are far from reality. Some commentators still paint Benedict as a stern man, as an inflexible and cold man, and summarize these characteristics with the adjective *German*. But as far as I am concerned, I repeat, he was a Bavarian pope, period. I want to say that he was a kind, sensitive man, gifted with a profound humanity, as well as with a great love of the beautiful. As for doctrinal matters, he held the rudder of Peter's boat with steady hands, and he was not concerned about the problem regarding the consent of public opinion. It is terribly unjust to describe and remember him as a merciless censor and an intransigent controller. Rather, he was a father, a true father who urged his children to question themselves about the most important issues for every person, beginning with the question of truth. We must be grateful to him for this.

ONE LAST, SWEET LOOK

Every time I passed through Rome from Korea, I went to visit him in the Monastery and I realized that his health was failing. Fixed in my heart is the sweet gaze with which he welcomed me on September 12, 2022, when I found him waiting for me in the living room sitting in an armchair. When I knelt to kiss his ring, I looked at his face and exclaimed: "Holy Father, how happy I am to see you again!" Bright eyed, he answered me with a voice full of emotion, "I am very happy too."

I experienced his agony in reflection and prayer, asking God to assist him in those sacred moments of his long life. When news of his death reached me, I felt certain that there was a great celebration in Paradise and that the Madonna went to welcome him at the gate to bring him to her son, Jesus, whom he had served with wisdom and humility. During Mass, which I celebrated mere moments later in one of the parishes in Seoul, I encouraged the faithful to ask for graces through the intercession of Benedict XVI, because we have another saint praying for us from Heaven!

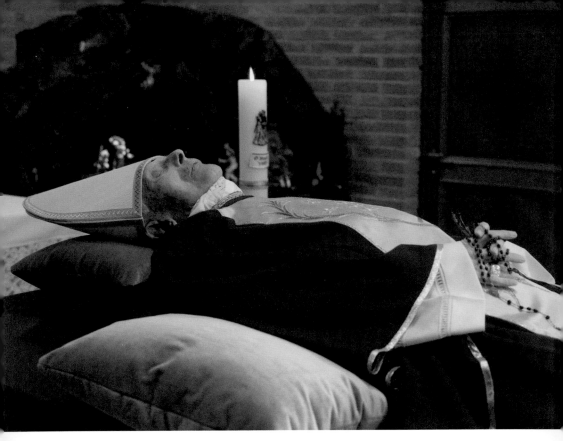

January 3, 2023, the
body of Benedict XVI
exhibited in the Basilica
of St. Peter. Over 65,000
people went to the Vatican
for a last farewell.

NOTES OF SORROW
AND GRATITUDE

The departure from this life of Pope Benedict XVI has aroused in my heart notes of sorrow and gratitude. As I recorded in these pages, he was a father to me, attentive and tender, wise but also extremely humble. As St. Joseph took care of the Holy Family with devoted obedience, so Joseph Ratzinger took care of the Church, especially when he was Pope.

Following the courageous act of resignation, he succeeded in continuing his tireless teaching on humility and love for the Church. His writings reveal a depth that is extraordinary and essential, both for today and for the future. He has been a true prophet, because he shared what he learned through his intimate life with the Lord.

In fact, during the last General Audience, held in a packed St. Peter's square on February 27, 2013, Pope Benedict entrusted us with words of reassurance: "Dear friends! God guides His Church, He always supports her, especially in moments of difficulty. Let us never lose this vision of faith, which is the only true way to look at the path of the Church and of the world. In our hearts, in the heart of each of you, may there always dwell the joyful certainty that the Lord is by our side: He does not abandon us, He stays close to us, and He surrounds us with His love." He closes his spiritual testament by saying: "I humbly ask: pray for me, so that the Lord, in spite of all my sins and shortcomings, may welcome me into the eternal dwellings. To all those who have been entrusted to me go my heartfelt prayers day after day."

As we mourn his loss, we thank the Lord for the gift of Pope Benedict XVI and his ministry. Together we implore the Lord to grant him eternal rest.

✠ ALFRED XUEREB

January 5, 2023, Pope Francis celebrates the funeral Mass of Benedict XVI, who died at age 95 on December 31, 2022.

PHOTOGRAPH REFERENCES:

Alfred Xuereb's personal photos:
13, 14, 19, 25, 39, 47, 87, 97, 118, 157,162, 178, 180, 181, 184, 185, 192, 193, 194, 199, 200, 203, 204, 209, 210, 240, 241, 244, 245, 259, 260, 265, 266.

Edizioni San Paolo photos:
6, 9, 75, 82, 101, 159, 220, 257, 258.

L'Osservatore Romano Archive photos:
4, 23, 27, 50, 53, 85, 86, 88, 90, 92, 103, 109, 111, 117, 123, 148, 149, 150, 164, 177, 179, 198, 205, 231, 243, 246, 247, 249, 255, 261, 270, 271, 272, 274, 275, 276, 277, 279, 281, 290, 291, 293, 295, 296, 301, 303, 307, 308-309, 310, 319, 320, 324-325, 326, 331, 332, 333, 338-339, 340, 348, 351, 352–353.

Catholic Press Photos:
16, 26, 127, 186, 201, 333.

Getty Images:
xviii–xix, xxi, xxii, 44-45, 61, 69, 73, 95, 121, 122, 125, 131, 132, 136, 146, 161, 221, 224, 323.

Shutterstock Photos:
31, 41, 57, 76-77, 93, 134, 228, 235, 285, 317.

Stefano Spaziani:
xi, 38, 312.

Sophia Institute

Sophia Institute is a nonprofit institution that seeks to nurture the spiritual, moral, and cultural life of souls and to spread the gospel of Christ in conformity with the authentic teachings of the Roman Catholic Church.

Sophia Institute Press fulfills this mission by offering translations, reprints, and new publications that afford readers a rich source of the enduring wisdom of mankind.

Sophia Institute also operates the popular online resource CatholicExchange.com. *Catholic Exchange* provides world news from a Catholic perspective as well as daily devotionals and articles that will help readers to grow in holiness and live a life consistent with the teachings of the Church.

In 2013, Sophia Institute launched Sophia Institute for Teachers to renew and rebuild Catholic culture through service to Catholic education. With the goal of nurturing the spiritual, moral, and cultural life of souls, and an abiding respect for the role and work of teachers, we strive to provide materials and programs that are at once enlightening to the mind and ennobling to the heart; faithful and complete, as well as useful and practical.

Sophia Institute gratefully recognizes the Solidarity Association for preserving and encouraging the growth of our apostolate over the course of many years. Without their generous and timely support, this book would not be in your hands.

www.SophiaInstitute.com
www.CatholicExchange.com
www.SophiaInstituteforTeachers.org

Sophia Institute Press is a registered trademark of Sophia Institute.
Sophia Institute is a tax-exempt institution as defined by the
Internal Revenue Code, Section 501(c)(3). Tax ID 22-2548708.